# Political Constructions

# Political Constructions

*Defoe, Richardson, and Sterne in Relation to Hobbes, Hume, and Burke*

CAROL KAY

CORNELL UNIVERSITY PRESS
Ithaca and London

CORNELL UNIVERSITY PRESS GRATEFULLY ACKNOWLEDGES
A GRANT FROM THE ANDREW W. MELLON FOUNDATION
THAT AIDED IN BRINGING THIS BOOK TO PUBLICATION.



First published 1988 by Cornell University Press.

International Standard Book Number 0-8014-2043-1
Library of Congress Catalog Card Number 88-3741

Printed in the United States of America

*Librarians: Library of Congress cataloging information appears on the last page of the book.*

*The paper in this book is acid-free and meets the guidelines for permanence and durability of the Committee on Production Guidelines for Book Longevity of the Council on Library Resources.*

# Contents

*Preface* vii

*Introduction* 1

1. POLITICAL ANALYSIS: THE MODEL OF HOBBES 19

Hobbesian Literary History *21*
Character *25*
Language *33*
Sovereignty *38*

2. DEFOE: ADVENTURES IN POLITICAL CREATIVITY 45

The Self-appointed Counselor *47*
Natural Law, Economics, and Providence: Defoe and Hobbes *66*
*Robinson Crusoe*: Political Man *75*
*Moll Flanders:* Political Woman *92*

3. RICHARDSON: PLOTS OF INTIMATE KNOWLEDGE 121

Travel between the Hedges *123*
Rules, Moral Language, and Vanity: Hume and Richardson *131*
*Pamela*: Love and the Love of Fame *141*
*Clarissa*: Trying Moral Discourse *159*

4. STERNE: SCENES OF PLAY 195

Compleasance *197*

*Tristram Shandy*: Playful Purposes *204*

*A Sentimental Journey*: Purposeful Play *246*

*Epilogue:* BURKE'S FEARFUL REFLECTIONS 265

*Index* 279

# Preface

The readings of Defoe, Richardson, and Sterne in this volume develop an interpretation grounded in British political philosophy and political history. The first chapter draws from Hobbes's *Leviathan* a model of political analysis that is illustrated and tested in the rest of the book. Each chapter on a novelist begins with a section of historically oriented biographical interpretation which outlines political issues particularly important to the author's fiction. Each of these chapters contains extended readings of two novels. The book concludes with a brief treatment of Burke's *Reflections on the Revolution in France*, which marks an important new phase of "political construction" in fiction and philosophy.

At the risk of reductive distortion, I offer the following schematic account of the book's argumentative strategy. This is not primarily a study of literary or philosophic influences on the novel; it is not primarily a study of the poetics of the novel. This book contributes to the criticism of fiction by constructing a new political thematics that draws on British, rather than continental, philosophy and takes into account basic elements of British political history from the English Civil War to the French Revolution. Hobbes is an appropriate philosophic guide for this period because it was the period of "the growth of political stability"—J. H. Plumb's anesthetic phrase for a consolidation of national authority which was widely accepted but often recognized as brutal. The establishment of national authority, taken for granted by most of us most of the time, was for authors of the seventeenth and eighteenth centuries often in crisis, often debated, and therefore more evident than it is to us.

I draw from Hobbes a political "problematic," a complex of interconnected topics which can serve as a corrective to the many and varied twentieth-century theories that neglect political institutions. Hobbes's theory of sovereignty does not require or recommend (indeed assumes to be impossible) a totalitarian governmental control over all social activities, but it does require consent to shared law and agreement about which institutions have final authority to make law. Hobbesian political interpretation does not reduce all explanation to some governmental operation or ignore the importance of nongovernmental forms of power. It is hypersensitive to power in any form. But nongovernmental institutions such as commerce, the family, religion, the arts and sciences, all look different—less coherent, less self-contained, less self-regulating—if you see them as operating necessarily within the framework of a sovereign state. And I hope to show that novels look different if you see their rhetoric, narrative, characterization, and plot in connection with Hobbesian insights into human competition and ignorance, which require the political solution of consent to authority.

In this book readings of individual works are designed not merely to illustrate but also to test in a variety of ways Hobbes's argument that a sovereign government is the essential institution of social life. Defoe's fiction offers, for example, the opportunity to test whether property relations underpinned by natural law are sufficient to structure society, a view that resembles that of Locke. I see Defoe not as an ideological forebear of nineteenth-century capitalism, but as someone who seeks to extend the power of the state, and his own power within it, by a variety of means, only one of which is commercial property. I compare Richardson's fiction to Hume's view that society is structured and stabilized by a variety of social systems, especially by the systematic operation of moral discourse. In the Sterne chapter, I consider the political implications of a liberal consumerist culture that seems to escape politics but depends on the political system. Political nostalgia becomes one of the nation's recreational resources, but it can also be exploited for political purposes. The topic of nostalgia leads to the coda on Burke's *Reflections*, which shows the transformation of Hobbesian and Humean materials that was passed on from the French revolutionary period to the nineteenth century.

The outcome of these tests is that the Hobbesian position wins conceptually and politically. Analysis of the novels reveals that structures which seem independent of or alternative to the state are described even by the novelists as interdependent with it, and the novelists help make the history in which England becomes the prototype of the settled state, the country that did not have a modern revolution. The institutional arrangements of the settled sovereignty, however, do not turn out to be what Hobbes recommended (he feared mixed or parliamentary government, religious diversity, the free press), and so the account of the ways sovereignty is understood and accepted must be complicated, as it is in the individual chapters.

My emphasis on particular problems of power and authority in each author is partly an expository device, since the novelists I treat share broad patterns of historical experience and political belief. But I think that the selection I make for each writer has the interpretive value of suggesting important short-range changes of political perspective. The three novelists I have chosen belong to three generations. Born at the Restoration, Defoe is in many ways a seventeenth-century man of politics, whose interest in natural law and political counsel is informed by his experience of revolutionary conflict over such matters. Richardson, born at the Glorious Revolution, formed early ties with the strident members of the Tory opposition, but absorption in business, which included profitable connections with Parliament, detached him from political activism and led him to social and literary means of reforming manners. Sterne was born near the death of Queen Anne and the fall of the Tory ministers, so he never knew a time before the Whig oligarchy. In the last decade of his life there were intimations of the breakup of this order, hints of a new imperialism and a new mass democracy, but there is no reason to believe that Sterne was particularly alert to them. His exceptional sense of national security makes possible his sense of play. That all three of these novelists, born over half a century apart, had dealings with the Walpole Whigs illustrates a remarkable fact of political history. Moreover, all three engaged in novel writing in resulting moods of political discouragement, indifference, or somewhat self-disparaging acquiescence. The novel does not fully rise to the status of a moral alternative to the satisfactions of political activity, but perhaps political dissatisfactions do give it a boost.

In some ways my chapters are cumulative, amounting to a shared framework of thought. All these novelists probably believed in religiously based natural law, in the importance of moral education, in the potential social advantages of commerce and the commercial press. In ways that complicated these beliefs, they all gave their allegiance (that is, obedience if not approval) to the sovereign institutions of mixed government in England, including the Hanoverian succession in the monarchy, the Anglican church establishment, and the political privileges of the landed aristocracy in local and parliamentary government. This group of beliefs and allegiances would figure in any description of the dominant eighteenth-century ideology.

It is not easy to defend conceptual choices of great magnitude. I am attracted to Hobbes's discourse on "opinion" rather than to more recent theories of "ideology" because Hobbes's emphasis on the dynamic will, the interplay of changing desires and fears, leaves conceptual space for the specifics of political experience and the potential of political activity. If he offers nothing like the utopian hope of freedom from alienation, Hobbes can serve to expose the conflicts covered over by concepts of human fulfillment. If he is lamentably suspicious of the institutions of "free speech" which we enjoy and wish to extend, his concepts of consent, command, counsel, and compleasance tell us something about how these institutions have worked.

In the course of composing this book, I have incurred so many debts that only the most conspicuous can be acknowledged here. I owe special thanks to Michael Seidel, Margaret Doody, David Bromwich, Bruce Robbins, and Gregory Vlastos, who have provided penetrating commentary on more than one stage of the manuscript. Earl Miner, Benjamin DeMott, and Fredric Jameson have also offered valuable criticism. My first outline was drafted at Princeton University, when Henry Knight Miller generously stepped aside and allowed me to lecture in the eighteenth-century-novel course. Students in this course and in its successors at Amherst College and Washington University have contributed greatly to my understanding of the novels and to my enthusiasm for them. Amherst College and Washington University have supported this project by funding uninterrupted periods for reading and writing.

My hopefulness about political construction has been nourished by a variety of institutions. At Princeton, interdisciplinary groups including the Christian Gauss Seminars in Criticism and the Friends of the Eighteenth Century mitigated departmental narrowness. At Washington University, the Literature and History program fostered collaborations that reached beyond our curricular ventures. I am grateful to Steven Zwicker for building this association and introducing me to colleagues in history from whom I have learned a great deal: Richard Davis, Derek Hirst, and Harold Ellis.

For me the most affecting examples of political activity have been drawn from the North American women's movement. Since joining the Graduate Women's Organization of Harvard University, I have benefited immeasurably from participation in feminist groups. Experiences in the well-organized and broadly based Princeton University Women's Organization, as well as in an inchoate women's group at Amherst College, have contributed to the meditations that fed this book.

These influences would not have been as helpful as they were if the understanding of them had not been shared with the loving and much-loved friend to whom this book is dedicated, Jonathan Arac. The taste for intimate friendship and many other things that motivate intellectual projects I attribute to my parents, Albert Kay and Lucie Breyer Kay, economists, novel lovers, New Deal Democrats, and friends.

CAROL KAY

*New York, New York*

# Political Constructions

# Introduction

In this study of eighteenth-century English fiction, I refer to a selection of canonized texts that cluster around the middle decades of the century, works by Defoe, Richardson, and Sterne which have come to be inevitable features of our literary history and our literary curriculum. Canon and curriculum have been and should be matters for debate in our profession, and I recognize that while I seek to expand the political understanding of our enterprise in certain ways, my book is also shaped by some conventional restrictions that have political import. I hope, nevertheless, that an analysis of "political constructions" will reach usefully beyond the books I have chosen to discuss.

By the word *construction*, I mean to emphasize what political philosophy shares with fiction: the conceptualization through argument and example of what is fundamental, what is crucial to social life.[1] I am not aiming for a complete historical description of social and political life, nor do I assume that novelists are aiming for such comprehensiveness in their representations, but rather that their constructions will be selective and exemplary—as will mine. To take fiction as exemplary is to assume that it may be understood rhetorically, and this is in keeping with the Horatian dictum, widely

[1]Throughout this book the terms *society* and *social* are used in two ways: (1) to refer to all systematic human interactions, including political institutions; (2) in a more restricted sense, in contrast with *politics* or *polity* or *political*, to mean non-governmental systems that can be conceived as independent (or partially independent) from government.

accepted in the eighteenth century, that art should give instruction and pleasure. Samuel Johnson took this tag from Horace as epigraph for his *Rambler* 4, on "modern fiction." For Johnson, more accurate, more specific representation of contemporary life means more rhetorical power, and that is a matter of social concern. Nevertheless, to say that eighteenth-century fiction teaches through example is not to say that we always know what it teaches. Consider how difficult it is to identify the teaching of Johnson's own *Rasselas*, even though the piece is usually taken as a didactic (my students always say pedantic) rather than imitative work. The difficulties and dangers, even the impossibility, of teaching and learning may be a part of the teaching of fiction and philosophy. And questions about the authority to teach open matters of form and theme to political meditation, even political interrogation.

For important reasons I have left the term *political*, surely the most important one, undefined. Thinking about that makes me nervous, since nothing is more explosively controversial than to define what is or (this may be even more explosive) what is not political. As the recent progress of feminist studies shows, what counts as political can change for a large number of people very rapidly. We should not expect to find a stable, universal definition for the political, much less a single, identifiable political realm. But accepting the mobility of the term can lead to the decay of its usefulness: is any matter of power and authority to be called political whenever anyone feels like it? Or to avoid that sloppiness, must we restrict the term to political activities and political analysis in the narrow sense identified by this Oxford English Dictionary definition: "the science and art of government; the science dealing with the form, organization, and administration of a state or a part of one and with the regulation of its relations with other states"?

My solution is something of a side step. I take from Hobbes's *Leviathan* a model of political analysis. The following passage from *Leviathan*'s chapter "Of the Difference of Manners" gives valuable clues for what counts in political analysis: "By MANNERS, I mean not here Decency of behaviour; as how one man should salute another, or how a man should wash his mouth, or pick his teeth before company, and such other points of the *Small Moralls*; but those qualities of man-kind, that concern their living together in Peace, and

Unity."[2] In the phrase "how a man should wash his mouth or pick his teeth before company," we hear an aristocratic disdain for considering anything less than what is crucially relevant to the survival of society. But nonetheless, Hobbes does place these humble matters before us. The common language, the deglamorized view of life, seem typical of him, and if the language trembles on the brink of satire, so does a great deal of novelistic description of unheroic everyday life. Hobbes's attitude toward social trivia must be complex, since the goal of his theory is to make the rules of social survival so well understood by sovereign and subjects that serious questions about them will be forever laid to rest, and most people will then be concerned only with matters of small morals.

We cannot infer from this passage a stable distinction between private and public, or social and political, since in Hobbes's theory the sovereign must have absolute sovereignty precisely because absolutely anything could become political, a matter for dangerous competition and contention, even how to pick the teeth. In other places in *Leviathan*, "how one man should salute another" is an especially sensitive area of behavior. It figures in the famous chapter "Of the Natural Condition of Mankind" under one of the three principal causes of quarrel that lead to the war of all against all, "Glory" or "Reputation": "for trifles, as a word, a smile, a different opinion, and any other sign of undervalue, either direct in their persons or by reflexion in their kindred, their Friends, their Nation, their profession or their Name" (I, 13, 185). The matter of how a man is to be saluted is in fact important enough to be listed as one of the rights of the sovereign, to specify what shall be the forms of civil honor.

Before returning to the matter of names and civil honor, I want to emphasize the advantage of choosing Hobbes as a model of political analysis: he offers both a restricted and a flexible understanding of politics. To choose Hobbes as a model of analysis is to center a definition of the political in the theory and institutions of state, those institutions that have final authority over the whole of society and the

[2]Thomas Hobbes, *Leviathan*, ed. C. B. MacPherson (Harmondsworth: Penguin, 1968), pt. I, chap. 11, p. 160. All further references, throughout the book, will be given parenthetically, by part, chapter, and page. Thus in this case: (I, 11, 160).

institutions that back the authority with power: the monarch and executive bureaucracy, legislature, courts, military, and police. Such a theory must be comprehensive in order to defend the necessity of such institutions and to account for differences in the exercise of their authority in different times and places. Although I am not drawn to Hobbes's monarchic sovereign, the perception that underlies the argument seems valuable: that any matter of human behavior might become a matter of concern to the commonwealth as a whole. Because of Hobbes's sensitivity to every possible source of conflict with authority, he provides a textbook on the sources of power, and he is especially sensitive to the powers of books and language. Furthermore, Hobbes is the premier of all political theorists for putting politics first of all the sciences, for seeing politics as the dominant, organizing feature of social life, and for denying that any other feature of social life—whether family, economics, language, or science—can provide self-regulating order.

The claim about the dominance of politics is the feature of Hobbes's theory that modern people are most inclined to disparage. Social scientists of many sorts offer accounts of social coherence that marginalize political institutions. Most confusing of all, Marxists, the people most likely to introduce "political analysis" into our literary curriculum, have traditionally considered the state no more than a superstructure erected on an economic base, although there have been some important modifications of that position. For both theoretical and historical grounds, I think it is worth pushing back on the other side of this argument. I do not see how the state will wither away, and I think that a reasonable requirement for even a utopian political theory is to envision how the functions of the institutions with final authority will be carried out. In our own historical setting, it would take considerable descriptive ingenuity to ignore the magnitude of state institutions, and though they were quite different in seventeenth- and eighteenth-century Britain (performing fewer functions and employing a smaller proportion of the people), I believe that the continuing controversies over the religious establishment and over the nature of allegiance made matters of public authority visible and important, in some ways more visible than they are to people like ourselves who live in more stable states.

New developments in Marxist analysis address some of my concerns and bring it closer to the needs of my study. In a critical discourse of ideology, I might call the competition between Hobbesian and non-Hobbesian tendencies "contradictions," and the dynamic domination of culture by the ruling institutions "hegemony" as conceived by Antonio Gramsci. Althusser's development of the "relative autonomy" of the political seems to do much of the business for Marxism that I am trying to do for liberalism by my adaptation of Hobbes. Althusser's admission that in some periods political structures are more dominant than economic structures would help make room for my historical claims about the importance of state formation in the seventeenth and eighteenth centuries. Perry Anderson has drawn attention to the rise of the absolutist state in the context of Marxist historiography. All of these developments bring Marxism closer to my analyses than to those of earlier commentators, whose "rise of capitalism" theses I debate in subsequent chapters. But in some ways these emendments of Marxism only reassimilate the philosophic tradition from which it emerged and make it more appealing for the politics of modern liberal states. For people who live in these states, particularly the United States, an elaborately revised Marxism may be only a long route round to political analysis.[3]

This book draws inspiration from an Anglo-American movement in political theory that began some three decades ago. At that time important challenges were made by political theorists to the dominance of the social sciences, including the antipolitical bias of older Marxism. Peter Winch's *Idea of a Social Science*, Hannah Arendt's *Human Condition*, and Sheldon Wolin's *Politics and Vision* are landmarks of this countermovement.[4] None of these people was a

[3]On hegemony, see Raymond Williams, "Base and Superstructure in Marxist Cultural Theory," in *Problems of Materialism and Culture* (London: New Left Books, 1980), pp. 31–49; for the major development of Althusserian ideas for political analysis, see Nicos Poulantzas, *Political Power and Social Classes* (London: New Left Books, 1973); on the absolutist state, see Perry Anderson, *Lineages of the Absolutist State* (London: New Left Books, 1974).

[4]Peter Winch, *The Idea of a Social Science and Its Relation to Philosophy* (1958; London: Routledge & Kegan Paul, 1976); Hannah Arendt, *The Human Condition* (Garden City, N.Y.: Doubleday, 1958); Sheldon S. Wolin, *Politics and Vision* (Boston: Little, Brown, 1960). For a sympathetic critique of the rigid opposition of social to political in these works, see Hanna Fenichel Pitkin, *Wittgenstein and Justice* (Berkeley: University of California Press, 1972), esp. pp. 193–218.

Hobbesist. But for the reasons I have outlined, the institutional struggle for attention to political philosophy brought Hobbes along in its wake. So when one thinks of the people who have contributed most to the academic study of the great texts of political philosophy—Leo Strauss, Sheldon Wolin, Quentin Skinner, J.G.A. Pocock—one inevitably thinks also of their work on Hobbes.[5] The struggle has not been exclusively within social science departments but also within philosophy departments that tended to depreciate moral and political philosophy. If our knowledge of the external world was the dominant philosophic topic, Hobbes's materialism disqualified him from serious consideration, so once again his is a very nice case for the study of institutions.

The sight of scholars in other disciplines justifying the study of great texts in their historical setting has a reassuring familiarity for literary scholars. But what can the struggle to resuscitate political philosophy contribute to the study of English literature? I think the carefully crafted texts of Hobbes and Hume and Burke should have no less claim on the attention of literary scholars than those of novelists. They should not be treated as background merely, nor merely as a source of themes. My dissertation, a detailed study of Hume's rhetorical and formal choices, preceded this work on the novel.[6] But the more precise and appreciative accounts of the formal choices of the great British philosophers which people in literature departments can contribute will not have much power (will in fact fall into dreadful inaccuracies) unless they also have a strong commitment to the interest of the philosophic arguments. One way to encourage this interest is to work with the arguments, test them out as descriptive frameworks for other books, as I do here. Will it inevitably be less interesting to do this with Hobbes than with Hegel or Heidegger?

[5]Leo Strauss, *The Political Philosophy of Thomas Hobbes* (1936), trans. Elsa M. Sinclair (Chicago: University of Chicago Press, 1963); Wolin, *Politics and Vision*, chap. 8, and *Hobbes and the Epic Tradition of Political Theory* (Los Angeles: Clark Memorial Library, 1970); Quentin Skinner, many articles, of which the most important is "The Context of Hobbes's Theory of Political Obligation" (1966), revised in *Hobbes and Rousseau: A Collection of Critical Essays*, ed. Maurice Cranston and Richard S. Peters (Garden City, N.Y.: Doubleday, 1972), pp. 109–42; J.G.A. Pocock, "Time, History, and Eschatology in the Thought of Thomas Hobbes," in *Politics, Language, and Time: Essays on Political Thought and History* (New York: Atheneum, 1971), pp. 148–201.

[6]"Philosophic Manners: The Writings of David Hume, 1727–51" (Ph.D. diss., Harvard University, 1975).

Some people may lament the permeability of literary studies by other disciplines. I do not know what a purely formal study of literature would look like, and I doubt that it is possible to create a literary theory independent of all other theories. I join a discourse already in progress on the social themes of eighteenth-century fiction and their philosophic bearing, but this discourse shares some of the biases that have marginalized political concerns in the other contexts I have described—an emphasis on epistemology rather than on moral and political philosophy, and an emphasis on social rather than on political institutions. I don't exactly want to win my arguments, to crush the opposition—no more epistemology, no more social science. I want to redress an imbalance and try out what these subjects look like in a political scheme. I find it possible partly to replay the twentieth-century debate about the political and the social by recasting it in terms of an implicit dialogue between earlier theorists. So Hume and Burke emerge for me as socially oriented theorists and historians of society, inspired by their perceptions of the organizing power of customary, natural-seeming social systems such as language, economic production and exchange, the family, and religion. I find it interesting to see how much ground they share with Hobbes (for instance, they all share the important premise that justice is an artificial creation, founded on opinion and belief), and I find it interesting to see how far they can succeed in providing alternative accounts to Hobbes's story of the ways social agreement is achieved.

One great advantage of replaying the twentieth-century debate with these figures is that I will not be inclined to let the political win out too easily from a desire for institutional revenge. None of these figures was a chairman of an academic department. One cannot read, let us say, the economic arguments of Hume without feeling the excitement of newly expanded powers of social description and the strong hopes for the moral well-being of societies experiencing the social development he describes. It would be foolish to charge Hume and Burke with the decline of politics, with the "fall of public man," since they were also important theorists of political party. With Hobbes and Hume and Burke, I can sketch a schematic account of political topics useful to the interpretation of the novel. Hobbes's *Leviathan* and Burke's *Reflections on the Revolution in France* mark the limits of the historical period in which I think it makes sense to locate our canonical eighteenth-century fiction, from the English Civil War to the French Revolution, from violent political conflict to social stability that is finally viewed as an alternative to violent revolution.

One way of understanding my book is to read it as an argument that challenges Ian Watt's *Rise of the Novel.* The categories by which Watt organizes intellectual history and social history—epistemology and bourgeois culture—I reposition within political philosophy and political history. My choice of authors and works largely coincides with that of Watt, except that I devote a chapter to Sterne rather than to Fielding, and I use a text-oriented approach in defining an intellectual history as well as a history of the novel. Sterne challenges political interpretation, while the importance of politics to Fielding's concerns has never been seriously doubted.[7] I interpret the "rise" of the novel to mean not merely the production of fiction about contemporary life, but also the rise to eminence of such fiction, so that the rise to prominence of individual authors illuminates the larger subject. Literary recognition confers status and authority upon authors, and the change in their sense of authority is marked in many ways besides the formal prefaces common in eighteenth-century fiction: for example, the rise in status and authority of central characters from first novel to second novel (from Pamela to Clarissa, from Joseph Andrews and Abraham Adams to Tom Jones and Squire Allworthy).

The place of novel writing in the careers of these authors also helps define the form of the eighteenth-century novel. In contrast to many nineteenth-century novelists, none of the eighteenth-century figures earns his living by novel writing and none begins his career

[7]Recent scholarship on Fielding's politics and recent interpretations of his thematics of authority give a picture that would fit well into this book but would not substantially change its view of the political topics of the eighteenth century. See Martin C. Battestin, "Fielding, Bedford, and the Westminster Election of 1749," *Eighteenth-Century Studies* 11 (1977):143–85, and his commentary in the Wesleyan editions of *Joseph Andrews* (1967) and *Tom Jones* (1979) (both Middletown, Conn.: Wesleyan University Press); Thomas R. Cleary, *Henry Fielding: Political Writer* (Waterloo, Ont.: Wilfrid Laurier University Press, 1984); Bertrand A. Goldgar, *Walpole and the Wits* (Lincoln: University of Nebraska Press, 1976); J. Paul Hunter, *Occasional Form: Henry Fielding and the Chains of Circumstance* (Baltimore: Johns Hopkins University Press, 1975); John Sitter, *Literary Loneliness in Mid-Eighteenth Century England* (Ithaca: Cornell University Press, 1982), pp. 189–202.

with the ambition to be a novelist. Yet in the movement from Defoe to Richardson, the possibility of earning fame solely by novel writing emerges, and finally Sterne stakes his reputation as an author on a single novel, the sort of investment in a form that signals its rise to importance and dignity. All of these authors make some kind of claim to teach their audience, but they define the authority won by their talents in different ways. Often the novel defines its political authority by setting up a comparison or contrast of itself with other sorts of discourse that make direct claims of power and influence, for example, sermons, laws and arguments in courts, and political oratory, or with genres not so clearly associated with the formal exercise of power but often thought to carry even greater authority, like satire, literary criticism, conduct books, philosophy, history, and scientific narrative.

A fundamental assumption of Watt's book is the interconnection of aesthetic particularism, economic and epistemological individualism, and privatization, all of which are subsumed under the term *individualism.* The importance he ascribes to individualism in the rise of the novel underlies his choice of *Clarissa* as the definitive novelistic text. This view by implication opposes the novel categorically to discourse about public things that might have an impact on political life. In my view, the relation of the novel to the political is an animating problem continually meditated and redefined by each major eighteenth-century artist. However isolated by unusual crises, even Richardson's characters work out their intense relationships within structures of social and political authority. Richardson explores problems of family love in the context of debates, sometimes nearly murderous debates, about authority and rights, and he frequently draws analogies to national politics. Matters of family management are not necessarily considered in the eighteenth century to be disconnected from the political welfare of the nation. The interconnection of bad manners and bad government is a common topic of eighteenth-century satires, though it is more widely recognized in the novels of Fielding than in those of Richardson. Richardson's decision to place his characters among the holders of large landed estates, the chief governors of England, rather than among businessmen like himself, gives his novels resonances for public life that they would not otherwise have.

The isolation of Pamela and Clarissa is by no means merely the unconscious reflection of a social trend. Deliberate decisions to refrain from appealing to formal political authorities help characterize the morality of the heroines and shape their fates; they choose morality enforced by social opinion over morality enforced by the legal system. I link Hume's moral theory with Richardson's belief in the social power of morality diffused through moral dialogue, and I argue that Richardson's stories show the limits as well as the uses of this sort of power. The letter form, so often celebrated as the appropriate stylistic registration of psychological individualism, does not seem to me intended primarily as the representation of inner consciousness. Richardson's letters are chiefly justifications offered to a figure of authority (Pamela writes to her parents, Clarissa to a friend who claims the right to protect her reputation). Each heroine wishes to use this sense of audience to draw her conduct in line with shared standards of behavior, and in each book the whole body of the heroine's writings can function to vindicate her questionable behavior to society. In spite of opportunities to study the accumulated archives of the protagonists, questions about the "real" feelings and intentions of Richardson's characters persist, especially in the critical commentary. Far from offering unimpeded access to the "inner" character that is associated with the novel form, Richardson shows that the relentless search for true, detailed knowledge of other people can play a part in violent competition for power. For this reason I have titled the Richardson chapter "Plots of Intimate Knowledge." Debates about character in Richardson's novels reveal the explosive Hobbesian potential in the optimistic, Humean scene of moral discourse.

The case of Sterne, the teleological fulfillment of Watt's argument, also fails to support his hypothesis that reality in the novel is supposed to reside in highly individualized consciousness. The situation of *Tristram Shandy* is defined not as reality but as a scene of play, as I call it in my chapter title. In his dedication Sterne tells the statesman William Pitt to take the book, not under his protection, but into the country with him. The main characters, Toby and Walter, are in retirement from their military and commercial careers; the clergyman Yorick is not at the center of the book and is rarely seen exercising his clerical functions. The eccentricity of the characters is indulged precisely because they are explicitly set at a distance from the exercise of any powerful authority. This is not Pope's retreat at Twickenham; Shandy Hall is a long way from London. The impotence of characters provides both pathos and charm. Things that in another context would be dangerous (for example, reading out an excommunication) are in this book harmless and amusing. The implication about English society at large which the book conveys is that there is room for play, because someone else (Pitt, for example) is running things, and further, that society is settled and stable enough so that there is a great deal of room for play in every life. The Catholic Dr. Slop comfortably falls asleep during the account of the horrors of the Inquisition in the sermon on conscience, and at the end he admits the sermon's aesthetic values. As originally delivered by Sterne, this sermon figured in the anti-Catholic propaganda intended to consolidate the nation against the Jacobites, but in the context of *Tristram Shandy* this function is attenuated. In the novel the sermon merely suggests that the scene of play is limited: some matters are crucial and subject to religious law interpreted by public regulation, rather than personal whimsy; but at the same time the contrast of the novel to the seriousness of the sermon defines a large place for play. The feeling of security proceeds in part from the sense that since the state is settled, Christian controversy has very limited interest to any of the parties involved (a view no doubt more comfortable for Anglicans than for Catholics and Dissenters).

The national settlement seems to allow Sterne what Hobbes denied, a stable, nonpolitical realm, not a private world of the self, but a leisure space for reading and writing which could never be troubled by questions of power. I am tempted to link Sterne with the invention of the aesthetic and the separation between art and politics which characterizes our own institutional situation, but this set of assumptions was not fully available to Sterne. Defining a special place for his art was a challenge to his strategic resources. Law, religion, politics, and war are invoked in order to differentiate these concerns from his novels. Even so he was not content to define his fiction as purely playful. In *A Sentimental Journey* he puts his clergyman at the center of the book (even though the clergyman is on holiday), and he more clearly links the capacity for play with the sort of moral imagination that can appreciate the value of an enemy's culture. Nostalgia in both of Sterne's novels for old-fashioned militarism at once defines the impractical, leisured atmosphere and operates as a repository of imagery for the confused politics of "patriotism" in the 1750s and 1760s. Hobbes had made a relatively modest trial of developing the aesthetics of political loyalty in the beautiful frontispiece to *Leviathan*. His presentation of the sovereign representative as an actor, the person of the state, implies the importance of the imagery of political identification. And he would have understood the vulnerability of treasured national imagery to appropriation by opposed political groups around Pitt, King George, and finally John Wilkes. Burke's reactionary nostalgia for customary associations, his elevation of English prejudices, forms an interesting parallel to Sterne's eccentricity and shows the decisive transformation of mid-eighteenth-century materials in the politically polarized revolutionary era.

Surveying one topic that I introduce in the Hobbes chapter—the power of naming—can help sketch the shape of the chapters that follow. One of Ian Watt's more interesting ideas is that the novel form is marked by the use of proper names, a sign in his view of the allegiance of the form to unique, individual experience. Identifying people by name is a matter charged with political significance of many sorts. Names, titles of honor, sometimes the absence of names, serve as signs of status and power in a society and as such can become sources of conflict. Hobbes was especially concerned to subject titles of honor to public regulation. Robinson Crusoe's expanded power on his island, which approached the power of Hobbes's sovereign, is shown by his expanded power of naming, granting himself titles ("lord of the manor," "king," or "emperor" to himself, "master" to Friday, and as Europeans appear and his authority is more confined again, he becomes "governor" for a short time). "Friday" is a name Crusoe has imposed, and it is an even more obvious exercise of arbitrary authority because Crusoe may have lost count of the days in the calendars of established nations. The conversion of Friday is not only an act of Christian charity which confirms Crusoe's own conversion, it is also an exercise of sovereign power, that authoritative regulation of the forms for honoring the deity which Hobbes had considered an essential part of sovereignty. So Friday's deity Benamuckee is renamed God and Christ.

The interest in the power of creating names is typical of what I identify as the central concern of Defoe's fiction, political creativity. Hobbes had both appealed to the reader's imagination for creating a more powerful artifice of society and had argued that this creativity must be radically limited in any stable state. Defoe, who as a dissenter was more than usually restricted in the exercise of formal political power, exploited with extraordinary zest many informal means of power: personal advice to kings and ministers, popular journalism, petitions, demonstrations, and rumors. The economic power that so many critics have thought to be Defoe's only concern was chiefly interesting to him as a means to political power. He represented the sort of subject Hobbes thought dangerous to sovereignty, the person inappropriately interested in the direction of the state. He was fascinated by the risks and opportunities in situations of political indeterminacy, like those that arise in overseas trade and colonization or in street demonstrations. Anonymity and the flexible assumption of different names aid the strategies for expanding one's power. Moll Flanders, the daughter of an unknown thief, lacks a name, and so it is easy for her to change her name. Even the reader never learns her name (neither the name of her mother nor of her last husband), only that she eventually attains, along with riches, a legal and respectable name as a landholder and wife in Virginia. The impersonations that characterize Defoe's journalism and fiction suggest that writing itself had for him the attractive indeterminate quality of allowing creations that might or might not have authoritative power over others, that might or might not be subject to political sanction, that he might or might not want attached to his own name.

The protracted conflicts in Richardson's *Pamela* and *Clarissa* could be understood as debates about the meaning of status words (*daughter, servant, father, master, suitor, husband, wife*) and as debates about the rules of behavior appropriate to each status. At stake is the possibility of losing one's name, not only the respect of society but even one's status. The ways the names of Pamela and Clarissa become legendary within their stories illustrate the importance of reputation to the fiction itself. When the good name of a Richardson heroine is threatened, her most characteristic means of power, the power of respected moral speech, must be safeguarded in elaborate ways by the power of the novel.

In *Tristram Shandy* the elaborate joking about the significance of names typifies the scene of play. The disaster of Tristram's name, brought about by confusions in the exercise of authority, causes pain to his father only, and only because of the oddity of his ideas. Other family members and the readers, more or less amused, develop sympathy for Walter's egregious suffering out of "compleasance," as Hobbes called his fifth law of nature, the striving of each person to accommodate the diversity of other people's affections. Hobbes worried about the irregular stones that might take up too much space in the edifice of state, but Sterne shows how to enjoy what is picturesque in Gothic irregularity of social architecture, his household of eccentrics. His recycling of odd old names (Tristram, Yorick, Ernulphus, Stevinus) shows the power of his fiction to convert reading to recreation.

Debates about the status of moral language and the language of honor engage the fundamental issues at stake in the shift from political philosophy to the social sciences and the history of societies. Hume agrees with Hobbes that moral language has no natural meanings, but he argues that it develops with widespread social interaction over time, not by the arbitrary impositions of clearly identifiable authorities. In the *Reflections* Burke sanctifies the gradual, at times irrational, growth of social creations as the necessary culture for stable government. Although Burke resuscitates religious imagery that suggests a mysterious and wise providential order in nature, the Hobbesian recognition of the basis of society in fragile human artifice underlies Burke's sensitive fears of a radical political revolution. Burke views the disrespect for title and marks of honors in France as a horrifying indication of social rending, the exercise of political authority that cannot, or at any rate should not, found a state.

I hope that this brief survey of my chapters shows that political interpretation based on pre-twentieth-century philosophy need not be blind to language or take it as a natural fact. If we want to develop a political thematics, the best theoretical move may be to approach language through a comprehensive moral and political theory rather than to append politics to a theory of language. Since the modern linguistics that has influenced new literary theory achieved much of its conceptual rigor by considering language as a system unto itself, a critic who wants to make political use of some feature of linguistic theory must elaborate it in complex and often unconvincing ways. The result may not be a more comprehensive social and literary analysis unified by language theory, but only an ingenious eclecticism that draws a variety of analogies among, let us say, linguistics and semiotics, Marxism and Freudianism. This analogical method offers many illuminations and has invigorated literary criticism, but it has also burdened criticism with a baroque mixture of different theoretical vocabularies which only the most adept can manage without a drastic loss of precision and which threatens to draw us even farther from any general audience.[8] I sympathize with the motivation behind this sort of theoretical criticism, which I see as the wish (perhaps an impossible project) to restore the comprehensiveness of the older moral philosophy without losing the gains made by the sharp theoretical distinctions of modern science and philosophy. But assembling a politics in this fashion has persistent theoretical weaknesses, the most important of which is the tendency in all the movements that feed current literary theory to underestimate the role of political institutions.[9]

[8]The most adept is certainly Fredric Jameson, who has the rare virtue of always analyzing the weakness of each element that he assimilates into his mixture. See *The Political Unconscious: Narrative as a Socially Symbolic Act* (Ithaca: Cornell University Press, 1981), esp. chap. 1.

[9]I have further addressed this issue in current criticism in "On the Verge of Politics: Border Tactics for Eighteenth-Century English Studies," *boundary 2* 12, no. (1984):197–215.

Most recently Michael McKeon has published an ambitious new work, *The Origins of the English Novel, 1600–1740* (Baltimore: Johns Hopkins University Press, 1986), which complicates the historical framework and expands the historical picture offered by Ian Watt, while preserving the dominance of epistemology and social theory and the subordination of political theory and political history that I have criticized. McKeon's work appeared after my book was complete, so that I do not give it the chapter-by-chapter attention it deserves. A schematic comparison, however, may be useful.

*The Origins of the English Novel* presents a "dialectical theory of genre" that accounts for the emergence of the monolithic category of the novel from diverse narrative modes. The enabling historical foundation of the novel for McKeon is the attempt to resolve analogous instabilities of epistemological and social categories, the crisis in the representation of "truth" and the crisis in the representation of "virtue." By contrast with McKeon's attempt at a comprehensive synthesis, my work should be seen as primarily critical in intent. I explore selective structures of power and authority, and with the aid of politically oriented theory and the evidence of political history, I push back on his sort of socially oriented synthesis.

In my Hobbesian analysis the particular instabilities McKeon describes can be placed among many others that require the political solution of consent to authority.

This book is an exercise in thinking with the categories I have drawn from a range of British political philosophy and British political history. It should be seen as parallel to and in some ways competitive with the political interpretation that has emerged from literary theory. The practitioner of "new new criticism" could find in this book some favorite topics and might be challenged by seeing them developed in a different idiom and in a different order of thought. I share with many critics an interest in social construction which includes questioning the coherence and continuity of constructions. I also share the hope that modern philosophy and science can be understood and used in ways that enhance the democratic potential of modern society, but I do not think that these good uses will be inevitable outgrowths of prior theory or social forms; they will be our laborious constructions.

Of all the movements that have recently nourished democratic hopes, feminism has affected my life most dramatically. Although this book is not a contribution to women's studies in the usual sense,

---

The specifically seventeenth-century crisis that the eighteenth-century structures (including the novel) "resolve" is civil war, for which category instabilities of many sorts provide inflammatory materials. Though we judge different institutions to be "dominant," I should emphasize that in my view the power of political institutions of governance must be understood in the dialectical way McKeon understands the power of economic institutions of production: that is, as complex historical organizations of social relations, not as simple causes that culture simply reflects.

McKeon's seventeenth-century focus biases his account of the novel in the direction of instability and against the growth of eighteenth-century stability that I detail. This bias leads him to underestimate the consolidation of aristocratic and Anglican power. McKeon looks to the large-scale social changes of capitalism, even though he acknowledges the limited applicability of this model to the eighteenth century. By contrast, my methods allow more weight to decade-by-decade political experience.

*The Origins of the English Novel* is especially weak when it frames accounts of "instabilities" into abstract narratives: "naive empiricism" challenges "romance idealism" and is in turn challenged by "extreme scepticism," which restores elements of romance idealism; "progressive ideology" challenges "aristocratic ideology" and is in turn challenged by "conservative ideology," which restores elements of aristocratic ideology. Almost all these terms derive from the vocabulary of nineteenth-century reaction against the Enlightenment, and they anachronistically project onto the earlier period the political polarization that occurred after the French Revolution; such anachronism tends to undermine the historical usefulness of McKeon's impressive erudition. My political construction, a combined canon of political philosophy and novelistic fiction, cannot provide a base broad enough for a comprehensive history, but it can serve to pry apart a critical consensus, nearly two centuries old, which obscures the philosophical interest and continuing relevance of these earlier writers.

it has something to say in every chapter about the role of gender typing in political conceptualization in philosophy and fiction. The identification of male novelists with female protagonists is fundamental to the whole history of the novel, and I link it with the modern revolution in moral philosophy which displaces the male soldier-citizen of the classical republic. The identification of women with nongovernmental forms of power, including the power of the novel itself, is important in the Defoe and Richardson chapters. In the Sterne and Burke sections, I treat a process that I have named "remasculinization," by which modern, "refined" men yearn for the vigorous militarism of a more sexually segregated society, while also competing with women for the prestige of civilized sensitivity. My use of Hobbes is inspired in part by a desire to ground in new ways the feminist arguments against the rigid opposition of public and private and by a desire to sustain specifically political activism within the feminist movement. Hobbes may help us take the state seriously, even though we take it in directions he would have feared.[10]

For citizens of the United States, who customarily evaluate political well-being in a language of rights, Hobbes is strong medicine—poison, some would say—and to adapt his insights for democratic theory as I seek to do will seem Quixotic at best.[11] But the British institutions thought to have inspired ours lack a foundational Bill of Rights, and the resulting differences in political conceptualization are pervasive. To recognize that our political culture is historically founded and that it grew in conjunction with a particular arrangement of sovereignty is to develop a Hobbesian perspective on anti-Hobbesian institutions. This perspective lacks familiar bound-

[10]The state generally appears in contemporary feminist theory as an agency of patriarchal oppression. In contrast to practical feminist efforts to use governmental means of reform, feminist theory has paid little attention to constructing a positive theory of the state. Nancy Fraser provides a hopeful new model in her critical adaptations of Habermas for feminist theory and oppositional welfare-state politics. See Fraser, "What's Critical about Critical Theory?: The Case of Habermas and Gender," in *New German Critique*, no. 35 (1985), pp. 97–132, and "Social Movements vs. Disciplinary Bureaucracies: The Discourses of Social Needs," Center for Humanistic Studies, University of Minnesota, Occasional Papers, Number 8.

[11]An interesting predecessor in this attempt is John Dewey, "The Motivation of Hobbes's Political Philosophy," reprinted in *Thomas Hobbes and His Time*, ed. Ralph Ross, Herbert W. Schneider, and Theodore Waldman (Minneapolis: University of Minnesota Press, 1974), pp. 8–30.

aries. It deprives us of the assurance that the political constructions we cherish are natural and inevitable, but it opens a wider vista of possibility for transforming old constructions and creating new ones. Feminist politics shows that improvements in equality and democracy require a dynamic understanding of politics. For a new recognition of human needs and desires we need not only a fair application of existing laws but also new laws, new kinds of laws, and new concepts of law in relation to other sorts of power.

# CHAPTER ONE

# *Political Analysis: The Model of Hobbes*

By MANNERS, I mean not here, Decency of behaviour; as how one man should salute another, or how a man should wash his mouth, or pick his teeth before company, and such other points of the *Small Moralls*; But those qualities of man-kind, that concern their living together in Peace, and Unity.

*Leviathan*, I, 11, 160

## Hobbesian Literary History

Reflections about civil war in Britain and the dangerous disputes about political authority which continued in the eighteenth century inspired many of the most talented authors to investigate "those qualities of man-kind, that concern their living together in Peace, and Unity." For this reason I take the philosophy of Hobbes not only as an influence on a particular discourse—political philosophy—but more important, as a provocation for reexamining the familiar themes of literary history. The history of the novel is particularly challenging, since the novel is now commonly associated with private, rather than public, life; with a social, rather than a political, order. We tend to think of the "political novel" as a special type, a risky hybrid, rather than part of the main tradition. A philosophically and historically enlarged understanding of politics is necessary before we can see the ways in which concern about the political order shaped fiction that is not usually classified as political. For this reason I have chosen to focus on Defoe, Richardson, and Sterne rather than on Fielding and Smollett.

In Britain of the seventeenth and eighteenth centuries there were some striking resemblances in the rhetorical situations of authors whom we have canonized in segregated pantheons as novelists and political philosophers. Their ambitions seem at once breathtaking and deeply troubled. Could the scrutiny of mundane, unheroic human behavior make the basis of an enduring book, a route to literary greatness? We may now answer in the affirmative for them, but we hesitate for our own time, not simply because we feel reduced by them to the status of aftercomers, but also because the problems that threatened them have not disappeared. Political practice so often presents a scene of degraded and trivialized relationships, including the debasement of language, that we tend to set it apart from what we greatly value. Yet politics is also the ground of our most heroic ambitions for great and lasting achievements, for human fulfillment in a good society. The political philosopher like Hobbes, who seeks to make of his subject an immortal book, engages in the redemption of politics in more than one sense.[1] This challenge resembles that of the novelist, who seeks to transmute the unheroic topics of everyday life into enduring art. A whiff of scandal, a tone of defensive justification, cannot be dispelled from these high enterprises. Their authors are in constant danger of being identified with the hack producers of such daily wastepaper as election propaganda, gossipy memoirs, adventure fantasies, plodding advice books. Their continual reference to common experience and the relevance of their books to practical decisions bind the attention of a wide audience but also raise up a host of critics who seek to protect the audience from such dangerous books. No wonder if modern novelists and political theorists withdrew from the claims of popularity or from the claims of immortality or from both kinds of ambition at once.

The term *masterpiece* has a dangerously elitist tone to modern democratic ears, and it has excused many lamentable omissions and distortions in our studies. But even a rectified, anticanonical historicism should allow a place for an account of the rise and fall of recognized ambition. So it seems appropriate to frame my analysis of political philosophy, as I do my analyses of novelistic fiction, by reference to particular canonized works. With the development of impressive scholarship on the history of political thought, the emphasis on masterpieces of political philosophy has been hotly debated in ways reminiscent of the old contest between scholars and critics in English departments.[2] I can no more claim to present through attention to a few major authors and major texts a comprehensive history of political thought than I can claim to offer a comprehensive account of eighteenth-century fiction. Nevertheless, I can through my

[1]For the irony of Hobbes's heroic ambition and his unheroic view of human life, see Sheldon S. Wolin, *Hobbes and the Epic Tradition of Political Theory* (Los Angeles: Clark Memorial Library, 1970).

[2]See the battle cry for a new history of political thought by Quentin Skinner, "Meaning and Understanding in the History of Ideas," *History and Theory* 8 (1969).

methods suggest some features of a more sweeping history of the period between the English and the French revolutions.

It is no accident that my framing texts of political thought, Hobbes's *Leviathan* and Burke's *Reflections on the Revolution in France*, were written in response to revolution. Revolutionary movements call for an expanded sense of politics, one that comprehends—or imagines, since a comprehensive view may envision more than any of us can know—a great variety of behaviors and beliefs while it imagines comprehensive change. Depending on the view of the observer, revolutionaries either penetrate to the political matter widespread in society or they pollute society with it; in any case, the view is transformed. This linkage, however, of political insight with revolutionary politics can become another reason that politics seems segregated and specialized in our ordinary understanding of social reality. "Political art" is commonly interchangeable with "radical" or "revolutionary" art. Irving Howe's *Politics and the Novel* announces its limitations when the author tells us that its title could have been "Revolutionary Politics and the Novel"—it might have been more revealing to say "Failed Revolutionary Politics and the Novel." The repeated modern treatment of disappointed revolutions makes Howe's chosen political novels seem faithful to the politics we understand, and perhaps because we read our history that way, such failures seem more novelistic than any imaginable novel of revolutionary success. I hope to do something more fundamental than supply the supplement Howe suggests, an account of those novels that portray "the normal interplay of group conflicts . . . regulated by democratic procedures,"[3] which would only reproduce the historical and institutional restrictions that trivialize our understanding of politics. To reread the fiction of Defoe, Richardson, and Sterne with the insights afforded by Hobbes is to test the continuing relevance of the revelations of a revolutionary time for a more stable society, and it is also to perceive social stability not as a given but as a goal, ardently pursued and arduously maintained, by authors as well as by other authorities. Burke extends and exemplifies these perceptions, but in ways that follow Hume in fundamentally transforming the Hobbesian heritage.

[3]Irving Howe, *Politics and the Novel* (1957; Greenwich, Conn.: Fawcett, 1967), p. x.

"Hobbesian heritage" strikes an appropriately hollow note, since the extent of Hobbes's influence by any strict standard of evidence is hard to measure.[4] Citing Hobbes with approval would have provoked censure, and on the other hand the common expressions of anti-Hobbesian fervor did not necessarily represent the fruit of careful study. Particular motifs that we recognize as Hobbesian in a text might have many possible sources. Because Hobbes's response to the political crises of the post-Reformation era was profound and not limited to the occasions of a few decades, his work can help us to develop the concepts of a historical period and thus make possible new kinds of particular descriptions. My choice of Hobbes rests on an even greater claim for his value. His analysis of the political component of social life laid out crucial problems for all of us who have followed, even though we disagree with him. Meditating on these problems and on the systematic relationship he gave them can improve our thinking whenever we wish to understand the world politically.

The strength of taking a single systematic account as our model of analysis, our source of political topics, is that when we find an author differing from Hobbes on some issue he considered crucial to his system, we will be alert to the far-reaching significance of the difference and stand ready to assess the power of imagination necessary for creating an alternative vision. Many readers who value novelistic fiction, that is, fiction that probes the minds of individualized characters who work out their relations in lifelike settings, consider that their favorite books offer an important challenge to the sort of universal system Hobbes intended to construct. An improved sense of what is at stake in the much-praised "inner view" of character that novels seem to offer will make us more careful to specify what sort of "view" particular novels offer and what sort of claims they put forward about the significance of their views.

[4]S. I. Mintz has collected evidence of the widespread outrage provoked by Hobbes, but Quentin Skinner has done a great deal to substantiate a widespread influence for Hobbes's theory. We need more research on the place of Hobbes in the political arguments of the century after he wrote. See S. I. Mintz, *The Hunting of Leviathan* (Cambridge: Cambridge University Press, 1962); and Skinner, "The Context of Hobbes's Theory of Political Obligation" (1966), revised in *Hobbes and Rousseau: A Collection of Critical Essays*, ed. Maurice Cranston and Richard S. Peters (Garden City, N.Y.: Doubleday, 1972), pp. 109–42.

## Character

New motives for description can affect the ways we value literature of the past. Twentieth-century readers, fully as interested in human psychology and behavior as were the authors of the seventeenth and eighteenth centuries, are often made uneasy by the emphasis on broad psychological laws in fiction that has at first seemed to present a recognizable world of ordinarily flawed characters, detailed contemporary scenes, and complicated narrators. The familiar conclusion from this frustration is that we have found an "early" modern period, crude in its first halting steps toward our favorite preoccupations, given to "overgeneralization," or lacking imagination for individual variation. Scholars try to correct this biased history, but in arguing for study of the past in its own terms seem committed to a radical separation between the past and the present. Even the most persuasively sympathetic scholars of the literary conventions or the "intellectual background" of an earlier period can short-circuit the curiosity and appreciation that could eventually flow from the perception of difference. The Christian world view, traditions of spiritual autobiography, satire, comedy, and picaresque, among others, have been invoked to explain why eighteenth-century fiction appeals to modern taste and then frustrates it. But explanations, if they are good ones, should not explain away. Putting the intellectual background into the foreground can help us respect the intelligence of past writers.

Hobbes deliberately chooses to write a science of generalized tendencies rather than a handbook for the study of particular individuals. He is not unimaginative about human difference; he founds his philosophy on a radical assumption about individuality: we vary so much from one another that individual intentions can never be reliably understood, cannot be known with the certainty necessary to form a firm foundation for political decisions. The Introduction to *Leviathan* directly rejects political wisdom based on knowingness about individuals, the courtier's special experience that might be associated with the views of Machiavelli or Bacon: "He that is to govern a whole Nation, must read in himself, not this or that particular man; but Man-kind" (Introduction, 83).[5] Readers of novels should be alert to the political interconnection between characterization and plot, the link between modes of understanding other people and the social narrative, the consolidation of a stable society or its distintegration. Because of this link the relation of narrator or implied author to audience comes under scrutiny in ways applicable to the rising ambition of fiction writers as well as to those of moral philosophers. Political philosophy according to Hobbes is not a specialist's enterprise. Anyone can check his general description by personal reflection, but no one can develop reliable insight into the particular directions passions take in individuals:

> for these the constitution individuall, and particular education do so vary, and they are so easie to be kept from our knowledge, that the characters of mans heart, blotted and confounded as they are, with dissembling, lying, counterfeiting, and erroneous doctrines, are legible onely to him that searcheth hearts. And though by mens actions wee do discover their designe sometimes; yet to do it without comparing them with our own, and distinguishing all circumstances, by which the case may come to be altered, is to decypher without a key, and be for the most part deceived, by too much trust, or by too much diffidence; as he that reads, is himself a good or evil man. [Introduction, 83]

Because we cannot read hearts, it makes sense for Hobbes to write about the passions in a chapter about manners. Hobbes's concern is not internal experience of feelings in themselves, but how people read one another, how motives are interpreted. Such interpretation will never amount to certain knowledge; it will always be a matter of debatable, uncertain opinion. In the introduction Hobbes directs the reader not to look knowingly at others, but to look inward. However, he reinterprets the injunction *nosce teipsum* to signify not self-scrutiny that leads to an independence from the opinions of others, but the sort of inward look that will discover the similarity of the passions in all people. Hobbes reworks the concept of "conscience" in a similar way: the original meaning, he insists, was shared knowl-

[5]My attention was drawn to this passage by Paul Cantor in a class on seventeenth-century literature at Harvard University, 1972–73. I owe a debt to this class, although I believe that Professor Cantor was trying to instill disapproval of Hobbes, rather than the enthusiasm that I contracted.

edge, and the word is applied only metaphorically to mean knowledge of "secret facts and secret thoughts" (I, 7, 132). Inner life that is entirely individual or private is politically irrelevant. In this sense, freedom of thought is ineradicable. But to found political action on the authority of one's private thoughts is as untrustworthy as to found it on crafty knowingness about other people: in each case sharing settled convictions about the inner life of individuals is an impossibility.

As the first part of *Leviathan* proceeds to read human nature, we learn more reasons why government cannot be founded on the knowledge of other people's minds, guided by clever people who have special insight. ". . . as for the knowledge of Fact . . . is originally, Sense and ever after, Memory" (I, 7, 131). No one can have direct sensation of another person's thoughts or feelings; they must be inferred from external signs. Furthermore, this judgment of character involves prediction about the future, which is unavoidably uncertain:

> The *Present* onely has a being in Nature; things *Past* have a being in the Memory onely, but things *to come* have no being at all; the *Future* being but a fiction of the mind, applying the sequels of actions Past, to the actions that are Present; which with most certainty is done by him that has most Experience; but not with certainty enough. And though it be called Prudence when the Event answereth our Expectation; yet in its own nature, it is but Presumption. [I, 3, 97]

An important part of Hobbes's project is to demystify prudence, foresight, wisdom, or prophecy; all are presumption. Not special powers of the mind, but simple frequency of experience makes "the best guesser," and this sort of guessing is a capacity shared with other animals. Science, the specifically human skills of naming, definition, and logical connection of propositions, leads to many wide-sweeping and reliable expectations; nevertheless, it amounts to only conditional knowledge of fact:[6] "No man can know by Dis-

[6]For Hobbes's scientific method, see M. M. Goldsmith, *Hobbes's Science of Politics* (New York: Columbia University Press, 1966); and J.W.N. Watkins, *Hobbes's System of Ideas* (London: Hutchinson, 1965). Although Hobbes tends to restrict the term *science* to matters of certain knowledge, and although he has political reasons for emphasizing the fallibility of all predictions or prophecies, his skepticism actually enlarges the importance of probable knowledge or prudence. Recent literary histories that emphasize probable reasoning in eighteenth-century aesthetic theory and

course, that this, or that, is, has been, or will be; which is to know absolutely: but onely, that if This be, That is; if This has been, That has been; if This shall be, That shall be: which is to know conditionally; and that not the consequence of one thing to another; but of one name of a thing, to another name of the same thing" (I, 7, 131). In a treatise that also seeks to found a science of politics on skeptical arguments, David Hume will brilliantly develop the distinction between matters of fact and relations of ideas that Hobbes has sketched. The development of epistemology has too often been detached from the history of moral and political philosophy, and studies of the novel which make links to philosophy typically perpetuate this error.[7]

One general portrait of human character will suffice Hobbes because there are no natural leaders: the radical limits on knowledge affect everyone. Even when people are convinced of their own superior prudence or science or inspiration by God, they are confronted by the impossibility of directly sharing this conviction with others. Prediction, even by the experienced, can always fail, since to "remember all circumstances that may alter the successe, is impossible" (I, 5, 117). The most convincing signs of science, the ability to demonstrate one's reasoning to another, depends on the degree of science in the minds of the judges: "The Sciences, are

---

practice fit well into the general pattern of my historical argument and can help to detail the historical picture that I schematize. See Eric Rothstein, *Systems of Order and Inquiry in Later Eighteenth-Century Fiction* (Berkeley: University of California Press, 1975); and Douglas Lane Patey, *Probability and Literary Form: Philosophic Theory and Literary Practice in the Augustan Age* (Cambridge: Cambridge University Press, 1984).

[7]Annotation throughout the succeeding chapters will have to carry the burden of this sweeping claim, but I will offer one particularly engaging example. A. D. Nuttall defines the really exciting problem of empiricism as solipsism and offers modern philosophy of language as its solution. Nuttall raises the arguments of Norman Kemp Smith about Hume's moral "naturalism," and he admits their plausibility, but he returns nonetheless to the skeptical arguments of Book One of Hume's *Treatise* because if we take Kemp Smith's view, Nuttall cries, "philosophy is forgotten." See Nuttall, *A Common Sky* (Berkeley: University of California Press, 1974), p. 97. Thus philosophy has been diminished to a few problems in epistemology. See also Norman Kemp Smith, *The Philosophy of David Hume: A Critical Study of Its Origins and Central Doctrines* (London: Macmillan, 1941), which has been fundamental for all later work on the constructive elements of Hume's philosophy and opens the way to understanding his history, politics, and aesthetics.

small Power; because not eminent; and therefore, not acknowledged in any man; nor are at all, but in a few; and in them, but of few things. For Science is of that nature, as none can understand it to be, but such as in a good measure have attayned it" (1, 10, 151). Even less do the signs of divine inspiration create superiority, since the only trustworthy signs of inspiration are those that conform to teachings of settled authority.

Whatever the natural differences in mental ability among people, the essential political problem and the main reason for human equality is the opinion of people about one another's wisdom. The perceptual system, given more physiological detail in Hobbes's other treatises, seems to necessitate vanity: one *knows* one's own wisdom; other people's wisdom is conjectural:

> For such is the nature of men, that howsoever they may acknowledge many others to be more witty, or more eloquent, or more learned; Yet they will hardly believe there be many so wise as themselves: For they see their own wit at hand, and other mens at a distance. But this proveth rather that men are in that point equall, than unequall. For there is not ordinarily a greater signe of the equall distribution of any thing, than that every man is contented with his share. [1, 13, 184]

What a delightful example of Hobbes's reading of the human heart! Intellectual vanity, the internal sense of superiority, is interpreted as a sign of equality. Reading general nature in oneself is an exercise in humility. Yet the impudent boldness of the philosopher seems to contradict the antiheroic lesson of humility. Skepticism poses special problems for the rhetoric of philosophy. The complex irony of the mock heroic is one resource, one temptation, of the skeptical philosopher or novelist who leads our charge into brick walls. Locke loved to allude to Don Quixote, who reminds us that the mock heroic and the mock pedantic often combine. Hobbes sallies forth at his best against commentators on great books of all sorts: on the common law, on ancient history, but especially against the vain "school-men" who found a "Kingdome of Darknesse" on Aristotle and the Bible.

Knowledge, shrunken to the small range of sense perception and memory, cannot serve as a complete guide to life, and indeed, in Hobbes's scene, human beings are creatures of appetite and aversion. Desire and fear regulate the "traynes of imagination": "From

Desire, ariseth the Thought of some means we have seen to produce the like of that which we ayme at: and from the thought of that, the thought of means to that mean; and so continually, till we come to some beginning within our own power" (I, 3, 95–96). Though beasts share with humans the aptitude for prudence, inquiry into causes, humans have a special, broad curiosity about the effects of anything imagined, a kind of curiosity not tied to immediate, practical needs: "for this is a curiosity hardly incident to the nature of any living creature that has no other Passion but sensuall, such as are hunger, thirst, lust and anger" (I, 3, 96).

The passions in humans are remarkably future oriented. Anxiety about preserving and safeguarding pleasures in the uncertain future fixes the attention on presumptions, fictions of the mind, rather than on present sensation, the only source of certain knowledge. The uncertainty of the future removes any possibility of a natural limit to desire; there is no *summum bonum* for the species or for individuals: "Felicity is a continuall progresse of the desire, from one object to another; the attaining of the former, being still but the way to the later. The cause whereof is, That the object of mans desire, is not to enjoy once onely, and for one instant of time; but to assure for ever, the way of his future desire" (I, 11, 160–61). Human desire is voracious, not because of the unsatisfying quality of pleasure or the impossibility of moderate enjoyment of pleasure, but because of the impossibility of security: "So that in the first place, I put for a generall inclination of all mankind, a perpetuall and restlesse desire of Power after power, that ceaseth onely in Death. And the cause of this, is not alwayes that a man hopes for a more intensive delight, than he has already attained to; or that he cannot be content with a moderate power: but because he cannot assure the power and means to live well, which he hath present, without the acquisition of more" (I, 11, 161).

Uncertainty about the course of nature alone would motivate anxious provision, but uncertainty about other people intensifies the dilemma. The restless seeking after power over the future provides an incentive to add the power of other people to one's own power, but without a settled agreement about sovereign authority, this ambition leads to fearful competition. Without a sovereign, the anxious, future-oriented nature of the passions would produce a state of war, without any extraordinary degree of greed or malice in human nature.

Hobbes's image of competition is not an economic model of competition for scarce natural resources, so that by developing insight into economic organization Hume, Smith, and Burke cannot see through Hobbes. Even in Locke's scene of society without government, a small population of subsistence farmers living on an abundance of land, the plot of the war of all against all is likely if one adds Hobbes's awareness of human anxiety. The desire to provide for the uncertain future and to secure oneself and one's property from equally anxious neighbors prevents purely economic arrangements from creating social peace unless there is a political settlement. The political settlement changes most crucially not the physical conditions of society but expectations, opinions about other people. The state of war is not so much a condition of literal unrelieved fighting as it is a condition of opinions about the future and about other people:

> For WARRE, consisteth not in Battell onely, or the act of fighting; but in a tract of time, wherein the Will to contend by Battell is sufficiently known: and therefore the notion of *Time*, is to be considered in the nature of Warre; as it is in the nature of Weather. For as the nature of Foul weather, lyeth not in a showre or two of rain; but in an inclination thereto of many dayes together: so the nature of War, consisteth not in actuall fighting; but in the known disposition thereto, during all the time there is no assurance to the contrary. All other time is PEACE. [I, 13, 185–86]

Pausing to examine this passage provides opportunity once again to enjoy the comic resourcefulness of Hobbes's skeptical analysis. The analogy of war to bad weather is a diminishing comparison that furthers the antiheroic aims of the work. The skeptic places human nature firmly within, not beyond, the rest of nature; he has compared human reasoning to the reasoning of animals and has found the human margin of skill in anticipation a grave danger. Yet the danger is without honor: we are deprived of the perception of war as a time for eminence, a critical opportunity to separate valuable from dishonorable intentions. No special mental or physical talents of any individual can resolve the war of all against all. The humiliation, however, is humorous and brings relief by stripping the scene of dishonor as well as of honor: "The Desires, and other Passions of man, are in themselves no Sin. No more are the Actions, that proceed from those Passions, till they know a Law that forbids them: which till Lawes be made they cannot know: nor can any Law be made, till they have agreed upon the Person that shall make it" (I, 13, 187).

As readers who do live under laws that generally forbid "invasions," we are habituated to disapproval. We never entirely abandon that attitude, and the odd contrast of our disapproving associations with the neutrality recommended by Hobbes heightens the sense of refreshment, of being on holiday, that the fiction of a world without law arouses. The flavor of disapproval reassures us that we are not without law, nor about to suffer the dreadful consequences of lawlessness. The pleasure the reader experiences in a scene of right to all things serves also as a proof of the passions, the sort of reading human nature in oneself which Hobbes recommends in the Introduction. The mixture of humor with disapproval could, and we have evidence that it did in many readers, shift in the direction of anger against Hobbes. Is it only his own peculiar nature that led to this theory? The generality of the theory, the conjectural nature of the description, is the major protection against moral disapproval. Gravity returns when Hobbes reminds his readers of the experiential models of society without a sovereign, especially when he mentions the analogy closest to home: civil war.

War resembles bad weather because both are founded on opinions about the future, not on certain perceptions of fact. Predictions about the weather are notoriously unreliable, but it is the nature of all opinions to be unrealistic, since no past experience is an adequate foundation for assurance. So there is no guarantee that these opinions will ever change: the Londoner feels justified in carrying an umbrella every day. Opinions about war, like many other opinions about people, have another reason for persistence, since they can create the fact that has been presumed. But precisely because opinion can be cut free from past experience, it may be flexible rather than intransigent. The humiliating limitations on human reason may be comic not because of the repeated, mechanical frustration of prudence by prudence, but because of a happy outcome, the creation of a new opinion. The unrealistic nature of the passions, their divorce from the certainties and pleasures of the present, is fostered for good or ill by a specifically human creation: language.

## Language

Hobbes first formally introduces language as an aid to presumption (I, 3, 98–99). In Chapter Four of Part I, "Of Speech," Hobbes identifies four major uses of speech: first, as an aid to the memory of conclusions about causes and effects, that is, to increase one's own range of presumption; second, to teach one's reasoning and presumption to others; and third, as signs of one's will, that is, to stimulate the presumptions of other people about oneself in order to gain their help. The fourth use of speech opens up a channel for human creativity rarely explored in *Leviathan*: "to please and delight our selves, and others, by playing with our words, for pleasure or ornament, innocently" (I, 4, 102). It is surprising to stumble across this notion of play in a work that seems to attach the concept of artifice exclusively to creations of power and authority. The analogy of the fine arts will be increasingly important to successors of Hobbes who are in search of a model of disinterested social pleasure, a model of society without an absolute sovereignty but also without contention. Hobbes does not tell us enough about play to discriminate it clearly from other motives. Indeed, for many theorists, play is generally purposive experience relevant to the use of power, like Hobbes's explanation of laughter as a "sudden glory."

The most powerful aid to reasoning that words give is generality. Experience is particular, but names and propositions made up of names can be universal. Language is irremediably social. Its generality is the means by which we convey our experience to others, whether experience of nature or of our own passions. But the social functions of generality can foster contention, since the generality of language implies a claim over other people, the claim that one's own conclusions and passions should direct the lives of others. The problem shows most clearly in the use of moral words, introduced into Hobbes's theory under the neutral title "Inconstant Names." Words of inconstant signification register approval and disapproval. Since passions differ, even in a single person, the meanings of words that register approval and disapproval shift: "For one man calleth

*Wisdome*, what another calleth *feare*; and one *cruelty*, what another *justice*; one *prodigality*, what another *magnanimity*; and one *gravity*, what another *stupidity*, &c. And therefore such names can never be true grounds of any ratiocination" (I, 4, 109–10).

This passage helps explain Hobbes's own freedom to redefine the associations of such words as *presumption* and *providence*, and it implicitly defends *Leviathan* in that its argument does not rest on the variations of approval and disapproval. The defense is necessary because variations in the meanings of moral words are not merely confusing, a chaos of individual meanings, but threatening and angering. Humans will invade for "a word" as well as for gain and safety (I, 13, 185). As Hume explains so brilliantly in the *Enquiry Concerning the Principles of Morals*, moral words are general in reference, and they imply a shared point of view even though they are used by individuals according to their feelings. This argument is used by Hume to explain how social peace and agreement are attained, without political means, as an unconscious effect of using moral terms. But Hobbes's political wisdom understands that the generality of moral terms makes them more, not less, dangerous expressions of individual feeling, since they aim to rouse and express general approval and disapproval. Using moral words involves a claim of power.

The fictional nature of words introduces Hobbes's argument about the necessity of sovereignty very early on in *Leviathan*. Justice is artificial because language is artificial: there are no natural, indisputable meanings of words. However, there are few motives to dispute about the names of physical objects, compared to the wide variations of intentions that motivate the use of moral words. Nevertheless, Hobbes makes clear that disputes even about the computation of numbers can arise, and when they do there is no solution but the establishment of an agreed-upon judge (I, 5, 111). Hobbes argues repeatedly that in the political realm logical demonstration is no guarantee of certainty.

Moral words, along with other signs of honor, are tools as well as signs of power: "what quality soever maketh a man beloved, or feared of many; or the reputation of such quality, is Power, because it is a means to have the assistance, and service of many" (I, 10, 151). Honor does not have a fixed, absolute meaning, but is grounded in opinion, opinions about the traits of individuals and opinions about the general signs of honor:

> The *Value*, or WORTH of a man, is as of all other things, his Price; that is to say, so much as would be given for the use of his Power; and therefore is not absolute; but a thing dependant on the need and judgement of another. . . . And as in other things, so in men, not the seller, but the buyer determines the Price. For let a man (as most men do,) rate themselves as the highest Value they can; yet their true Value is no more than it is esteemed by others. [I, 10, 151–52]

The market analogy should not deceive us into thinking that Hobbes looks to the self-regulating mechanisms of markets and conventions to solve disputes about what is honorable. Because honor is a source of power, it is the object of continual competition, and in a state without law it is a cause of war (II, 17, 225–26). Possessing honor and conferring honor can present challenges to sovereignty, and in a well-settled state the sovereign has authority over signs of "dignity," just as he does over the definition of moral words like *just* and *unjust*.

Authority over language, especially over the language of honor, is crucial for ensuring that religion makes peace, not enmity, among people. Religion is a creation of language, a specifically human institution. The extensive curiosity about causes and effects which is fostered by the use of language leads those "who make profound enquiry" to the postulate of an eternal first cause (I, 11, 167). But since the mind cannot conceive the infinite, all names applied to the first cause, even "God," are marks of honor. For those who "make little or no enquiry into the natural causes of things" and suppose several kinds of invisible powers, propitiating the spirits by ceremonies and words of honor seems even more important. Because of the opinion that great power is attached to these acts of honor, politicians have always interested themselves in religion. This concern is even more important for Christians, who believe that God has instituted laws "not only of behaviour toward himselfe, but also towards one another; and thereby in the Kingdome of God, the Policy, and lawes Civill, are a part of Religion" (I, 12, 178). Since laws are promulgated in words and words have no natural meaning, God's laws, like human laws, are subject to disputes that can only be resolved by an agreed-upon judge: "All Lawes need Interpretation" (II, 26, 322).

The most fundamental sovereign authority is the right to interpret language. The sovereign defines "justice" by the promulgation of laws, and since all laws need interpretation, the authority to interpret all laws, past and present, written and unwritten, must be a part of sovereignty. Public commentary on law, whether comments on natural law in moral philosophy or comments on sacred law or civil law, carries a possible claim against sovereign authority and must be subject to the sovereign power (II, 26, 325–26). Indeed, all public speech has a potential effect on the social peace and must be subject to sovereign authority:

> it is annexed to the Soveraignty, to be Judge of what Opinions and Doctrines are averse, and what conducing to Peace; and consequently, on what occasions, how farre, and what, men are to be trusted withall, in speaking to Multitudes of people; and who shall examine the Doctrines of all bookes before they be published. For the Actions of men proceed from their Opinions; and in the wel governing of Opinions, consisteth the well governing of mens Actions, in order to their Peace, and Concord. [II, 18, 233]

Even Hobbes's own book is not law, however true it may be (II, 26, 322–23). Only a sovereign who understands its arguments and exercises his "entire Soveraignty, in protecting the Publique teaching of it" (II, 31, 408) can make the book law. Only then is science power, since few can hold Hobbes's principles as certain knowledge demonstrated by reasoning, but everyone will hold it if it is made authorized opinion. Hobbes locates the image that has become the touchstone of the postrevolutionary epistemology, the blank tablet, in an explicitly political context: "the Common-peoples minds, unlesse they be tainted with dependance on the Potent, or scribbled over by the opinions of their Doctors, are like clean paper, fit to receive whatsoever by Publique Authority shall be imprinted in them" (II, 30, 379).

Hobbes's effort to establish his submission to sovereign authority is carried on in a chapter that defines three different kinds of precepts: commanding (the right only of the sovereign), exhorting, and counseling (II, 25, 302–11). The presence of a middle term between counsel and command reintroduces the problem of Hobbes's own work. Exhortation is a kind of counsel, but it shares with command the stylistic traits of personal interest and the intention of affecting the passions of a multitude by analogies, metaphors, examples, quotations from respected authors, and inconstant names. Counsel, by contrast, uses simple, clearly defined, logically arranged reasoning about consequences, directed to the interests of the sovereign. The scene of counsel is a private audience, not the address to a multitude.

The logical form of Hobbes's treatise would seem to place it in the category of counsel, but the attempt to exemplify the way his science could become general opinion, a kind of civil religion, leads Hobbes to similes and metaphors and other attempts to stir the passions, all of which mark an exhortation that encroaches on command. Is the audience for *Leviathan* select and private, or is *Leviathan* already a popular work intended to mold the opinions of the populace? Perhaps a more popular form of address is necessary, because after the execution of Charles I in 1649 Hobbes considers Parliament the sovereign. Or perhaps Hobbes considers that there is no sovereign, as he was to argue in *Behemoth*, so the audience for the counsel of *Leviathan* is all people, since the right to define has reverted to all users of words. Political controversy of the seventeenth century helps develop the large readership and the popular trade in books, pamphlets, and journals that affect the writing of novelists and philosophers, even those who are most suspicious of these developments.

The problem of identifying the audience for philosophy, and along with that decision the appropriate rhetoric and form, affects the history of the discourse. Difficulties in making these choices shape the careers of such authors as Locke, Shaftesbury, Berkeley, and Hume. The collected works by any one of these authors resemble a kind of debate among forms: the formal, extended arguments of the scientific treatise or the philosophical history confront the shorter, more casually connected, more conversational forms of essays, letters, and dialogues. Authors sometimes try to indicate a definitive choice by establishing a personal canon that excludes a form (as Hume excluded his *Treatise*) or by relegating it to anonymous status. The tension can be seen even within individual works. Indeed, Parts III and IV of *Leviathan* shift the form of the work considerably. Because Hobbes presents no explicit excuse or sign that the work as a whole will be diverse and loosely connected, and because the sequence of part titles—"Of Man," "Of Commonwealth," "Of Christian Commonwealth," "Of the Kingdome of Darknesse"—seems to promise continuity, the second half appears extraneous and is generally ignored.[8] The conscious, troubled effort of novelists to define their authority parallels the effort of political philosophers in the seventeenth and eighteenth centuries. A defensive preface is not the only way authors define the authority of their books; important clues can be found in length, the continuity of sections, closure, modes of reporting dialogue or addressing the reader. Histories, memoirs, diaries, epistles, essays, dialogues, satires, sermons, and political speeches provide a variety of models for authoritative address which can be defined as resources or rivals by novelists as well as philosophers. The sense of difficulty, the conscious questioning about authority in the writings of this period, contribute to thir enduring interest.

## Sovereignty

After Hobbes has pictured the dilemma of endless contentions over uncertainties without an agreed-upon authority, the advantages of obeying such an authority are clear; the question remains: how do the restless, uncertain, contentious people of Hobbes's theory achieve agreement about authority? In some respects this question cannot be answered. The failure to find a convincing image of the change of opinion necessary for establishing civil society has been identified as a fundamental flaw in Hobbes's argument. How do people overcome their fearful anxiety, their dangerous anticipations, sufficiently to trust mutual promises to lay aside the right to all things? Since obligation comes into existence only under civil society, what binds people who enter into the first agreement? Must there be after all a natural morality, an obligation to observe promises and therefore a natural standard by which to judge even the sovereign?[9] Locke thought so, and he places the problem of contention in the execution of justice, not in the understanding of it.

[8]On the significance of these sections, see Pocock, "Time, History, and Eschatology in the Thought of Thomas Hobbes," in *Politics, Language, and Time: Essays on Political Thought and History* (New York: Atheneum, 1971), pp. 148–201.

[9]See A. E. Taylor, "The Ethical Doctrine of Hobbes," *Philosophy* 13 (1938): 406–24; Howard Warrender, *The Political Philosophy of Hobbes: His Theory of*

In some respects the dilemma arises only because readers interpret Hobbes's narrative historically. The analytic-compositive method he so admired favored a narrative composition of analyzed constituents, but the narrative was "conjectural," to use Dugald Stewart's helpful term. In fact history, motivated by arguments about precedents, was a direct object of Hobbes's attack, though the special case of law, the Christian revelation, led him to pursue a historical form of argument in Part III of *Leviathan*. Hobbes admits that there was never such a time or condition as the war of all against all which he has described, and so we may presume that there was never such a time or condition as the social contract. In some ways the gigantic gap between a world without law and a settled government conveys an important lesson of Hobbes's teaching. His analysis intends to reveal not a single identifiable historical act, but a continuous underlying assumption of people in civil society. Increasingly his term *contract* seemed too conscious, explicit, and particularized an image of this assumption. Hume's description of convention without promises like two men pulling the oars of a boat (*Treatise*, III, II, ii) corrects the impression. But close attention to the ways Hobbes defines the kinds of contracts erodes the sense of historical particularity. The contract to transfer or abandon rights may reach into the future, unlike a contract to transfer a thing. Indeed, the abandonment of all rights reaches into the whole future. Signs of contract are not only express words, but also inferences: "Signes by Inference, are sometimes the consequence of Words; sometimes the consequence of Silence; sometimes the consequence of Actions; sometimes the consequence of Forbearing an Action; and generally a signe by Inference, of any Contract, is whatsoever sufficiently argues the will of the Contractor" (I, 14, 193–94). Most human activities during the peace of civil society are signs of the social contract.

But the explanation of Hobbes's fictions still leaves in doubt the historical action of creating government, a problem facing England in Hobbes's time. Without civil authority, the only general motive to observe promises is fear, fear either of visible or invisible powers. Convictions about invisible things are impossible to share directly and are very likely to differ without civil authority to harmonize

*Obligation* (Oxford: Clarendon, 1957); and Brian Barry, "Warrender and His Critics," in *Hobbes and Rousseau*, pp. 37–65.

opinions. So promises based on such fears are hard to rely on. Fear of other people is only a strong motivation to observe promises in civil society, since without civil society "the inequality of Power is not discerned; but by the event of Battell" (I, 14, 200), that is, only a battle can establish which party most people will aid. Fear of other people is only a motive to peace in a state of peace. Hobbes's emphasis on fear has led some to believe he argued that a sovereign rules chiefly by force: might makes right. Though Hobbes considers the military power an important part of sovereignty, and he does argue that fear of physical violence is an incentive to forming and obeying government, sovereignty cannot be established by might. No one person can gather enough strength to safe from murder by stealth: only consent can motivate obedience in the dark.

Examining the creation of the sovereign authority at first intensifies the mystery of the transition from war to political society. It hardly seems to be created at all. The absolute right of the sovereign is neither created nor granted by the social contract, for then it could be revoked, as in Locke's theory. According to Hobbes the absolute right of the sovereign is the natural right to all things that the agreed-upon sovereign has not been required to resign. Nevertheless, something else belonging to the sovereign is created. Part I of *Leviathan* ends noticeably and oddly with the introduction of a new term to describe a new power: personation. How does personation fit into Hobbes's previous definition of human perception and passion? Personation or representation is fundamentally an act of naming: the sovereign acts in the name of the state.[10] This name has the fictional quality of all names and confers the powerful belief of generality.

The etymology of *person*, a mask or disguise for the stage, is suggestive. It narrows the gap between natural and artificial persons, since both are "actors," speaking and performing in the name of someone, whether in one's own name or in the name of someone else. In either case, the person is identified by appearances. The analogy to the arts suggests that personation is motivated not only by the quest for power through the creation of an effective agent, but

[10]See Hanna Fenichel Pitkin, *The Concept of Representation* (Berkeley: University of California Press, 1967), chap. 1.

also by aesthetic pleasure. Things that were diverse assume unity, things or persons that could not speak or act now leap into life: "there are few things, that are uncapable of being represented by a Fiction" (I, 16, 219). The capacity for pleasure in creating and observing artificial persons seems to be something Hobbes wants to foster. The memorable frontispiece of the sovereign man composed of many men, the continuous analogy of the state to a natural body, seem to appeal to this pleasure. The possibility of identifying with the power of the state even when one's own power is limited seems important to Hobbes's system. The power of the commonwealth is not something merely acknowledged as a means of self-preservation; it is also something that can be celebrated: "The Libertie, whereof there is so frequent, and honorable mention, in the Histories, and Philosophy of Ancient Greeks, and Romans, and in the writings, and discourse of those that from them have received all their learning in the Politiques, is not the Libertie of Particular men; but the Libertie of the Common-wealth: which is the same with that, which every man then should have, if there were no Civil Laws, nor Commonwealth at all" (II, 21, 266).

Hobbes wishes to avoid this confusion about liberty, which could prompt the sort of individualistic heroism he associates with the readers of the classics. So when he celebrates the heroic qualities of the commonwealth, he shifts from the analogy of the artificial man to a metaphor of nonhuman power, the leviathan: "This is the Generation of that great LEVIATHAN, or rather (to speake more reverently) of that *Mortall God*, to which wee owe under the *Immortall God*, our peace and defense" (II, 17, 227). These images excite a pleasure in the image of power without raising imitation and competition, since as the epigraph from Job teaches, there is no comparable power. If these images are playful, they are nevertheless purposive, since they channel creativity into social activities that are uncontentious.

Hobbes at times rouses the suspicion not merely that actions and expressed opinions are formed by civil society, but that the inner feelings, the person behind the mask, is shaped by social needs, like stones shaped to fit together in an edifice (I, 15, 209). His analogy leaves in question the agent of the "mutual accommodation." "Compleasance" is a law of nature, something everyone should strive for, but like other laws, the obligation can only take effect in a state of settled sovereignty. And we may remember that elsewhere Hobbes has compared his own activity to the planning by an architect for a more durable building, designed on better principles than existed before (II, 20, 261). When we put the two passages together, we glimpse a writer who wishes to reform human nature, not just read it. Perhaps the sovereign is the builder who planes down oddly shaped stones or casts the unshapable ones away.

In the letter of dedication that begins *Leviathan*, Hobbes placed himself outside the edifice of authority, as a defender, not as a constructor in any sense. His antiheroic image of the defense of Rome is clacking geese, not a generally respected source of utterance. His distance from the individuals who hold power makes him "simple and impartiall." The uncertainty about sovereignty in Britain helps explain in another sense his ignorance of those in power, but this source of simplicity does not necessarily imply distance. The dedication to Francis Godolphin, the brother of a friend who was an eminently worthy member of society, and Hobbes's position in Paris in the court of Charles, suggests that being outside the walls of the seat of power may be an image of closeness, not of distance. The geese after all were sacred, and their clacking was authorized, or perhaps won for them, their title of honor. In any case, the loud, noisy image does not suggest speech that carefully discriminates between counsel and command. The "due submission" Hobbes offers in his letter has a wide latitude when the sovereign is uncertain. The unusual freedom of interpretation, especially of the interpretation of Scripture in Parts III and IV, has no parallel in his earlier work.

As we move away from the time of civil war, few authors show the signs of interpretive freedom Hobbes exercised. The modern successors of Hobbes shift the investigation of the psychology of authority and obedience from political to sociological and historical categories. Obedience is seen not as a conscious action of consent, but as the less conscious operation of conventions absorbed in family life and in work, institutions that shape natural-seeming shared meanings through impersonal systems of signs, especially language and money. David Hume is a key figure for understanding the transition from political philosophy to the social sciences, and in the perspective of his writings and even more for us as inheritors of the sociological tradition, Hobbes can look remarkably unsatisfactory.

Hobbes was not entirely ignorant about modes of social organization which have not been formally legislated. He well understood that some of the pleasures and reassurances provided by the commonwealth could be supplied by smaller groups, and that social groups organize authority in ways important to the political order. The importance he gives to the institution of religion should win him a place in the history of the social sciences. More can be learned about Hobbes's view of social subgroups in the chapter "Of SYSTEMES *Subject, Politicall, and Private*" (II, 22). The elaborate detail of the chapter should not obscure Hobbes's teaching about different social groups: family, status groups, business organizations, parties and religious sects, and government officials ("bodies political"). The power and authority of such groups are only conducive to social peace if the groups are subordinate to one political authority. Otherwise they serve to foster dissension and conflicting claims of sovereign representation.

The absolute authority of Hobbes's sovereign does not entail totalitarian government, the systematic control of social organizations by public laws or by the sovereign's appointed officials. Hobbes wished only to establish the right of the sovereign to make any law, to judge what is necessary for the public peace. There are many indications that Hobbes does not expect the sovereign to interfere extensively with social groups: in fact, he seems to recommend a prudent accommodation of the sovereign's laws to existing attitudes in society. Many crimes are "things commonly so valued," but common value is given currency by the authority of the sovereign (II, 27, 352). The sovereign may be prudent in observing the common understanding, but he is not obliged to observe it. Family life, an important locus for the novel, seems to be a particular object of respect for Hobbes, and sometimes it is given a primary place in his historically oriented accounts of the origin of government. But his skepticism about all forms of natural authority raises useful questions about authority in the family and the place of the state in regulating that authority. Hobbes therefore can help us ask questions about the place of the family in fiction.

Habit or custom, whether experienced as unconscious conditioning or invoked as an argument of right by precedent, provides no secure means of resolving disputes. Perhaps the social sciences only seem a satisfactory substitute for Hobbes's science of politics in very peaceful times, in well-settled states; and, as Hobbes would have understood, the assumption about social peace made by the social sciences serves to reinforce the peace of peaceful states.

If the British authors of the eighteenth century do not feel under threat of anarchic war, as Hobbes did, they nevertheless are not secure about the public peace. Political questions such as the ones Hobbes asked were quite audible. J. H. Plumb's image of "the growth of political stability" is helpful, but it requires important modifications, such as those sketched by E. P. Thompson and other practitioners of the new social history or, on the other hand, by Linda Colley's new work on the Tory opposition.[11] In an era aware of the possibility of violent disagreements about authority, not just political controversy, but also crime appears as a kind of challenge different from the settled understanding implied by such terms as *deviance* or *dissent*. The eighteenth century is located between two violent revolutions. The first is English and the second is French, though with the help of Burke's anxious vision, the French Revolution could seem a torch to light another English civil war. Jacobite uprisings are still in mind when the fear of Jacobins replaces them. Disputes about the religious establishment continue to raise questions about sovereignty even if debates or demonstrations do not proceed to general armed conflict. One major goal of the authors of this period is to create a scene of dispute that would not result in Hobbes's choice of plots, either total war or else submission to absolute authority.

[11]See E. P. Thompson, *Whigs and Hunters: The Origin of the Black Act* (New York: Pantheon, 1975); Douglas Hay et al., *Albion's Fatal Tree: Crime and Society in Eighteenth-Century England* (New York: Pantheon, 1975); Linda Colley, *In Defiance of Oligarchy: The Tory Party, 1714–1760* (Cambridge: Cambridge University Press, 1982).

# CHAPTER TWO

# *Defoe: Adventures in Political Creativity*

They mistake sometimes the Precepts of Counsellours, for the Precepts of them that Command; and sometimes the contrary; according as it best agreeth with the conclusions they would inferre, or the actions they approve.

No man can pretend a right to be of another mans Counsell.

*Leviathan*, II, 25, 302, 303

## The Self-appointed Counselor

As a Dissenter, a failed businessman, and a pamphleteer who had sat in pillory, Daniel Defoe would hardly seem a likely candidate for being recognized as a respected authority in politics or literature. Yet he earned the personal attention of a king, the patronage of several powerful ministers, popular honors from the citizens of London and Edinburgh, and the admiration of an ever-growing body of readers. His fascinating career reminds us that power seeking can be conducted in a surprising variety of ways. Defoe was a seventeenth-century political activist who helped bring about the eighteenth-century "growth of political stability" which then cramped his style. His notorious ingenuity in impersonation has a great deal to do with his double (and dubious) aim: to create a more imposing edifice of state and to find new kinds of space for himself within it.[1]

Defoe's religious status made him acutely aware of the possibility of contention and of the arbitrary, artificial nature of the public law. His experience, however, was only a more intense form of the general experience. After the separation of the English church from the authority of the pope, English Protestantism was left indistinctly

[1]Sources of biographical and historical information for this chapter include John Robert Moore, *Daniel Defoe: Citizen of the Modern World* (Chicago: University of Chicago Press, 1958) and *A Checklist of the Writings of Daniel Defoe* (Bloomington: Indiana University Press, 1971); James Sutherland, *Defoe: A Biography* (Philadelphia: Lippincott, 1938); J. H. Plumb, *The Growth of Political Stability in England, 1675–1725* (Harmondsworth: Penguin, 1973); W. A. Speck, *Stability and Strife* (Cambridge, Mass.: Harvard University Press, 1977); Geoffrey A. Holmes, *British Politics in the Age of Anne* (New York: St. Martin's Press, 1967) and *Augustan England: Professions, State and Society, 1680–1730* (London: George Allen and Unwin, 1982); George Harris Healey, ed., *The Letters of Daniel Defoe* (Oxford: Clarendon, 1955).

defined. Disagreements about church government, forms of worship, and the doctrines of belief were carried on as a part of legitimate politics. Because decisions made by the sovereign power kept changing, the line between legal and illegal religion was unclear. In such an atmosphere, Archbishop Laud's introduction of a more restrictive church discipline was a considerable incentive to rebellion. Yet the civil war did not teach, as the returning monarch supposed, the wisdom of wide toleration. The hopes of many Protestants were disappointed by the members of Parliament, who were resentful of their own past experience of exclusion under Independent and Presbyterian authority and who had been panicked by an untimely revolt of Fifth Monarchy Men. In 1662, a year after Defoe's birth, his parents would have seen their clergyman, Dr. Annesley, along with several thousand other clergymen, expelled from the church by the Act of Uniformity, which required the use of a designated prayer book, an oath of passive obedience to the king, and episcopal ordination. Perhaps the Foes (as his parents were named) followed their clergyman through his various clandestine meetinghouses until he was licensed to hold services in his own home. The Test and Corporation acts severely restricted the political activities of nonconforming Protestants by requiring the Anglican sacrament for public office in Parliament, army, navy, and local government; degrees from Oxford and Cambridge, designed for training establishment clergy, were out of the question for nonconformists.

One might wonder why these laws of conformity were obeyed, since the earlier ones had provoked revolution. The same sorts of disagreements continued with the same sorts of aims. Dissenters did not rejoin the Anglican church in overwhelming numbers and so remained a substantial part of the population. Furthermore, the late seventeenth-century monarchs, who had at least a part of sovereign authority, preferred wide toleration. The divided sovereignty between king and Parliament would seem especially likely, as Hobbes argued, to encourage insurrection. One must imagine that many people (including monarchs) came to an understanding not very different from Hobbes's arguments in favor of the authority of a sovereign government to determine the establishment of religion: religious disagreements among Christians had not been resolved by arguments or war, yet obedience of a common authority was necessary for stability. Dissenters accepted the terms of the public peace and continued to hope for a peaceful change of law. A large number participated in government by conforming in the narrowest, most technical interpretation of the law, "occasional conformity," that is, taking the Anglican communion once a year. Some office holders may simply have broken the law without being brought to trial because their fellow subjects wished them to serve; some brought to trial were acquitted by sympathetic juries. Though broad toleration could not be passed in Parliament, social practice would not enforce the rigid exclusion dictated by the statutes, especially in localities where dissenting communities were strong, like the City of London. Efforts to intimidate juries in order to enforce laws such as the Conventicles Act succeeded only in establishing restraints on judges' power over juries. Relaxed enforcement of laws allowed not only a great deal of participation in government, but also the development of alternative institutions, like the dissenting academies, so that there was little incentive for armed revolt against the laws, or even for vigorous political pressure.

Defoe belonged to the first generation raised during the rocky adjustment of attitude about fighting to define the national church. He joined the revolutionary opposition to the Catholic monarch James II in order to bring a Protestant, the Duke of Monmouth, to the throne, a strategy that might have earned gratitude for the help of Dissenters and so won more political rights. But the gamble was lost, Monmouth was defeated and executed, and the notorious Judge Jeffreys handed out much more severe sentences than had been the norm at the Restoration.

Unlike some Dissenters' opposition to James, Defoe's was not mollified by the suspension of the Test Act and the Declaration of Indulgence for Dissenters and Catholics. In pamphlets of 1687 and 1688, Defoe urged Dissenters to reject the new civil liberties because they were promulgated by illegal royal authority without the consent of Parliament. In spite of constant opposition to James, Defoe had a lifelong admiration for the Marquis of Halifax, even though in the reign of Charles II Halifax had led the victory over the Whig attempts to exclude James from the succession; and on the other hand, Defoe distrusted Whig politicians such as Shaftesbury who sought the support of Dissenters to gratify personal ambition.

Defoe wanted to weld the dissenting interest to a new consolidation of the national interest.

When the nation became united in resistance to James, Defoe was prominent in welcoming William's invasion. Although the peacefulness of the 1688 Revolution is always stressed, the threat of violence behind it, the defection of the army, was extremely important, and in Ireland the change led to protracted battle that resulted in even worse civil disabilities for Catholics. Defoe never had to fight to secure William's rule, but he defended him in numerous tracts and poems. In Defoe's own account he became an unofficial adviser to William, a position won through unsolicited support in a long, satirical poem, "The True-Born Englishman" (1701). Perhaps Defoe had hoped to win important office under a Protestant monarch who favored toleration, but once again Dissenters' hopes to regain political rights were frustrated by an intransigent Parliament, so Defoe could not enjoy the usual benefits of royal favor. Although he never again participated in revolution, Defoe continued to practice a high-risk variety of politics.

How could Defoe gain political influence without elective office or important royal appointments? His location and popularity in the City of London helped him, because the City exerted a special influence on national government.[2] As a wealthy center of trade, the City affected the welfare of the nation. Very few "money men" sat in Parliament, but powerful merchants could influence elections and advise the ministry or Parliament. Newly organized financial institutions, especially the Bank of England, formalized and symbolized the interrelation of government and trade.[3] Though Defoe did not belong to the group of wealthy merchants, he was well acquainted with them and perhaps was thought by William's ministers to understand and influence them. Institutions of City government were more democratic than elsewhere in the nation; political controversies

[2]See Dame Lucy Sutherland, "The City of London in Eighteenth-Century Politics," in *Aristocratic Government and Society in Eighteenth-Century England*, ed. Daniel A. Baugh (New York: Franklin Watts, 1975), pp. 157–75.

[3]For the development of financial institutions, see P.G.M. Dickson, *The Financial Revolution in England* (New York: St. Martin's Press, 1967). For the development of economic theories in relation to political and economic crises, see Joyce Oldham Appleby, *Economic Thought and Ideology in Seventeenth-Century England* (Princeton, N.J.: Princeton University Press, 1978).

were more open and violent and fostered habits of political opposition. Even ordinary London people could influence the government because they lived near the Houses of Parliament. The city crowd could and did threaten individual legislators or even gather to threaten the assembled Houses. The much-cherished right to petition, a formal means of addressing the government available to the politically disadvantaged, could easily slide into mob violence; for this reason, Hobbes had urged strict regulation of petitioning.

Defoe exploited the latitude of the right to petition by carrying at least one dispute very close to armed insurrection. In 1701 Defoe won fame in the City of London by entering Parliament with sixteen armed men as self-appointed spokesman for the nation. They presented *Legion's Memorial*, a work probably written by Defoe, who in later years often signed his pamphlets "Legion" to recall this triumph. The memorial demanded parliamentary support for William's aggressive efforts to curb the power of Louis XIV, an expensive military policy that the landed proprietors in Parliament did not want to finance. The memorial also demanded and obtained the release of previous petitioners (the "Kentish Petitioners") who had been arrested by parliamentary authority. Though the categories of merchants, Dissenters, and London crowds do not form a single social group, their interests, as in this case, often overlapped. Their informal, sometimes dangerous, methods of pressuring Parliament can explain a great deal of the antagonistic writing against London and the merchants. Hobbes's antagonism to the City of London, to merchants, and to the right to petition are closely connected.

Only briefly was Defoe able to add the power of personal fortune to his other means of gaining influence in the nation. In 1692 Defoe's business failed, and he incurred a debt of £17,000 from which he never entirely recovered. Typical of his risky engagement in public life, part of this debt came from insuring ships for William's navy. To aid the bankrupt insurers, Parliament passed a number of acts that allowed special arrangements with creditors to avert imprisonment. Like the political disabilities of Dissenters, Defoe's civil status as a debtor was uncertain, subject to shifts or even a decisive, favorable political redefinition. In neither case were his hopes fulfilled. Although he eventually attained a comfortable yearly income from government funds, investments, and earnings from his writing,

Defoe's economic position remained insecure. At the very end of his life Defoe once more had to go into hiding to elude the prosecution of a creditor. Without the power of great wealth, shadowed by the threat of imprisonment for debt, Defoe is the more impressive for his resourceful discovery of routes to power.

The City was a center for a special kind of trade that had been particularly encouraged by the political and religious controversies of the seventeenth century: the popular press. Experience confirmed Hobbes's argument that government is founded on opinion. Defoe's most persistent efforts to act as counselor to his nation were his pamphlets, books, and newspapers. Defoe's contemporaries shared Hobbes's suspicion of the threat to sovereignty that could come from unlicensed use of these means for shaping opinion. Members of Parliament and the ministry sought to exploit the power of the press while limiting their political opponents' access to it. The extensive use of anonymity in the period is a clue to the continuing threat of arrest.

Anonymity was not a secure protection from legal persecution.[4] It was not often truly secret, and it also gave opportunities for complicated kinds of risks, especially the sort of satiric impersonation that appealed to Defoe. Defoe was arrested in 1703 for *The Shortest-Way with the Dissenters* and in 1713 for a series of pamphlets, including one with the provocative title *And What if the Pretender Should Come? or, Some Considerations Of the Advantages and Real Consequences Of the Pretender's Possessing the Crown of Great Britain.* In each of these pamphlets Defoe impersonated and exaggerated the "high-flying," anti-Dissenter wing of the Tory party, intending by the hoax to draw out their approval of his feigned Jacobitism and thereby to discredit them. But these violent, revolutionary-sounding tracts provided his political enemies (Tories in 1703, Whigs in 1713) with a pretext for misunderstanding him and launching prosecution. In 1704, rescued from prison by the favor of Robert Harley, a moderate

[4]E. P. Thompson investigates anonymous threatening letters written by members of the lower classes as a form of social protest and compares such limited and yet criminal acts of rebellion with the "wars of insinuation and character assassination" conducted in the public press under pseudonyms: "The free born Englishman crept about in a mask." See "The Crime of Anonymity," in Douglas Hay et al., *Albion's Fatal Tree: Crime and Society in Eighteenth-Century England* (New York: Pantheon, 1975), p. 272.

Tory minister, Defoe became a political agent and propagandist for the ministry, first for Harley, then for the Whig Godolphin, then for the Tory government of Harley and Bolingbroke, who obtained for Defoe a pardon for the tracts of 1713. In this nine-year period (1704–13) Defoe conducted his journal the *Review*.

After Queen Anne died in 1714 and the Tory ministry that Defoe served fell from power, Defoe was convicted of libel (once again for exposing a Jacobite). To avoid a severe sentence, he agreed to work secretly for the Whig ministry while maintaining the appearance of an opposition Tory journalist who sought a moderate relation to government. These doublings and redoublings of impersonation probably allowed Defoe considerable room for strategies to express his true convictions, including criticisms of the ministry. His many assertions about writing from his true convictions may be more than disingenuousness. In 1717, when the Whig ministry that Defoe served split into two factions, Defoe continued in the employment of Sunderland's ministry, meanwhile writing pamphlets supporting Townshend and Walpole, who had resigned from it. These pamphlets widened the gulf between the Whig ministers and so helped undermine the treason proceedings they were conducting against Defoe's old Tory patron Robert Harley, whom he was defending in a number of anonymous works. When Harley was released, Defoe wrote a pamphlet recommending Whig reconciliation and scolding them for fumbling the prosecution against Harley.[5]

The political motifs of Defoe's career are more persistent and important than the shifty pursuit of personal interest or personal loyalty. From his early participation in rebellion to his voluntary entry into political pamphleteering, City leadership, and personal advice, Defoe shows a restless desire to shape his nation, a desire perhaps only augmented by the massive restrictions on the formal channels for what I have called political creativity. Hobbes's political theory fundamentally argued that people have created their nations and can make them better, while at the same time it warned continuously against the vainglory of "men that have a strong opinion of their own wisdome in matter of government" (I, 11, 164). The capacity to

[5]On this murky period, see Geoffrey M. Sill, *Defoe and the Idea of Fiction, 1713–1719* (Newark, N.J.: Associated University Presses, 1983), pp. 121–47.

identify with the power of the state, rather than a desire to seek limitless personal power, was essential to Hobbes's psychology of civil society. But in practice it is difficult to differentiate this identification with the state from a desire to direct the state.

Defoe's career would have been impossible if Hobbes had won his argument and widespread fears of the anarchic potential of political controversy had resulted in complete government control of the press. On the other hand, Defoe's career demonstrates the limits on the "free" press enforced by governments with only moderate powers of patronage and prosecution. The idea of legitimate, organized political parties, including organized opposition, grew up together with increasing security about the allegiance of most subjects to their government. But in Defoe's lifetime this security was never entirely anchored, and his "exaggerations" roused public conflict, not because he miscalculated his irony, but because extremism and repression were dominant features of his political landscape. In his many efforts to expose as Jacobites those Anglicans politically opposed to Dissenters, Defoe was trying to use an antirevolutionary, nationalist position on the Protestant succession to lay the foundation for reform of the political settlement. This position, however, was ultimately most successfully occupied for twenty years by the Court Whigs under Robert Walpole, who managed the Jacobite threat to justify a system of one-party government which stultified reform while it stifled partisan conflict. After 1714 Defoe clearly understood that the Jacobite threat would be used cynically by Whig ministries to persecute legitimate opposition, but he could not altogether escape the logic of this process.[6]

However much Dissenters like Defoe accepted the overall bargain represented by the seventeenth-century settlement, they had certainly not lost all hope of changing its terms and coming into power. In his unfinished last work, *The Compleat English Gentleman*, Defoe had no embarrassment about offering his own education in the dissenting academy of Charles Morton as the model for all

[6]Linda Colley has argued against J. H. Plumb that Walpole's one-party rule destabilized the political system by excluding from national and local government a sizable proportion of the Tory elite, who were therefore provoked to experiment with revolutionary politics. See Colley, *In Defiance of Oligarchy: The Tory Party, 1714–1760* (Cambridge: Cambridge University Press, 1982).

gentlemen, the natural rulers of England. The idea seemed so sensible partly because the dissenting education as Defoe described it was not for a life at the periphery of society, but for a life at the center of national government:

> He had a class for eloquence, and his pupils declaim'd weekly in the English tongue, made orations, and wrot epistles twice every week upon such subjects as he prescrib'd to them or upon such as they themselves chose to write upon. Sometimes they were ambassadors and agents abroad at forreign Courts, and wrote accounts of their negotiations and recepcion in forreign Courts directed to the Secretary of State and some times to the Soveraign himself.
>
> Some times they were Ministers of State, Secretaries and Commissioners at home, and wrote orders and instruccions to the ministers abroad, as by order of the King in Council and the like. Thus he taught his pupils to write a masculine and manly stile, to write the most polite English, and at the same time to kno' how to suit their manner as well to the subject they were to write upon as to the persons or degrees of persons they were to write to. . . . In a word, his pupils came out of his hands finish'd orators, fitted to speak in the highest presence, to the greatest assemlies, and even in Parliament, Courts of Justice, or any where; and severall of them came afterward to speak in all those places and capacities with great applause.[7]

Defoe's teacher, Reverend Morton, a distinguished scientist, sought greater scope for his talents in emigration, Locke's solution to the problems of people who do not fit into a specific society. Though Defoe finds expansive overseas opportunities for his fictional characters, and though he claimed to have been offered opportunities of this kind, his own solution was quite different. *An Essay upon Projects* (1697) shows the role Defoe envisioned for himself from early in his career.

As the first work that he publicly acknowledged (the Preface was signed by his initials) and a work reissued when he was under threat for the publication of *The Shortest-Way with the Dissenters, An Essay upon Projects* has a strong claim to mark his identity as a writer and as a public person in a broad sense. In spite of his extensive indebtedness of only five years before, when the essay had been drafted, Defoe writes his Preface as someone entitled to address the

[7]Daniel Defoe, *The Compleat English Gentleman*, ed. Karl D. Buelbring (London: David Nutt, 1890), pp. 219–20.

public. Though his chief title to attention, he insists, is the value of the projects themselves, the Preface is addressed to Dalby Thomas, one of the commissioners for managing His Majesty's duties on glass, "under whom I have the honour to serve His Majesty." The address identifies Defoe in a modest way with government administration, which was expanding greatly in this period to meet the needs caused by William's wars.[8] His small office was won, in the first place, by the sort of volunteer administrative zeal that the work itself shows. Defoe had perhaps helped devise modes of taxation; he had already appeared before the Privy Council and the House of Commons to testify. Defoe's journalism supported the mixture of volunteer and remunerated government service, testimony before Parliament, and personal influence on ministers and (by his own account) a monarch. These activities added up to a satisfying and effective life for someone barred from sitting in Parliament and from holding city office.

The sort of project that inspired Defoe required a strong national executive.[9] The foundation for the whole *Essay upon Projects* is laid in the first proposal, for increased banking activity regulated by government. The longest and most elaborate of the projects ("Of the Highways") creates a system of taxation and investment, a semi-judicial commission of review and appeal which combines business-

[8]According to Plumb, "The number of men employed by the government grew faster between 1689 and 1715 than in any previous period of English history and perhaps at a rate not to be equalled again until the nineteenth century. The value of government business grew equally fast, and in so doing touched directly the lives of more people than ever before" (*Growth*, p. 118). In describing the growth of size, power, professionalism, and independence of the Treasury, Plumb notes the involvement of amateurs (like Defoe) in devising new taxes to support William's wars (p. 121). Geoffrey Holmes reinforces this view in *Augustan England*, pp. 239–61.

[9]Manuel Schonhorn has drawn attention to Defoe's interest in building strong executive government, his hero worship of William III and other strong warrior kings, and his hostility to Parliament. See "Defoe: The Literature of Politics and the Politics of Some Fictions," in *English Literature in the Age of Disguise*, ed. Maximillian Novak (Berkeley: University of California Press, 1977, pp. 15–56. I think Schonhorn mistakes the bearing of his evidence in suggesting that Defoe let go of the constitutional ideal of mixed government confirmed in the 1688 Revolution. Defoe's efforts to shore up executive effectiveness and help various ministries manage Parliament did not amount to a move toward "a unitary executive sovereignty" (p. 22). Defoe accepted Parliament as an essential feature of English government, however much he might deny the myths about its antiquity, its supremacy, or the virtuous "independence" of its members. Defoe's traditional analogies of kingship to fatherhood do not amount to a patriarchalist derivation of monarchical right from fatherhood.

men and local representatives. The essay begins with a stirring appeal: England should view the creation of good highways as an opportunity to rival the Romans in military and governmental power. The chief model of central government (and perhaps its origin, as Locke had argued) is military organization. Defoe's lifelong admiration for William was partly based on an admiration of his military prowess, and he memorably argued against his countrymen's fears of a standing army, in *An Argument Shewing, That a Standing Army, With Consent of Parliament, is not Inconsistent with a Free Government* (1698). He reassures readers of his *Essay upon Projects* and of the standing army pamphlet that all will be legitimized and safeguarded by acts of Parliament and ultimately by the character of the British nation, jealous of its liberties. A proposal for a military academy in the *Essay on Projects* could be seen as an attempt to find a compromise between a national army and the local militias, expert professionals and high-born amateurs, a plan to diffuse military expertise throughout the nation without arousing fears of absolutism. Defoe's desire to create bold projects and new national facilities made an identification with strong centralized government inevitable, and we should therefore understand why Defoe should find it easy to switch his loyalty to successive administrations.[10]

[10]Although Defoe did not reject political virtue, some theories of it were not acceptable to him. J.G.A. Pocock describes Defoe's rejection of the neo-Harringtonian version of Machiavellian virtue, the idealization of the Gothic origins of the landed aristocracy and of Parliament. Defoe defends public credit and the standing army, the bugbears of the neo-Harringtonian opposition. Yet Pocock claims that Defoe's discussion of credit admits much of what his opponents decried, the "female" inconstancy of credit, its dependence on opinion and passion. The image of credit expands to comprehend a view of society as a world of opinion, "a mobile, somewhat Hobbesian, universe in which every object was potentially a source of either profit or loss, a subject of both hope and fear." Yet Pocock thinks that Defoe was not ready to solve the problems of mobile opinion by resorting to a theory of managerial sovereign authority. See J.G.A. Pocock, *The Machiavellian Moment: Florentine Political Thought and the Atlantic Republican Tradition* (Princeton: Princeton University Press, 1975), pp. 432–61, esp. 452–59.

This valuable account of Defoe's search for a political ethic might have been less tortuous if the focus in neo-Machiavellian discourse had been less confining. In a later essay Pocock admits that the long history of discourse on republican virtue has been paralleled by an equally (if not more) influential discourse on law and that in seventeenth-century England these different tendencies were chiefly represented by Harrington on the one side and Hobbes and Locke on the other. See "Virtue, Rights, and History: A Model for Historians of Political Thought," in *Virtue, Commerce, and*

Party loyalty was not a marked feature of political life in this period; in fact, it would have been widely recognized as a corrupt, antipatriotic principle. Defoe's hero, Lord Halifax, had publicly defended "trimming" your sails to the political winds to keep the ship of state afloat. Robert Harley, Defoe's patron after 1703, boldly tacked about to enjoy power with Whigs and Tories alike. Defoe's notable loyalty to Harley involved an idealization of Harley's capacities as a political manager, a moderator of factions who could be all things to all people. His long memorandum to Harley on the methods for becoming a prime minister in the mold of Richelieu (*Letters*, 29–50) shows Defoe's preference for strong executives in spite of typical British suspicions of French-style centralism. Similarly obnoxious to British political prejudices was Defoe's recommendation that Harley as secretary of state form with the lord treasurer and a few other ministers an "inner cabinet" more secret, unified, and effective than the large cabinet council (*Letters*, 34–36). Plumb considers just such a development a contributing factor in the growth of political stability. Like so many other acts of political management, the reduction of cabinet was effected by Walpole, but it had been pioneered in the reign of William III by Sunderland, a Whig patron of Defoe's, who like Defoe called a large, contentious cabinet "monstrous" (*Growth*, 109–11). Like the private conduct of executive business, the private collection of political information recommended by Defoe had the flavor of the French court. As Harley's secret emissary to Scotland, Defoe described himself as a Richelieu, who had "my spyes and my Pensioners in Every Place" (*Letters*, 211).

Though his fellow subjects valued stability as Defoe did, increasing local autonomy and memories of Stuart tyranny made Defoe's style of governmental project unfeasible. The lack of effective central authorities to solve the large-scale problems of crime, riots, and poverty in the 1740s, 1750s, and 1760s troubled Fielding and Johnson as well as

---

*History: Essays in Political Thought and History, Chiefly in the Eighteenth Century* (Cambridge: Cambridge University Press, 1985), pp. 37–50. As I shall argue, Defoe's political theory clearly conforms to the juridical paradigm, including Pocock's association of the history of jurisprudence with economic theory. Defoe's corollary interest in government as an affair of managing opinion might have been clearer to Pocock if he had recognized that Defoe was writing in support of the ministry from 1711 to 1714, as well as from 1698 to 1701.

Hume, who was to describe the goals of liberty and security as competitive principles in British government. Defoe did not dare to polemicize on behalf of the expansion of executive powers. He achieved his greatest rapport with the popular politics of his period on occasions in which he could describe his objectives in terms of preserving English liberty, as in his opposition to James's illegal exercise of the dispensing power and to Parliament's imprisonment of the Kentish petitioners. Yet his popular poem in defense of William III, "The True-Born Englishman," is daring in its definition of what is English: it rejects the widespread myth about the Saxon ancestry of the English aristocracy, and it courts what might seem like a denigratory identification of William with William the Conqueror. Defoe's satiric exposé of the fickleness of the mongrel English breed opens up the imagination to the positive dynamism of William's new leadership.

The happiest coincidence of Defoe's constructive imagination with his country's ambitions was the Union of Scotland and England in 1707. All of Defoe's skills as a journalist, public man, and private adviser were marshaled for this effort. Though Defoe was acting informally and secretly as the ministry's agent. his efforts were, as so often the case, largely voluntary. The opportunity to bring together a number of his goals must have been gratifying: more effective centralization of government; firmer support for the Protestant monarchy; the union of Protestants in nonsectarian national goals, including the goal of economic development; the pleasures of clandestine and public forms of politics. Defoe supported the Union in his English paper, the *Review*; sent back secret, detailed reports to Harley; helped members of the Scottish Parliament work out the new schedule of tariffs; advised ministers in cases of conscience; made himself and his opinions popular in Edinburgh; and wrapped up the episode with a large, formal history of the Union.

When we think of the problem of individualism in Defoe's life, we should think of the problem of competition as Hobbes conceived it, not the laments about individualism familiar in nineteenth- and twentieth-century anticapitalist culture criticism. The desire for a large personal role in creating the institutions of his society was more important to Defoe than individualistic business competition. Later critics of capitalism often decried its hidden, unconscious politics.

The power that wealth brings was the open, not the hidden goal, of Defoe, and the more enthusiastically celebrated because other types of access were closed. In 1705 Defoe chose a setting on the moon for *The Consolidator*, in which he could elaborate an extended imagination of Dissenters uniting all their economic power in ways that would be legal, Defoe continuously insists, but immensely debilitating to Anglicans. The antagonism to great merchants shown by such satirists as Swift does not proceed from a vague conservative opposition to bourgeois taste; it is founded on the potent political influence Defoe envisioned. Defoe's fantasy role for himself is not the profiting merchant, but the adviser and counselor of the whole operation. The project is only fit for the lunar setting of the work; no such national political organization as he recommends would have been allowed in England.

However inventively Defoe could move or evade the entrenched Anglican power, after he had been deserted by everyone except William Penn when he was imprisoned in 1703 it surely became clear to him that he could not act even as a semiofficial adviser to Dissenters. The informal routes to power have their dangers and dissatisfactions. If the public counsel of the pamphleteer and journalist was not accepted, he was exposed to public hatred and contumely, and his recorded positions could not be entirely erased from the public mind. The journalist who attempts to speak to or for the public, in spite of all expressions of respect and hesitancy, may seem like a dangerous usurper if he fails to persuade; and if he should also be suspected of being a clandestine adviser to the government, one not subject to public questioning or public pressure, he might especially provoke outrage. Such was the case in Defoe's opposition to Occasional Conformity, which was announced in a pamphlet of 1698, *An Enquiry into the Occasional Conformity of Dissenters, In Cases of Preferment*.

Although the course of history confirmed Defoe's advice to resist James's Declaration of Indulgence, his position on Occasional Conformity was less successful with Dissenters. The attempt to challenge influential Dissenters, even in the most polite terms, as in the *Letter to Mr. How* (1701), created great anger. When Tories followed up Queen Anne's strong endorsement of church establishment in her coronation speech with a bill against Occasional

Conformity, Dissenters could only be confirmed in their fears that Defoe was on the Anglican side. His strategies and intentions were, in fact, hard to assess, since they were not the product of group debate and group commitment. His curious pamphlet *An Enquiry into Occasional Conformity. Shewing that the Dissenters Are no Way Concern'd in it* (1702) pursues a strategy of embracing the bill as a measure that will sift the chaff from the Dissenters and thus strengthen them. Though there is every reason to believe that Defoe strongly disapproved of the act and hoped to discourage Parliament by this satire, in the light of his previous writings against Occasional Conformity it was likely to be understood as support for the bill. No wonder Dissenters were confused by the irony of *The Shortest-Way with the Dissenters*, and dissenting ministers refused to visit Defoe when he was imprisoned.

At the very least he was gambling in a dangerous game without the full backing of his interest group. His hope seems to have been to create opposition to the bill and to the laws on conformity generally by creating political tension and polarization. In defense, Dissenters would close ranks and pursue their long-term interests with more fervor, while high-flying Tories would be lured into betraying their true extremism and so prompt moderate Anglicans to dissociate themselves from persecution. Indeed, in *The Consolidator*, Defoe seems to credit his project with some success in the long term (the bill was after all defeated), though it is clear that his services went unrecognized by Dissenters. Dissenters would have been even less grateful to Defoe had they known that he advised Harley in 1704 to strengthen his position by encouraging "trusty hands" to introduce a new bill against Occasional Conformity. Defoe's plan was to punish Whigs who were forming alliances with Tories against Harley by trapping them into supporting the bill, then defeating it decisively, and thus alienating from the queen and the electorate those who had supported it (*Letters*, 69). Surely the risk would have seemed too great to most Dissenters (in fact, just such a coalition of Whigs and Tories did succeed seven years later in passing a bill against Occasional Conformity), and Defoe's presumption in offering such advice without consulting the people most affected would have been infuriating.

The distinction between informal means of power and devious

manipulating is not very clear. Indeed, Defoe had recommended to Harley a virtuous "dissimulation" in the public interest (*Letters*, 42). Increasingly, as Defoe pursued clandestine forms of influence, especially after the fall of Harley with the death of Queen Anne, his credit as a public advocate was threatened, and the scope of his effectiveness was limited. Disguised as a follower of Harley's thrown into opposition and tempering the tone of Tory journals for a succession of Whig ministers, Defoe had a role very different from that in which he spoke for the nation in *Legion's Memorial* of 1701. When we try to picture the place of Defoe's conduct books and novels in his career (1715–30), it might not be an exaggeration to say that he was seeking the satisfactions of popularity that he could no longer find in political activism.

Political counsel, the generic aim of his journalism, was not the organizing assumption of Defoe's conduct books and novels. But the exemplary status of the narrators and characters offered in some ways a more potent strategy of persuasion, a strategy to induce the identification of reader with fiction that drew more on the constructive element in Defoe's imagination and less on his somewhat self-entrapping gift for paradoxical turns of argument. Controversial topics like religious toleration could be entertained in fictional modes that did not seem controversial and so would not immediately polarize the audience. Yet Defoe's immersion of debates or projects in lifelike stories sometimes results in confused impressions of his purposes, especially for modern readers, who expect clearer generic demarcations separating argument, report, and narrative fiction.

Alan McKillop offered valuable insights into the close relationship of Defoe's journalism to his novels, citing passages in which "Defoe used the word 'story' to mean not 'narrative' but 'discussion,' account,' or 'report,' somewhat as the word is now used in American journalism."[11] This observation could furnish evidence for Lennard Davis's more recent argument that Defoe's literary practices show marks of an undifferentiated "news/novels discourse," which was split apart in the course of the eighteenth century into news and fiction by politically motivated legal and ideological pressures.[12] Davis

[11]Alan Dugald McKillop, *The Early Masters of English Fiction* (Lawrence: University of Kansas Press, 1955), p. 8.

[12]Lennard J. Davis, *Factual Fictions: The Origins of the English Novel* (New York: Columbia University Press, 1983). The chapter "Defoe: Lies as Truth" (154–73) is

could also be seen as developing Ian Watt's principle of the "formal realism" of the novel, "the primary convention, that the novel is a full and authentic report of human experience."[13]

Unlike Watt and Davis, however, McKillop stressed the motivating argumentative structure in Defoe's fiction and journalism. Defoe "does not share our interest in the exact analysis of narrative intent. His way is to cite detail in support of an argument or moral, and it is hard to say when the detail becomes feigned narrative" (*Early Masters*, 8). Impersonation of a single character's point of view orders the novels, yet "impersonation in Defoe is frequently connected with editorial writing and argument rather than with fiction" (9–10). Even at the most advanced stage of Defoe's art, "the deliberating and discussing of policies and plans by the characters, the elaborate weighing of pros and cons, as in conference or committee, carries over into the long narratives a method typical of the pamphlets, in which we hear the writer asking incessantly and persistently, 'In the light of these considerations and circumstances, what shall we do?'" (10).

The argumentative features of Defoe's writing allow G. A. Starr to connect him to traditions of casuistical works by divines and journalists. But this sort of argumentative training, Starr admits, does not lead to coherent plot structure; it rather tends to confirm the episodic, situation-by-situation quality of Defoe's fiction (*Defoe and Casuistry*, 50). Defoe does not organize a rhetoric of fiction, in Wayne Booth's sense. No critical account can make every page seem necessary and harmoniously integrated into overarching structures of plot and character development which teach an implied author's values.[14] One must instead identify the sort of occasion that draws out Defoe's persuasive imagination.

---

marred by the lack of any assessment of the political content of Defoe's writings so that Davis's term *lie*, along with his term *ideology*, becomes a structural category emptied of intent. For a more satisfactory account of Defoe's attitude toward lies as truth, see G. A. Starr, *Defoe and Casuistry* (Princeton, N.J.: Princeton University Press, 1971), pp. 190–211.

[13]Ian Watt, *The Rise of the Novel* (1957; Berkeley: University of California Press, 1962), p. 32.

[14]It seems parochial to deny the term *novel* to Defoe's long narrative fictions and to reserve it for works with unified dramatic plots, called "represented actions" by Sheldon Sacks. A wide variety of fictional forms were called "novels" in the eighteenth century, and indeed the novel has been a generically absorptive form

In all of his novels, as in his political life, Defoe is fascinated by situations in which law and the principles of authority are unclear, situations in which there are exceptional opportunities for innovation, argument, and artful negotiation, but also exceptional dangers and fears. Such uncertainties give dramatic tension to individual episodes, animate extended dialogue, and provide a connecting mood or attitude throughout the narratives. Defoe's typical protagonists—international travelers, criminals, and women—are particularly subject to situations of conflicting or uncertain laws, whether positive law, natural law, divine revelation, or convention. As Starr says, "It is in an ethical no-man's-land . . . that Defoe seems most at home" (*Defoe and Casuistry*, viii). But Defoe's characters do not merely deliberate and decide, they exert power to change their circumstances or to deal with changes in nature or in other people. Starr admits that Defoe's novels are not so casuistical as his conduct books, because he chose characters who are hurried along by events (50). Defoe's typical resistance to decisive endings, even when he has sketched in a plot that should end with secure personal status, is a clue to his profound sympathy with the more insecure, power-seeking phase of the narrative.

Yet we should not think that Defoe shared our antipathies to social organization. The modern equivalents of the social projects that fired Defoe's imagination paradoxically resemble the sort of bureaucratic structures that make modern people yearn for adventures on desert islands. In the late seventeenth century, however, the impotence or inefficiency of public agencies was more obvious than the possibilities of continuous social supervision that haunt us. Even record keeping was for Defoe a matter of inventiveness and personal risk. In the preface to the *Essay upon Projects*, he offers to help the govern-

throughout its history. Attempts to classify the structural features of Defoe's novels, like Ralph Rader's label "simulated naive incoherent autobiography" and Michael Boardman's further application of Rader and Sacks, have genuine descriptive value, even though they are haunted (as we all are) by the models of nineteenth-century fiction that influence our generic expectations. See Sheldon Sacks, *Fiction and the Shape of Belief* (Berkeley: University of California Press, 1964), p. 15; Ralph Rader, "Defoe, Richardson, Joyce, and the Concept of Form in the Novel," in *Autobiography, Biography, and the Novel* (Berkeley: University of California Press, 1973); Michael Boardman, *Defoe and the Uses of Narrative* (New Brunswick, N.J.: Rutgers University Press, 1983).

ment by providing more accurate information about the value of estates for the land tax. One of his chief pieces of advice to Harley was to collect information about politically influential people throughout Britain, and some of his surviving secret reports seem to do exactly that (*Letters*, 36–37, 57–58). Defoe's *Tour through the Whole Island of Great Britain* is a single-handed substitute for a national geographical and economic survey. But it's more fun to invent public agencies than to be administered by them; it may be that Defoe would not have had much interest in the ordinary, day-to-day direction of public administration, even if more opportunities had been available. Harley and Godolphin offered Defoe a regular public position as a commissioner of the Customs in Scotland, an appropriate post since he had helped the Scottish Parliament work out the new customs duty, but he was easily convinced that he would be of more use in the irregular, self-invented secret service that had taken him there.

Hobbes leaves uncertain the extent to which restlessness and insecurity can be cured in political society. One of the chief analogies for the state of nature is the continuing suspicion among citizens that leads to locks and bolts and armed guards. Hobbes advised monarchs to discourage the competition for high honors nourished by the ideals of ancient literature and those of the feudal aristocracy. His suspicion of even the modern goal of commercial competition, great mercantile wealth, shows that he fears the sort of restless competition that civilized activities foster. And Hobbes would have considered impossible the political culture that gained acceptance in Defoe's lifetime, a culture that tolerated violent controversy within the constraints of an antirevolutionary politics.

The fundamental uncertainty about converting human restlessness to constructive use persists in Defoe's fiction. Defoe's fictional probe is perhaps the less revealing since the exemplary status of his characters is unclear; the much-celebrated "individualism" of his format makes it difficult to decide whether Crusoe and Moll are extraordinary in their power seeking or typical. Defoe's repeated assurances in his prefaces that his stories offer incredible variety suggest that he expects the desires that activate his characters' adventures to rouse some kind of fellow feeling in his readers, if not an entirely approving sort of sympathy. After all, as Hobbes knew, his picture of restless self-seeking fit the traditional Christian imagery of sinful earthly vanity. The growing popularity of Defoe's novels in the twentieth century suggests that with increasing stability of Western societies, more people share Defoe's hunger for adventures in creativity than Hobbes's fear of anarchistic competition. And because we take our state organizations for granted, or because we fear their massive power, it is easy for us to underestimate Defoe's hunger to invest creativity in a state that could survive the shocks of competition and could structure life in ways that would more fully deserve his allegiance.[15]

## Natural Law, Economics, and Providence: Defoe and Hobbes

Of all the canonized eighteenth-century English novels, Defoe's fiction comes closest to central features of Hobbes's theory. In the most informed, insightful, and plausible treatment of Defoe's moral philosophy, Maximillian Novak persistently underlines the Hobbesian elements in Defoe's writings, sometimes explicitly attributing them to Hobbes, sometimes attributing them to other writers or to Defoe's originality.[16] Novak's insights help frame the questions involved in the rest of this chapter, which explores the extent to which Defoe's fiction can be seen as illustrating Hobbes or challenging him.

Rather than following the common course of tracking Defoe's ideas to Locke, we should recognize that Defoe constructed an "eclectic originality" from the pool of intellectual influences which also nourished Locke: "Like Locke, Defoe was strongly influenced by the two main streams of political thought during the latter half of the seventeenth century: the doctrines of Hobbes and his disciples and those

[15]Alick West has written the Marxist analysis of Defoe that comes closest to this chapter, since he emphasizes Defoe's investment in the creation of the state as well as in the institutions of trade. But for West, these structures and Defoe's understanding of them are always bourgeois, and the conflict between restless passion and governmental order is always attributed to the contradictions of capitalism. See "Daniel Defoe," in *Crisis and Criticism and Literary Essays* (London: Lawrence and Wishart, 1975), pp. 178–228.

[16]Maximillian Novak, *Defoe and the Nature of Man* (Oxford: Oxford University Press, 1963).

of his opponents, perhaps best represented by Richard Cumberland" (Novak, *Defoe and the Nature of Man*, 2). Cumberland's arguments against Hobbes circulated widely through Pufendorf's quotations from his writings, especially in *De Jure Naturae et Gentium* (Novak, 14). Pufendorf's long-lasting international importance was an important source of information about Hobbes, as well as about arguments against him.

The idea of fundamental law, common to all nations and accessible to reason without the injunctions of divine revelation or positive law, had deep roots in Stoic and Christian thought. New pressures on the formulation of natural law philosophy were felt during the seventeenth century, fueled especially by the controversies within states about religious authority and by conflicts among states over religion, commerce, and colonization. It was a particularly urgent task of moral philosophy to detach a morally based theory of law from the debated theses of theology and biblical interpretation, or at least to identify the least debatable theses of theology in which to ground a theory of law. For it must be remembered that even "modernized" natural law theorists like Grotius and Pufendorf rested their arguments on religious beliefs about the divine origin of universal reason, which dictates moral obligations.[17] While severing the tie to theology in his assault on rationalism, Hobbes built upon (or, rather, reconstructed) the natural law tradition to create a universal political theory that similarly emphasized human equality in a state of nature and the consent or contract that brings government into being. Therefore, writers in the natural law tradition often sound Hobbesian, and indeed coincide with Hobbes on many points.[18]

[17]The quoted term is George Sabine's. See "The Modernized Law of Nature," in Sabine's *A History of Political Theory* (New York: Holt, 1937), pp. 415–34. The classic source for the subject is Otto von Gierke, *Natural Law and the Theory of Society, 1500–1800*, trans. Ernest Barker (Cambridge: Cambridge University Press, 1934), 2 vols. For a more recent account of the background of seventeenth-century natural law theory in sixteenth-century Thomists of the Counter-Reformation, see Quentin Skinner, *The Foundations of Modern Political Thought* (Cambridge: Cambridge University Press, 1978), 2:135–84. For a discussion of natural law in John Locke, see John Dunn, *The Political Thought of John Locke* (Cambridge: Cambridge University Press, 1969), pp. 187–99.

[18]Several provocative and widely debated studies argue Hobbes's essential dependency on natural law. See Howard Warrender, *The Political Philosophy of Hobbes: His Theory of Obligation* (Oxford: Oxford University Press, 1957); and A. E. Taylor,

In Defoe's state of nature, humankind is fearful and weak (Novak, 23). Self-preservation is the first law of nature, embedded in the passions as well as in reason (Novak, 19).[19] Crusoe's anxious condition on his island was a state of war in Hobbes's sense, because it was not just a determinate time of battle but "a continual state of mind" (Novak, 36). Competition in power threatens everyone and motivates the establishment of government (Novak, 18). But one never entirely resigns one's right to self-preservation, even under government.[20]

It is worth pausing to note that these Hobbesian elements that Novak has extracted place the moral psychology of Defoe's writing in a political framework of thought. Other critics have noted the "restless seeking of power after power" in Defoe, but they reorient these themes by modern ego psychology and, perhaps also, by existentialism. Thus one critic writes that Defoe's novels "raise the issue of self and identity prominently. . . . The narrative is used to attest to there being more to a narrator's life than a meaningless flux of disparate experience. Autobiography becomes an attempt to create life and

---

"The Ethical Doctrine of Hobbes," reprinted in *Hobbes Studies*, ed. K. C. Brown (Cambridge: Harvard University Press, 1965).

[19]Novak is mistaken when he asserts that "in proclaiming self defense as a law of nature as well as a right, Defoe was more radical than even Hobbes" (*Defoe and the Nature of Man*, p. 19). Compare *Leviathan*, I, 14, 190: "And consequently it is a precept or general rule of Reason, that every man, ought to endeavour Peace, as farre as he has hope of obtaining it; and when he cannot obtain it, that he may seek, and use, all helps and advantages of Warre." The gloss calls this passage "The Fundamentall Law of Nature." Defoe and Hobbes agree that self-preservation is the primary law. Defoe might have disagreed with Hobbes's deduction of a right to "all helps" to self-preservation in a state of nature.

[20]Novak does not mention that for Hobbes, as for Defoe, one can never make a binding covenant against one's own self-defense. In cases of starvation (*Leviathan*, II, 27, 346) or threatened execution (I, 14, 199) or in a losing war (II, 29, 375), obligations to the laws of the commonwealth cease. One cannot infer an extensive right to revolution from these passages, but they do show that Hobbes assumed that there are certain natural psychological limits to the authority of government and that it would be prudent not to drive too many people up against these psychological walls. Defoe defended a right of revolution against James II, rather than the common, less radical course of describing James's departure as an abdication. Like Locke, Defoe assumes that there is a contract between people and magistrates, as well as the Hobbesian social contract of all people with one another, and like Locke Defoe asserts that there is a dissolution of government when governors break the law (see "The True-Born Englishman," pt. II, ll. 808–27). But after 1688 Defoe denied that the Protestant monarchs threatened self-preservation in any way that could justify revolution in Britain, and he seems distinctly more favorable than Hobbes to using war as a tool for national power and unity.

soul."[21] Another quotes Hobbes appropriately and imaginatively to illuminate Defoe's novels, but she moves them away from the constructive values of Hobbes's commonwealth toward Rochester's cynicism and nihilism. The result is to turn a political psychology toward the metaphysical: "Although Defoe's characters seem to be acting purposefully in the world, they are always, in actuality, merely reacting to the terrors of their own finitude."[22] There is in her view of the books no true, progressive mastery of the environment, for "the inescapable reality is always death" (Birdsall, *Defoe's Perpetual Seekers*, 39). For discriminating between a metaphysical and a political analysis in this case, it is useful to remember the distinction Leo Strauss found in Hobbes's theory: natural death comes to everyone and so the far of it need have little political bearing, but commonwealths are created to insure against violent death at the hands of other people.[23]

Certain features of Defoe's natural law theory could be taken as principles of a natural sociability that would eliminate Hobbes's war of all against all: notably the recognition of property preceding the establishment of government (Novak, 15), the existence of family society in the state of nature (Novak, 16), and the natural law of gratitude (Novak, 113–28). To Novak's list of natural laws prominent in Defoe's fiction, I would add the very important law of keeping promises, abiding by contracts, an essential part of natural law theory. Where does Hobbes stand on these widely recognized laws or conditions of nature? For him natural laws, like the general rules governing property and moral virtues such as gratitude, are not laws but "theorems" (*Leviathan*, I, 15, 217), conclusions of reason about important qualities of character and behavior "that dispose men to peace" (II, 26, 314). They do not become laws until a commonwealth

[21]Everett Zimmerman, *Defoe and the Novel* (Berkeley: University of California Press, 1975), p. 5. See also Homer Obed Brown, "The Displaced Self in the Novels of Daniel Defoe," *ELH* 38 (1971):562–90.

[22]Virginia Ogden Birdsall, *Defoe's Perpetual Seekers* (Cranbury, N.J.: Associated University Presses, 1985), p. 20.

[23]Leo Strauss, *The Political Philosophy of Hobbes: Its Basis and Genesis*, trans. Elsa M. Sinclair (Chicago: University of Chicago Press, 1966), pp. 6–29. Note especially the contrast between Hobbes's moral basis of political obligation in the specifically human fear of violent death and Spinoza's reduction of right to might in a naturalistic framework of argument (pp. 28–29).

is settled and the sovereign declares them part of the positive law. Though we may view these theorems as laws commanded by God and binding in a state of nature, they have little reliable influence on human conduct until there is a human sovereign authority to interpret and enforce them. Fair property dealings, promise keeping, gratitude, and other natural laws Hobbes lists (*Leviathan*, I, 15) could be seen as his attempt to outline a desirable political culture for states, but the first two laws (of self-preservation and of the social contract) are the fundamentals. Similarly, in several passages Hobbes recognizes the probable historical origin of society in family structures (II, 20, 253; II, 22, 285). He only denies that parental authority is the legitimate foundation of political authority, rather than consent, and that parental authority supersedes the sovereign authority in case of conflict. Instead, according to Hobbes the positive law licenses the specific form of family life, which may differ from nation to nation (II, 20, 253–54).

Novak's account of Defoe approaches the Hobbesian view that the natural laws of sociability require the firm foundation of government.[24] Novak notes how precarious property is in the *Farther Adventures of Robinson Crusoe* until the Spanish captain takes on the role of magistrate (54–56). One couplet from Defoe's *Jure Divino* seems especially Hobbesian:

> The Wit of Man could never yet invent
> A Way of Life without a Government. [Novak, 57]

Similarly, other lines from *Jure Divino* show patriarchal family society degenerating into feuds until agreement to form a stable state is reached (Novak, 17). Defoe's understanding of gratitude strikes Novak as surprisingly utilitarian and political, and he compares it to the relevant section from *Leviathan* (119–21). Novak's brief treatment of the natural obligation to keep promises shows naive Moll Flanders learning that her lover's marriage promise needs to be guaranteed in political society by a written contract (99–101).

It makes sense that Defoe's moral philosophy should give a large

[24]Starr has noted that in casuistical writing that may have influenced Defoe, natural law arguments are rejected as grounds for disobeying positive or divine law. Although natural law theory has a potential revolutionary use, that cannot be said to be its main function in the eighteenth century.

place to the institutions of government, considering his enormous investment in political writing aimed, after 1688, at marshaling national allegiance against rebellion and national support for strong and creative administrations. It also makes sense to follow Novak in identifying Defoe's economics with mercantilist concerns about national wealth and state power rather than with nineteenth-century-style laissez-faire capitalism.[25] Joyce Appleby has argued that English mercantilism (that is, "a large body of public law directed at state economic goals") emerged for the first time in the 1690s, in a period of economic dislocation caused by King William's war. In this crisis laissez-faire free-trade arguments of merchants seemed inadequate to the landholders and manufacturers for meeting the problems of employing the poor, protecting English manufactures, and competing for world markets. Throughout the eighteenth century, balance-of-trade arguments (with are implicitly statist) suppressed free-trade arguments, as merchants joined the politically dominant landed class in policies thought to be in the national interest.[26] Defoe does not emerge as a laissez-faire theorist;[27] instead, through-

[25]Maximillian Novak, *Economics and the Fiction of Daniel Defoe* (Berkeley: University of California Press, 1962).

[26]Joyce Oldham Appleby, *Economic Thought and Ideology in Seventeenth-Century England* (Princeton: Princeton University Press, 1978), pp. 242–79. Appleby denies that these political divisions of the 1690s represent the standard oppositions of class analysis (land versus money correlated with old morality versus new economics). She emphasizes that the landowning classes accepted ideas about the values of economic activity, especially the development of banking and of the productivity of land. The split in the 1690s was caused by a divergence of interests between, on the one side, landlords and manufacturers who were tied to the whole economy as employers and sources of tax revenue, and on the other side, merchants, bank promoters, and stock jobbers "whose speculative ideas moved as freely as their capital" (p. 265). One reason that the mercantilist position was articulated in terms of an outmoded "balance of trade" argument rather than in an argument about the authority or responsibility of states to control economic freedom was because of the explosive political association of state control with Stuart monarchical pretentions. Appleby invites us to consider the eighteenth-century suppression of free trade arguments as one more effect of the entrenchment of Whig oligarchy. It is worth noting, once more, that the development of central governmental authority in the eighteenth century—those arguments and policies that I have called Hobbesian—were at the time, for important political reasons, cloaked in antiabsolutist garb.

[27]Geoffrey Sill has shown that in 1713 Defoe defended the lowering of trade restrictions with France, but not on laissez-faire capitalist grounds. Defoe's arguments were oriented to the balance of trade and other national interests, and they were made to protect the Tories from Whig attacks on the Peace of Utrecht. Sill objects to Appleby's account of the development of eighteenth-century ideology, but

out his career, he urged political responsibility for the economic development of labor and of markets.[28] He did not identify himself with the narrow group interests of merchants, nor did he participate in the antipolitical, amoral ethos usually attributed to "economic man." Defoe, like his creation Robinson Crusoe, is better understood as "political man."

As we have seen, Defoe's psychology of political man is structured by morally based natural laws headed by the primary law of all, self-preservation. It makes little sense, therefore, to seek in Defoe's fiction, as many critics do, an inevitable and protracted conflict between motives of economic self-interest and moral law. Ian Watt maintained that "the conflict between spiritual and material values . . . was perhaps more obvious in the eighteenth century than at any other time."[29] Yet he immediately cited counterevidence showing that such religious authorities as Bishop Warburton and, indeed, even Defoe himself, did not see an inevitable clash between utility and salvation. Watt nonetheless asserted the negative evidence to be positive evidence for his thesis, since the conflict between religion and capitalism was presumably so deeply rooted in the social structure and so threatening that it could not be acknowledged. With such procedures a critic is bound to underestimate very seriously the consciousness of historical agents expressed in their religion, morality, and politics, in order to maintain dogmatically a crude schema supposed to derive from social history.

In a more recent book, John Richetti quotes with approval Martin Price's version of the supposed conflict of Puritan and bourgeois, which is now more respectfully but less plausibly attributed to Defoe's own consciousness of "the frequent conflict between the

---

his evidence neatly fits her argument. Defoe should be seen as aligned with mercantilism and the consolidation of national power whether managed by Harley and the Tory ministry or later by Walpole and the Whigs. Defoe's personal loyalty and short-term political objectives, of course, had some effect on particular acts of advocacy. See Sill, *Defoe and the Idea of Fiction*, pp. 16–18, 30–55.

[28]Peter Earle also associates Defoe with the mercantilist emphasis on high employment, protective tariffs, and competition for world markets, but considers him somewhat unusual in wishing to maintain English wages at their relatively high level. Earle's description of Defoe's hostility to technical innovation and his emphasis on social stability fit the political picture I have been drawing. See Peter Earle, *The World of Defoe* (London: Weidenfeld and Nicolson, 1975), pp. 107–57.

[29]Watt, *The Rise of the Novel*, p. 83.

demands of commercialism and those of spiritual salvation."[30] Richetti then asserts, in an unrecognized contradiction, that scholarship about Defoe's "fairly coherent views on God, man and society" illustrate this insight about the incompatibility of religion and economics. Richetti relies on C. B. Macpherson's arguments about "possessive individualism" to reduce political philosophy of the seventeenth century into evidences of a market economy (despite residual traces of religion) and hence, by a further reduction, into an essentially capitalist vision. So, though Richetti's Hegelian framework allows him to see more connections than do most critics between the psychological themes of selfhood and the political themes of mastery, his analysis tends to collapse into the formulaic opposition between social experience, conceived as fundamentally economic, and outdated religious ideology: "The narrative problem . . . is to allow Crusoe to enjoy freedom and power without violating the restrictions of moral and religious ideology which defines the individual as less than autonomous" (*Defoe's Narratives*, 63).

It would make more sense to claim Defoe had a religious optimism about economics. Since economic activity and many other forms of self-preservation and self-interest show fundamentally moral motives, particular conflicts with positive or divine law can be resolved by a redirection of the same energies by an individual or a society. The devil may play upon desires for economic security, but he didn't invent them. Perhaps many twentieth-century people are so haunted by a nineteenth-century evangelical image of morality as necessarily sacrificial that they cannot recognize self-interest as a moral motive. Self-interest is a feature of most moral systems, including various kinds of Christian morality, and it does not make the writing of Defoe inevitably "secular."

Defoe had a fully religious sense of self-interest. He believed that human beings can and should help themselves by detecting God's special, as well as general, Providence in the patterns of individual

[30]Martin Price, *To the Palace of Wisdom: Studies in Order and Energy from Dryden to Blake*, quoted from page 264 of the 1965 New York edition by John Richetti in *Defoe's Narratives: Situations and Structures* (Oxford: Clarendon, 1975), p. 5. This passage and the rest of Richetti's *Crusoe* chapter are enthusiastically endorsed by Leopold Damrosch in *God's Plots and Man's Stories* (Chicago: University of Chicago Press, 1985), p. 189.

and national history. Defoe's fiction was shaped partly under the influence of various religious genres that teach the ways of Providence, such as spiritual diaries and autobiographies, exemplary lives, collections of providential events, and allegorical fiction.[31] Moreover, there is good evidence that Defoe believed in manifestations of the supernatural in special premonitions and dreams, apparitions caused by God, angels, intermediate (semiangelic) spirits or the Devil, in bibliomancy, second sight, and day fatalities.[32]

We need not set aside or deny Defoe's well-documented beliefs about revelation to conduct political interpretation of his fiction. Our inquiry should be: what bearing do beliefs about supernatural phenomena have on the social transactions pictured by Defoe? To use Hobbes's terms, do they help people live in "peace and unity," to trust one another and avoid conflicts? Do they serve to authorize those who have special insight into Providence over those who lack it? Claims to interpret providential signs often provoked sectarian controversy; disputes within what J. Paul Hunter called "the Providence tradition" illustrate Hobbes's analysis of the political problems caused by claims of special revelation. Though Hobbes suggested many base motives for people who claim supernatural inspiration, he does not deny the possibility of God acting directly to affect a person's senses. Instead he argues that people have no way of sharing these special experiences with others and so no means of inducing belief in their religious inspiration, except by the exercise of authority that has already been recognized on other grounds. Hobbes does not believe he lives in a world of purely secular motives any more than does Defoe. For the human psychology of both fear and power seeking generates questions about a deity and how to honor and influence that deity. Neither would have considered practical our rigorous separation of church and state. Religious belief is a part of political interpretation.

Reading people and predicting the future by means of natural laws, providential signs, or some other means is an activity of the

[31] G. A. Starr, *Defoe and Spiritual Autobiography* (Princeton: Princeton University Press, 1965); and J. Paul Hunter, *The Reluctant Pilgrim* (Baltimore: Johns Hopkins University Press, 1966).

[32] Rodney M. Baine, *Daniel Defoe and the Supernatural* (Athens: University of Georgia Press, 1968).

reader as well as of the characters of Defoe's fiction. The diverse institutions of literary criticism do not arbitrate interpretations of fiction with the unified authority that Hobbes recommended for his sovereign interpreter of law. Perhaps Defoe was drawn to fiction for this relative freedom from political supervision, and drawn especially to create novels of "incredible variety," as he boasted in his prefaces. In the long narratives Defoe opened for his readers a wide field of possible interpretation, as he opened for his protagonist-narrators a wide field for the exertion of their powers. So we will learn something from Defoe's novels about how power works, even if we remain unsure about what use of power he most recommends.

## *Robinson Crusoe*: Political Man

Defoe's first, most popular, novel allows its hero the most extravagant adventures, with the widest latitude of personal creativity. But the moral significance of Crusoe's desires and opportunities is confused from the very beginning, overcast with guilt, yet not clearly criminal. Is it wrong for him to leave his home? Did he abandon a calling? Not exactly, since as a third son he had not been "bred to any Trade,"[33] though his father designed him for the law. His father advises against leaving home, will not consent to it (different from forbidding), but does not curse him. Instead he delivers a prediction that "God would not bless me" (6). The statement may only have the status of strong prudential advice: God will not bless what is against your interest. Twice during the stormy first voyage, the prediction recurs to Crusoe's memory like a curse about to be fulfilled, and that fearful interpretation receives confirmation from the captain of the ship:

> *Young Man*, says he, *you ought never to go to Sea any more, you ought to take this for a plain and visible Token that you are not to be a Seafaring Man.* Why, Sir, said I, will you go to Sea no more? *That is another Case*, said he, *it is my Calling, and therefore my Duty; but as*

[33]Parenthetical references to *Robinson Crusoe* and *Moll Flanders* give page references to the Oxford World's Classics editions: Daniel Defoe, *The Life and Strange Surprizing Adventures of Robinson Crusoe, of York, Mariner*, ed. J. Donald Crowley (Oxford: Oxford University Press, 1981); and Daniel Defoe, *The Fortunes and Misfortunes of the Famous Moll Flanders*, ed. G. A. Starr (Oxford: Oxford University Press, 1981).

> *you made this Voyage for a Trial, you see what a Taste Heaven has given you of what you are to expect if you persist; perhaps this is all befallen us on your Account, like* Jonah *in the ship* of Tarshish. . . . Upon that I told him some of my Story; at the End of which he burst out with a strange kind of Passion. . . . *And Young Man,* said he, *depend upon it, if you do not go back, where-ever you go, you will meet with nothing but Disasters and Disappointments till your Father's Words are fulfilled upon you.* [15]

Unlike Hobbes, Defoe believed in the possibility of reading providential signs in surprising events or strong impulses of mind, "listening to the voice of Providence," as he called it in one section of *Serious Reflections of Robinson Crusoe*:

> I cannot doubt that the invisible hand of Providence, which guides and governs this world, does with a secret power likewise influence this world, and may, and I believe does, direct from thence silent messengers on many occasions—whether sleeping or waking, whether directly or indirectly, whether by hints, impulses, allegories, mysteries, or otherwise, we know not; and does think fit to give us such alarms, such previous and particular knowledge of things that, if listened to, might many ways be useful to the prudent man to foresee the evil, and hide himself. [191][34]

This passage echoes and confirms many like it in the original narrative.

As readers of *Robinson Crusoe*, we confront Hobbes's problem: whose authority shall we trust in reading providential signs? What phenomena should be viewed in this way? The passage in the *Serious Reflections* admits that the signs of providence are "so imperfect, so broken, so irregular, that men may either never be able to pass any right judgment of them, as is sometimes the case, or make a perfect judgment of them, which is often the case, and so the end of the intimation be entirely defeated without any fault, neglect, or omission of the man." Doesn't Crusoe's "impulse" to travel count as a "token"? After all, fortune smiles on Crusoe's second journey, and he gains the patronage of a generous sea captain as well as a vague form of paternal support: "This 40l. I had mustered together by the Assistance of some of my Relations whom I corresponded with, and who,

[34]Parenthetical references give page numbers from *Serious Reflections during the Life and Surprizing Adventures of Robinson Crusoe*, in *Works of Daniel Defoe*, ed. G. H. Maynadier (New York: Sproul, 1903–4).

I believe, got my Father, or at least my Mother, to contribute so much as that to my first Adventure" (17).

Defoe is unwilling to identify his hero's wanderlust as a clear violation of the Fifth Commandment. Even in the case of a more decisive prohibition, it is not certain that Defoe interpreted the Fifth Commandment as a God-given paternal authority to determine a child's occupation. Defoe's later reflections on the original narrative try to sort out this problem: Parents have a duty to introduce their children into the world, though they should consult "the inclinations and capacities" of their children (*Serious Reflections*, 68). Children need not follow callings chosen by parents, but Crusoe's fault was in avoiding any steady occupation.[35] Novak is right to stress that the natural law of gratitude includes gratitude to parents. But Hobbes, who also recognized gratitude as a natural law in his own sense, points out that in a commonwealth fathers resign absolute power over their children, though "it was never intended, they should lose the honour due unto them for their education" (*Leviathan*, II, 30, 382).[36]

Our difficulty in interpreting the bearing of the Fifth Commandment on Crusoe's life, like our difficulty in interpreting the bearing of providential signs that may or may not back it up, is entirely in keeping with Hobbes's skepticism about interpretation when we lack a sovereign interpreter. Whatever respect is due to a father's advice, it is not the sovereign law. Crusoe's refusal to inherit his social life from his father is typical of the plots of many novels and brings them close to the vision of post-Hobbesian political philosophy. Family life may be an important influence and training ground for social life, but fundamental rights and duties cannot be derived from parental authority. Crusoe's adult ties to his adoptive relations, the captain and his widow, and the Brazilian partner, turn out to be much more important than the ties to his original family.

[35]Hunter notes that in the guide tradition children have a duty to attend to paternal advice, but this does not mean that "parental choice is the ultimate determinant of one's station" (*The Reluctant Pilgrim*, p. 37).

[36]Novak contrasts Hobbes to Defoe on the grounds that Hobbes traced the obligation of children to generation (*Defoe and the Nature of Man*, p. 122). But in fact Hobbes argues that generation and nourishment placed parental dominion in the mother, unless positive law ruled otherwise (*Leviathan*, II, 20, 253–54). Note that Crusoe's mother is more favorable to his journey.

Almost immediately in the narrative, Crusoe's resistance to his father's advice becomes conflated with resistance to understanding the role of Providence in his life, a refusal to reflect seriously, to recognize providential intimations.[37] This sin has a much clearer status, since Crusoe's path to conversion and the recognition of God's hand in his life provide elements of structure in the book. The broad relevance of the spiritual problem, "stupidity" or ignorance of Providence, tends to mitigate the suggestion that leaving home or seeking a different way of life is in itself sinful, or indeed that any other act in the book is sinful in itself, apart from neglecting God.[38]

The blurry moral meaning of the original act of disobedience, and of similar sequences throughout his novels, makes some readers feel that Defoe is writing too hastily to lay a firm foundation for his moral fable, or else that the spiritual parts of the book are not very well thought out, merely "Sunday religion," conventionally obligatory but extraneous to the exciting interest of his fiction. Other readers defend the artful construction required to capture the mixed motives of his mundane characters. Without making judgments about Defoe's techniques of composition or the sincerity of his inner faith, I would only urge that the murkiness that proceeds from invoking rules of behavior and standards of judgment, which are then uncertainly applied by characters and readers, is Defoe's best atmosphere. Like Hobbes's state of nature, the moral terrain of Defoe's fiction is not entirely fluid; there are recognized principles of behavior, at least laws of nature, laws of religion, and individual contracts. But rarely does a sovereign interpreter pronounce judgment on the character, the sayings, or doings of the narrator-protagonist; and the social scenes, though they rarely represent a state of war, are makeshift affairs without much stability, because the political order does not serve all the needs of society or continuously enforce its laws. Yet the indecisive stage of moral discourse and the unstable situation are most appropriate to the energies of Defoe's characters.

The arguments that Crusoe's father has used to keep him at home

[37]Starr has argued that Crusoe's "original sin" is not so much a specific act of disobedience as a symbol of the rebellion against Providence, "the natural waywardness of unregenerate man" (*Defoe and Spiritual Autobiography*, p. 79).

[38]There is one unambiguous sin before Crusoe's conversion: his conforming to Catholicism in Brazil.

(the prospect of "a Life of Ease and Pleasure") do not suggest that his problem was a moral conflict over the value of status and wealth; this is not the story of someone punished for material greed, haunted by guilty conflict with religious asceticism. What takes Crusoe away from "the middle Station of Life" is the thirst for adventure and distinction, an appetite that Defoe, like Hobbes, associates with both aristocracy and criminals: "He told me it was for Men of desperate Fortunes on one Hand, or of aspiring, superior Fortunes on the other, who went abroad upon Adventures, to rise by Enterprize, and make themselves famous in Undertakings of a Nature out of the common Road; that these things were all either too far above me, or too far below me" (4). The gentleman-highwayman figure who appears so often in eighteenth-century fiction (for example, in *Moll Flanders, Tom Jones, Humphry Clinker*) demonstrates the association of a certain sort of restless passion with high birth and crime. The wide scope of the landed proprietor, the chief beneficiary of English liberty, may be desirable for certain large spirits who do not happen to be endowed with appropriate status or the means to support that status. For most of these figures, emigration, Locke's safety valve, provides the possibility of attaining greater liberty and property. Defoe at times suggests that pirates draw from the ranks of exceptionally skilled seamen for similar reasons: the life of lawful seamen is too narrow in both senses: too rigidly disciplined and too impoverished. He might have learned more as a seaman and risen in the ranks, but Crusoe ships out as a gentleman.

What does bind people together, if not blood relations? In the dilemma pictured by Hobbes, the restless seeking after power makes a person want to add the power of others to his own, but this desire creates a fatal competition that reduces everybody's power. After a prosperous first voyage, Crusoe's second voyage to the coast of Guinea ends by enslaving him. Since he never consents to this debasement and clearly does not consider himself bound by law to his master, he assumes powers not lawful at home: he appropriates his master's boat, holds the power of life and death, enslaves another person, forcing one servant to swim away at gunpoint and the other, a boy named Xury, to pledge obedience.

Since no settled positive laws bind them, the relation between Crusoe and Xury tells a great deal about what fundamental human qualities Defoe believed underlie society, "those qualities of mankind, that concern their living together in Peace, and Unity." Though force and the desire for self-preservation motivate Xury to obey, consent even for slaves is essential for Defoe, as for Hobbes, and Defoe generally prefers to formalize covenants. Crusoe makes Xury swear by his God, the only guardian over promise keeping in a state of nature. For Defoe keeping promises seems to be an almost irresistible, fundamental human tendency, even without secure means of enforcement. Without trust, international trade would have been much more difficult, and a surprising number of people in Defoe's novels go to great lengths to keep faith, as he points out in *Serious Reflections* (19–24). In his fiction there is also a great deal of maneuvering to induce people to give their word or, on the other hand, to avoid the bond of an oath.

Defoe grants his protagonists a quality Hobbes denies in the Preface to *Leviathan*, one that adds a more secure trust to the general tendency to credit promises: skill in the assessment of character. Although the Moor and the boy Xury speak the same words, that they would "go all over the world" with Crusoe, he will not trust the Moor and he does trust Xury. He reads Xury's character in his face: "The Boy smil'd in my Face and spoke so innocently that I could not mistrust him" (23). In this respect Defoe's characters are politicians more on the Machiavellian model than on the general scientific principles of Hobbes. Nevertheless, reading character in physiognomy is not an entirely reliable skill in Defoe's view. His protagonists make mistakes, like Moll's entrapment by the Lancashire frauds. In *Jure Divino* Defoe prays for a mark from heaven by which to read hypocrisy, but a footnote admits, "This is a wish only."

The obedience of Xury is secured not merely by one oath but by continuing benefits of food and drink, to which he responds with generous gratitude, and Crusoe takes pleasure in his pleasure. The first smile of gratitude is confirmed by many more. Their commitment quickly grows to exceed a mere quid pro quo. Xury proves his loyalty, as Friday does later in the book, by offering to risk his life to provide for them both. And once again the ability to detect the true internal meaning of the external sign is crucial to Defoe. Crusoe may suspect Xury's motives for offering to go onshore alone, but "the Boy answered with so much Affection that made me love him ever after.

Says he, '*If wild Mans come, they eat me, you go wey*'" (25). Xury's superior skill in skinning animals is displayed willingly for his master's benefit. Voluntary exchanges like this one, more on the order of gifts than equivalent exchanges under compulsion of necessity, characterize Defoe's world. Later the Portuguese sea captain rescues Crusoe for charity, not pay, and receives an unexpected present from the widow of Crusoe's first patron. A similar sort of mutual generosity marks the end of the whole story. Indeed, *honesty*, as the word is used in the *Serious Reflections*, refers more often to generosity than to mere fairness.

Exceptionally reliable promise keeping, magnanimity, the power of reading faces and providential signs are human resources pictured by Defoe which we might expect to efface the Hobbesian vision of human competition in a situation of radical uncertainty. But in Defoe, as in Hobbes, when these manners make for peace and unity, they are blended with self-interest and self-preservation rather than set into a drama of protracted moral conflict. So we do not find the sort of patterned complexity of character or the sort of plot development that we recognize as novelistic. The blending of interest with other motives is often clumsy, even though the unassimilated lumps of justification in the texture of the narrative provide material for endless critical discoveries of complexity.

Explicit promises provide important guarantees to Defoe, but he shows that problems of trust can be resolved without the shared language that makes formal contracts possible. On the coast of Africa a group of natives seems able to understand a natural language of gestures: Crusoe makes signs for food and they bring food, but they are afraid to approach his boat and he is afraid to approach shore. The deadlock is resolved by the grateful trust induced when he kills the animals that threaten the Africans. Furthermore, in return for the meat they are happy to part with the skins and a larger quantity of provisions. A certain element of magnanimity seems essential for breaking the deadlock. Nevertheless, the natural language of magnanimous deeds and symbolic gestures, like Crusoe's saving Friday and Friday's original act of submission by placing Crusoe's foot on his head, is not sufficient for a continuously shared social life. In spite of a number of mutual services, Crusoe does not trust Friday with the use of guns until he can speak fluently in English and they have had religious discussions, so that they can understand promises and the religious sanctions for each other's oaths.

Defoe does not seem entirely at ease with the institution of slavery, though he also does not seem to question it fundamentally. Since both Xury and Friday come from slaveholding nations and readily consent to a similar relation with Crusoe, they seem to excuse an Englishman's participation in the institution of slavery. This is not an institution an Englishman would be proud to invent. Crusoe, by contrast to Xury and Friday, cannot be induced to consent to slavery either by self-preservation or by gratitude to his gentle Turkish master, and we may remember Defoe's assertion of a right of revolution against tyranny in *Jure Divino.* In spite of the racist implications of the contrasting political attitudes, Defoe seems anxious to transform the situation of slave owning from one of brutal and continuous force to one more like any other kind of mastership, stabilized by mutual benefit and affectionate gratitude. Friday is taught to call Crusoe "Master," but is his title "servant" or "slave"? The sale of Xury is not presented as heartless, part of the story of the hardened sinner, but as an act of gratitude to the Portuguese captain. It depends on the consent of the boy, under humane arrangements for liberation after ten years if he converts to Christianity, an arrangement that does not seem too different from that of indentured servants. Indeed, in the *Serious Reflections* Crusoe praises the generosity of the Portuguese captain in paying for Xury, since he "was not my slave by any right, or if he had, became free from that time and the life of Xury, which he had saved, as a servant, was his own" (24). Crusoe later learns that parting with Xury was imprudent, since labor was desperately needed in Brazil. He relates this imprudence to other providential punishments for his irreverence, but he never seems to consider selling Xury as in itself sinful. Similarly, when he sails out from Brazil once again to Guinea, he blames his "inclination of wandering abroad" for the disastrous shipwreck, but there is no suggestion that he was punished for any sin in his intended slave trading.

Defoe does not seem to believe that Christians are entitled to enslave non-Christians on the grounds of religion alone. As Crusoe carries on the long debate with himself about his revulsion from cannibalism, he comes to the conclusion from principle and then, as an afterthought, from policy that he should leave judgment in God's hands. His breach of the decision not to slay or enslave the cannibals is justified by a special dream, providential circumstances, self-defense and the defense of Friday—or perhaps beliefs about these things merely explain rather than justify his change of mind. In Crusoe's original meditation on revenge against the cannibals, he brings to mind the universal abhorrence of Spaniards created by their unjustifiable brutality toward the idolators in the new world who practiced human sacrifice. In *Serious Reflections*, however, Defoe has Crusoe justify the Spaniards as the instruments of Providence in order to introduce his suggestion that Christians of different persuasions should settle their differences by uniting in a new crusade against the pagan (223).

How do we weigh these contradictions?[39] In the first case Crusoe's prudential fears about being outnumbered seem to determine him against making war on the cannibals, just as self-defense motivates his change of mind; and in the *Reflections* prudential regard for Christian unity at home may underlie his desire to arouse his readers against the pagans, or perhaps he intends to support some international project involving an alliance with Spain. Do these considerations make unimportant the meditations in *Crusoe* on judging the morality of other nations? The fictional voice, alternately affected by different principles and subject to shifts of situation, seems to lack force, if we expect an example of moral decision making or a drama of psychological conflict.[40] After one of these moral meditations the

[39]Novak suggests that contradictions between the *Reflections* and *Robinson Crusoe* show that "the closer Defoe's name became associated with *Robinson Crusoe* the more orthodox he became in religious matters." See *Defoe and the Nature of Man*, p. 46.

[40]See Michael Boardman, *Defoe and the Uses of Narrative*: "In *Robinson Crusoe* there is frequently not only no fusion of personality with the other elements of the story, there is no purposeful contradiction" (p. 54). Boardman considers Crusoe's account of Providence calling on him to save Friday "a bit of extraneous casuistry" (p. 61), so perhaps he has trouble taking Defoe's ethics seriously. E. Anthony James describes the shifts and inconsistencies of Crusoe's attitude toward killing the cannibals as evidence of Defoe's deliberate artistry in representing "the values of a narrator who is pious enough, but who is practical above all else, and adept at making his piety a medium of self interest which is always supreme." So James considers Crusoe's analogy to Spanish persecution in America a "lame" rationalization of his fear of attacking the cannibals, and his sense of providential call in saving Friday a rationalization of his decision to obtain a slave to help him leave the island. See *Defoe's*

narrative seems to rush along impelled by the changing desire or need of the protagonist in changing circumstances, with few backward glances at the complex consequences of such a difficult decision and very little ardent justification, so that the speaker seems either incoherent or shallow. For these reasons, connecting Defoe to a tradition of casuistical writing seems wrong in spirit, however many illuminations of his sources it may provide.[41] The extended moral debates or meditations in Defoe's fictions do not structure the narrative so much as they open up the opportunity for Defoe to explore issues that troubled him and his audience, to try out controversial poses while avoiding possibly embarrassing commitments to them. This quality of argumentative experiment characterizes much of his pamphlet writing and helps to explain why he preferred writing with a fictional mask, as well as why he was continually misunderstood.

The similarity of the episode with Xury and the episode with Friday raises fundamental questions about Defoe's art. The detail of the two episodes does not function in a contrast between the damned and the saved state because there is no condemnation of the sale of Xury; the parallelism seems mere repetition to fill out the volume. Since Defoe wrote his fiction rapidly, one can imagine him stumbling across good material and reworking it at greater length without either removing the earlier version or feeling obliged to account for the repetition by weaving thematic significance into it. In a similar way, his narrators will recur to a past episode and fill it out. Sympathetic critics are ingenious in providing the rationalization that Defoe has inconveniently overlooked, by filling out the sketchy structure of character change. But most memories of *Robinson Crusoe*, most abridgments or dramatizations, simply leave out the Xury episode rather than use it to underline a contrast of the later episode with the earlier one: it is not typically seen as part of a rational, memorable structure.

This sort of redundancy can provide important clues to what inspired Defoe to his most powerful creations in fiction. The tension between the desire for supportive associations with other people and

---

*Many Voices: A Rhetorical Study of Prose Style and Literary Method* (Amsterdam: Rodopi NV, 1972), pp. 187–92, esp. p. 189. For an account more respectful of Crusoe's ethical reasoning, see Hunter, *The Reluctant Pilgrim*, pp. 182–84.

[41]Starr admits this problem, *Defoe and Casuistry*, p. 50.

the fear of them is one of his most important motifs. The tension is felt most acutely when the ordinary rules of settled society which organize expectations about human associations are not in force. The brief, local interest of the dramatic decision to trust Xury and the interesting problem of finding terms of trust with the Africans is expanded, intensified, and imaginatively reworked in the most memorable scenes on Crusoe's desert island. The loneliness of separation from fellow-Europeans is extended to the loss of all human company. Crusoe's deep yearning for society and deep anxieties about it are beautifully exemplified by the fearful thrill of hearing his name pronounced in a voice of exasperation by his parrot. This paradoxical feeling is most completely exploited in the most memorable episode: the appearance of the naked footprint on the beach.

Starr and Hunter have argued persuasively that this episode figures importantly in the spiritual plot of the book.[42] The terrible fears Crusoe experiences test his conversion, cause him to backslide: "Thus my Fear banish'd all my religious Hope" (156). But Crusoe restores himself with a renewed sense of his sinfulness, and once again the providential memories of the biblical reassurance "call upon me in the day of trouble," restore his calm, send him to pray, and turn him to another consoling text. Trust in Providence does not prevent personal effort for Defoe; it inspires perseverance regardless of limited foresight. During his spiritual confusion, when he neglects to pray, Crusoe is also tempted in despair to destroy the works of all his labors. Later, somewhat more composed, though fearful even in prayer, he produces new fortifications that are of later use in expanding his society. What seem like extravagant precautions later prove eminently practical. The restlessness of Crusoe makes his book Hobbesian as well as Augustinian. After the social setting has been well arranged by political contracts, the human psychological equipment becomes socially productive.

The plots of economic accumulation, political power, and spiritual salvation are not mutually exclusive, but attending to the political themes of the books accounts for features that other views ignore. The special qualities of the desert island make possible activities that

[42]Starr, *Defoe and Spiritual Autobiography*, pp. 114–15; Hunter, *The Reluctant Pilgrim*, pp. 181–82.

give a strange sense of accomplishment. Although the creation of an island solitude can be associated with religious meditation, Defoe seems anxious to deny this symbolic meaning to the island adventure. In the *Serious Reflections of Robinson Crusoe* he argued that one does not need a literal solitude for reflection. On the other hand, though the details of economic production occupy a great deal of space in the account, one can't associate the attractions of the island setting with the bourgeois success story. Crusoe's earnings from the island are modest, and more than outweighed by the losses to his Brazilian estate in his absence. The material accomplishments on the island are made believable, reduced from heroic status, by the many failures, the sense of waste in reinventing agriculture and the crafts, and a union rather than a division of labor. The paradoxical sense of satisfaction felt by Crusoe and the reader, even in the midst of frustrating effort, comes from the extraordinary autonomy that Crusoe conceives not merely as liberty, the freedom from interference, but as rule: "I was Lord of the whole Mannor; or if I pleas'd, I might call my self King or Emperor over the whole Country which I had possession of. There were no Rivals; I had no Competitor, none to dispute Sovereignty or Command with me" (128).[43]

Much of the dramatic suspense created by the first footprint is generated by the threat to sovereignty once other people join Crusoe. As for Locke, so for Defoe human labor has established a title to property, and Crusoe explains, in much the same way Locke did, that consumption sets a natural limit to property (129). Nevertheless, Crusoe's behavior is Hobbesian. Uncertainties about an unknowable future, fears of natural disaster and human invasion, make Crusoe overproduce, and the narrative consistently confirms his wisdom. As in Hobbes's theory, the respect for property does not in itself solve questions of governance. It is not because they recognize his title to the island as a property owner, that Friday, his father, and the Europeans who come to the island initially obey Crusoe. Self-preservation and gratitude are their primary incentives to consent to obey him. The title to property follows along with other rules established by Crusoe as the sovereign authority. The power to feed his

[43]For the thematics of rule in *Robinson Crusoe* and the *Farther Adventures*, see Novak, *Defoe and the Nature of Man*, pp. 50–60.

subjects wins gratitude, which helps secure the contract that force and his leadership in war initially won.

Like Hobbes's sovereign, Crusoe wields extensive authority. He is commander-in-chief and the sovereign lawmaker in morality. Among his first acts are commanding Friday to slay their mutual enemy and forbidding his cannibalism. Crusoe is the sovereign over titles of honor: he names Friday and teaches him to use the title "Master." Friday's name is a particularly revealing token of arbitrary authority, since Crusoe has long since lost synchronization with the calendar kept in European nations.

As sovereign Crusoe exerts authority over religious worship, substituting his own titles of deity, God, and Christ for Friday's divinity "Benamuckee." Perhaps at first the act of conversion is seen in the context of Crusoe's personal salvation (he says the attempt deepened his own religious understanding) rather than as an act of sovereign power. But later in the narrative it becomes clear that the religious settlement is an act of sovereign power, when Crusoe comments that he has "allow'd Liberty of Conscience throughout my Dominions" (241) to the Catholic, the pagan, and the Protestant. Once again the exemplary status of the fiction is in doubt when the reader might wish to know Defoe's true opinions. He brings up liberty of conscience "by the Way." Defoe was not willing to argue for complete religious liberty in Britain on the grounds either of individual conscience or sovereign authority.

Crusoe's extensive power cannot be invoked as a general argument for unlimited monarchical sovereignty in other contexts. The exotic setting could emphasize how unlikely such power is at home, in spite of the universal desire for it. "All men would be tyrants if they could," is Defoe's echoing refrain in *Jure Divino*. Even on the island, in extraordinary circumstances, the independent authority of conventional social ties is respected. Though in need of food and drink himself and sympathetic to the Spaniard, Crusoe allows Friday's reverential preference for ministering to his father to govern his actions after the battle with the cannibals. Indeed, Crusoe sends Friday with extra bread and raisins for his father. Crusoe is careful to show respect for the captain's authority in front of his sailors.

Back in Britain even the restless Defoe acknowledged the importance of governmental respect for traditional social authority. From

Scotland, Defoe sent back the warning to Harley that the appointment of justices of the peace in Scotland should include traditional clan leaders, even at the cost of party unity, since violations of hierarchy would damage respect for justice (*Letters*, 240–41).[44] Though sovereign authority is superior to these authorities, conflicts with them should not be unnecessarily provoked. Prudence about the lack of a majority religion, not the rights of conscience, dictates toleration on Crusoe's island; and prudence, not universal science, dictates Crusoe's Hobbesian version of absolute monarchy. For many theorists including Locke, military leadership explained the historical growth of absolute monarchy without justifying its perpetuation.[45]

It may be that Crusoe does not labor to convert Friday's father and the Spaniard because with the new hope of escape and with the introduction of Europeans an ambition to rule is not a chief motive. Now Crusoe congratulates himself on being "like a king." It is, however, only a "merry reflection" (241). In conversation with the Spaniard about the risk of using Catholic sailors for their escape, the terms of obedience to Crusoe that the Spaniard offers have the quality of an individual, not a social contract. Because they are not under the laws of any established government, the contract is unenforceable, but the Spaniard offers to swear the men to a written oath upon the Bible. In addition, he advises that they plant enough food to provide for the new men, whose obedience may be shaken if they do not see immediate benefits from it. Once again, to the tendency (if not universal habits) of gratitude and promise keeping, Defoe adds special insight into character. The captain assures Crusoe that his men are "all of them very honest civil men."

When the English arrive on the island, Crusoe's efforts to gain authority over them are even more limited, since he shares a common law with them. Providential hints warn Crusoe to show caution in approaching the English seamen, who turn out to be mutineers. But when the English captain, freed by Crusoe, greets him as if he

[44]Contrast Schonhorn's view that Defoe "seems never to have been able to comprehend the subtle influences of culture, custom, precedents—the unconscious conditioning of political order" (p. 48). Defoe "comprehended" the influence of traditional culture, includng the ways it is invoked in political polemic. He did not worship custom; he expected that political leadership would mold it in dynamic ways.

[45]Schonhorn ("Defoe," pp. 27, 35–37) has demonstrated Defoe's theory of providential legitimation of monarchy by trial in war.

were an angel (254), Crusoe refuses to pretend to any special status as the arm of Providence. He asks only that the captain not claim any authority on the island, that he take orders from Crusoe when supplied with arms, and that he take Crusoe and Friday to England free of charge. The captain's gratitude for providential deliverance mingles with his desire for self-preservation and the need to accept Crusoe's leadership in maneuvers against the mutineers. In reducing the mutineers to submission, the captain and Crusoe awe them into submission by some political playacting. The sham tactics are justified not only by self-preservation but by the recognized authority of the English captain. As the understanding of authority shifts from personally created authority on the island to authority granted by constituted nations, it is interesting to note that the captain, not Crusoe, invents the title "Governor" for Crusoe by which he can awe the mutineers.

As Crusoe falls in with the game, he pretends first to be an official under the governor of the island. Then with the captain's help Crusoe appears in clothes appropriate to his role as governor and engages with the captain in a mock dispute over his right to punish the mutineers. Instead of hanging them, Crusoe offers to leave them the island. Other than extracting a promise from them to treat the Spaniards kindly when they arrive, there are no formalities of conveyance, suggesting that as an Englishman among Englishmen, Crusoe now has no more property in the island. At the end of the book, Crusoe refers to a return to the island in which he effects a more elaborate property settlement, without any explanation of his right to do this—though the discovery of the island and the creations of his labor might have satisfied Grotius and Locke that it was his property. Even then, he basically only ratifies the property arrangements that the settlers have already made. The title to authority has become vaguer and less imposing, probably because Defoe did not want to put forward Crusoe's absolute monarchy as anything more than a phase of civilization or an abstract model of political energy.[46]

[46]Sill agrees that Defoe deliberately moves his hero away from monarchical rule. He argues that in the *Farther Adventures* Crusoe becomes an ideological "emblem" as a figure who absorbs clashing interests and subsumes them to the interest of collective enterprise (*Defoe*, pp. 166–70), However, Sill's final emphasis on moderation, self-restraint, and retirement betrays the restless energy of Crusoe, who refuses

The contrast of Crusoe's activities on the island with his return to England and Portugal is striking. He receives a fortune as the passive recipient of an income managed by others, secured by the complex laws of each nation and the personal fidelity and skill of his managers. The dispersal of the money in gifts is his chief means of exerting his power. The status of a landed proprietor who enjoys a secure position of power within the confines of settled states is now available to Crusoe because of his wealth and his property in Brazil. But the great imaginative investment of the book in creating forms of power outside established polities makes it unsuitable to install Crusoe in such a position as if it were the final goal of the book. He is uncertain where to settle, and there is a final adventure with wolves in the Pyrenees, a pale version of Crusoe's role as generalissimo on the island, an adventure without political consequences. The weakness of this episode can alert us to the nature of Defoe's interest in his island. The island offered few dangerous encounters with animals or exciting discoveries about new kinds of plants. The exploring passages function in the tale of anxious provision, not as the natural-history interests of a travel book.

How shall we interpret the open-endedness of *Robinson Crusoe*?[47] It is partly the strategy of a writer for pay, who wants to keep open the possibility of future profits. But even structures motivated in this way emit thematic impulses. If Crusoe's initial desire to travel was morally wrong, there are no particular hints of it at the end of the book. The motif of the prodigal son is not pronounced at the end: Crusoe's father is dead, so there is no scene of repentant return. Instead, Crusoe returns to the captain's widow, who has always encouraged and never disapproved of his journeys. Crusoe cheerfully lays out some of the proceeds from his Brazilian estate to remove his two nephews from the "middle station of life": one is bred up as a gentleman, the other is encouraged to become an adventurous sea captain. It is interesting to find in the *Farther Adventures* that Crusoe's wife, however sadly, interprets his dreams about returning

---

during most of his life to settle for the England Defoe knew. Moderation might be the lowest common denominator, the minimum restraint on the partisanship of the new Whig ministry, but it is a great distance from the creative energy Defoe celebrated in William's reign.

[47] Sill and Alkon take the end of the *Farther Adventures* as the end.

to the island as a providential directive. This continuation seems intended to remove any aura of sin from adventures, while preserving the story of Providence. The interest of "further adventures" promised at the end of the first volume seems political, not economic or spiritual. Defoe offers stories about the difficulties of union among the colonists, battles, the growth of the population. Crusoe's alluring dream that opens the *Farther Adventures* pictures Crusoe dispensing justice on the island and executing criminals, official acts of authority that he never attempted in the first volume. Though Crusoe is interested in provisioning the colonists, he does not view this as a personal investment, but as a political responsibility.

In *Robinson Crusoe* Defoe indulges in the imagination of extraordinary powers exerted outside the boundaries of settled society. The topic must have been especially appealing to someone who did not enjoy full civil rights, who had been imprisoned and continually threatened with prison, and yet who was such an ardent entrepreneurial statesman. Though the situation was imagined and far different from Defoe's own, a similarly grand exercise of individual power was not impossible in his time. International trade and international conflict continue to present situations of legal indeterminacy in which individual agreements have far-reaching effects. One of Hobbes's models for the state of nature is the relationship of nations. A period of active trade and colonization, when communication was not rapid, allowed many opportunities for the sort of creativity Crusoe enjoyed. However, outside the supports of settled nations, Crusoe's creations do not promise to have long life.

In a witty article Michael Seidel has proposed a reading of *Robinson Crusoe* as an allegory of political "exile" during the years of the Restoration monarchies (in one early edition Crusoe's exile extends from 1659 to 1687) when Defoe thought England was in captivity and in need of energetic resistance to patriarchal authority, a time for the resumption of the subject's sovereignty in order to resettle the monarchy.[48] It is difficult to read Crusoe's temporary return to England as a symbol of the triumphal landing of William of Orange, and this poor fit suggests the way Defoe saw his political setting at

[48]"Crusoe's Island Exile," in Michael Seidel, *Exile and the Narrative Imagination* (New Haven: Yale University Press, 1986), pp. 19–43.

the time of writing *Robinson Crusoe*, thirty years after the Glorious Revolution. Many problems that had seemed crucial in the seventeenth century were not solved, in spite of the great national settlement that Defoe had celebrated. The dates of Crusoe's reign indicate the nostalgia Defoe must have felt for earlier, more heroic times, when one could associate social restrictions with tyranny and self-assertion with the rights of Englishmen. The confused status of the political teaching of *Robinson Crusoe*, the combination of pleasure and pain in the exercise of power and the fragility of political construction, has something to do with Defoe's yearning for a powerful, principled, popular voice, like the voice of *Legion's Memorial*, which spoke for a nation in support of a strong warrior king, and with Defoe's recognition that such a voice was no longer possible for him. The persuasive indirection of a woman's voice and a confinement of political will to "feminine" strategems seem more appropriate to Defoe's situation after 1714. It is to Defoe's credit that his imagination of the "feminine," dependent position of power is not an imagination of weak will.

## *Moll Flanders*: Political Woman

Born to a condemned criminal and taken up by a gypsy band, Moll Flanders starts her life almost as detached from settled society as Robinson Crusoe on his island. Throughout *Moll Flanders*, as in *Robinson Crusoe*, the lack of an economically secure, legally defined position in society is a terrible threat and yet also a powerful incentive, an opportunity for creativity. Yet Moll's most unattached position is her point of maximum weakness at the outset of her tale, whereas Crusoe's distressing island solitude is also sovereignty. In choosing a female protagonist, Defoe did not abandon his investigation of restless power seeking. His narrative shows nothing like the ideal of feminine debility that Mary Wollstonecraft complained of at the end of the century. Nevertheless, in *Moll Flanders* the inventive resourcefulness that Defoe loved is confined within structures of subordination, deference, and dependency.

Even Locke's theoretical escape hatch of emigration fails to provide Moll with anything like Crusoe's island autonomy. America twice offers Moll the opportunity for enlarged power, but it also proves the site of conflicting authoritative claims that gather about her with threatening force. In the culminating achievement of her career, Moll furnishes a considerable estate in the colonies and so joins the class of landed proprietors, the fundamental base of political power in a nation as most eighteenth-century people conceived it. But Moll will never be lord of the manor; she remains a wife whose authority is delegated, dependent on her husband's lazy trustfulness. Her story, like Crusoe's, is said to amaze people, but she cannot tell it in her real name, much less begin with the history of her name, as Crusoe does. Defoe's "editorial" preface insists on the dependency of Moll's authorial efforts on his own literary and moral values. In a way different from Robinson Crusoe, Moll needs a sponsor and censor.

At no point in her story is Moll pictured entirely without power, but she must exercise power in relation to higher authorities. Money is a crucial tool of her advances toward security, though the reputation of wealth without the substance will sometimes do. But without a clear, honorable legal status, wealth is often insecure and sometimes unusable. Moll is like Defoe: her most important skill is the artful management of the opinions of other people. The talents of impersonation and persuasion that Crusoe showed briefly in managing the mutineers are greatly expanded in Moll's story as the authority to rule is commensurately reduced. In *Moll Flanders* Defoe explores the Hobbesian situation of counsel rather than the situation of command. Even Moll's opportunities for contracting are rhetorically and strategically molded by the considerations of subordination that characterize counsel.

The account of counsel in *Leviathan* is strangely relevant to the investigation of the power of women in their households. Because of his hostility to Parliament and the trials of political controversy, Hobbes recommends that a sovereign take counsel in private. He extends the conventional analogy between the sovereign and the head of a household to recommend this containment of political dialogue: "Who is there that so far approves the taking of Counsell from a great Assembly of Counsellours, that wished for, or would accept of their pains, when there is a question of marrying his Children, disposing of his Lands, governing his Household, or managing his private Estate, especially if there be amongst them such as wish not his prosperity?" (II, 25, 310). Hobbes's scene of political counsel has several resemblances to counsel in a gentleman's household. It is "secret" rather than public, and it has an emotional ambience of trust rather than of suspicion and agonistic debate. The good counselor speaks in the interest of the authority he advises—or rather, he "pretendeth only (whatever he intendeth) the good of him, to whom he giveth it" (II, 25, 303); for this reason the counselor should avoid all signs of passionate personal interest, especially figures of eloquence. Unlike those who deliberate in a democratic assembly, the counselor has no right to give counsel but must wait to be asked for it. This view of political counsel limits all members of society, even men who aid in the important processes of governance, to the deferential manners of women and servants, and this transformation is in keeping with Hobbes's persistent effort to debunk classical ideals of masculine virtue.

Yet this crucial chapter of *Leviathan* does acknowledge the necessity of continuing dialogue between governors and subjects in a society, and the ground rules that specify subordination also offer some protection to the inferior parties in the discussion. Since the person in authority has authorized the counselor's speech by requesting advice, he should not punish anyone for it, no matter what they advise. And though the counselor should be brief and not hold forth like a public orator, the "frequent interruptions" (II, 25, 309) that Hobbes thinks will be made by the person in authority suggest a process of give and take that facilitates committed involvement while it allays suspicion. Moll, like Defoe, exploits the large territory opened up by counsel and the latitude of its rules.

The story opens with Moll's concern to find a minimally secure social position, a parish settlement. She dimly remembers herself as a small child taking the initiative in leaving the gypsies, and though the authorities of Colchester have no legal responsibility to provide for her, somehow her case comes to be widely known, and the compassion of the magistrates moves them to settle her with a parish nurse. The first dramatized scene shows Moll not quite eight years old persuading her nurse not to send her out to service, as the magistrates had ordered. At the end of the conversation Moll comments, "I had no Policy in all this" (12), but her term underlines the singular effectiveness of such a young child.

From the beginning Moll relies on the ability to create in another person a strong belief in her loyal affection. The child has more latitude than the adult would have to show her affection and her fears about the commandments of the authorities, but her impulsive tears effect the opening move typical of Moll's later successful negotiations. She leads the other, stronger, party to inquire about her desires and so authorize the scene of counsel. Moll's response to her nurse's questioning is a vivid account of her (all too realistic) fears about life at the bottom of the domestic hierarchy. First Moll explains that she is crying because she does not know how to do housework and because the maids will beat her, even though she is too young to do much. When the nurse promises that she will not be sent out to service until she is older, Moll goes on crying because she has to go at any time. Finally the nurse asks, "why, what? . . . is the Girl mad? what, would you be a Gentlewoman?" Moll answers yes and goes on crying. First she provokes laughter by her improbable answer and then tears by her childish promise to pay her own way by her needlework and by going without food if only the nurse will let her stay. This piquant exchange, related to the mayor, becomes a "story" that makes him and his family laugh. After they come to prattle with the child about being a gentlewoman, the story becomes even more delightful when the nurse learns that Moll thinks a certain "Madam," who does not go out to service but mends lace is a "gentlewoman." We begin to see that telling a story about oneself and becoming a story that others enjoy can be a substitute for the allusiveness and figures of rhetoric that Hobbes stripped from the language of counsel when he made it private. And telling a story about yourself, when it has been requested, meets Hobbes's most substantial recommendation about counsel: that it be based on relevant experience. Even women and children can meet this standard.

Moll's mistake about what she wants to be seems ominous, given her eventual life of crime, and more than a hint of pride comes into her account of being made a pet by the leading families of Colchester. But her mistake is poignant, since she wants to earn an honest, independent living and does not realize how small is the chance of supporting herself by needlework. Nevertheless, the leaders of the town patronize her. They teach her special skills and give her business, and they supply her with clothes and money enough to support her when she goes off the public maintenance.

But as in so many situations of Moll's later life, her independent efforts can be made only in a structure of dependency. When the old nurse dies, Moll is destitute until a genteel family that she had visited takes her in at the top of the servant hierarchy. Along with the daughter of the house, she begins to acquire the education of a gentlewoman.

Critics disagree about Defoe's judgment of Moll's desire to change her status.[49] Even if we decide that Defoe did not view her ambition as immoral, we needn't necessarily conclude that he favored this sort of effort for every servant. The problem of uppity servants brought out the conservative in everyone, including Defoe. But Moll rises first through patronage. Eighteenth-century England was a place in which personal patronage was a kind of wild card in the game, a rule that could suspend other rules. Patronage gained pardons for criminals, educated members of the lower orders, granted government jobs, officerships, clerical livings, and even seats in Parliament. Rising in the social hierarchy by patronage confirms, rather than challenges, the authority of the higher orders who do the patronizing. It is hard to believe that Defoe, who worked so many years with ministerial patrons, should disapprove of this sort of encouragement, yet his relation with Harley demonstrated the difficulties of actually attaining and maintaining the benefits that patronage seemed to open up. Moll's comfortable home and workplace are suddenly swept away with the death of the nurse, so that Moll is in danger of losing both the earnings her attractiveness and skill had won her and also the setting in which she could earn more. This is one of Moll's problems: she must gain the credit of trusting others and the power that comes from patronage yet still develop enough independent resources to protect herself.

Welcomed into the home of genteel people, her natural talents enable Moll to learn gentlewomanly skills more quickly than the daughters of the house, and in ways that further equip her to appeal to them. But this sort of attractiveness in a young woman has an effect on people different from the appealing quickness of a child. The story of Moll's seduction by the elder brother of the house and its consequences is one of the most extended and effectively drama-

[49]Starr, for instance, sees it as the spiritual sin of vanity in *Defoe and Spiritual Autobiography*, p. 127.

tized episodes in the novel. It is important for initiating the spiritual story of sin and redemption: the initial vanity, the lack of serious reflection, the opportunities to repent, the hardening in sin, the final repentance. The seduction also initiates, or rather prefigures, Moll's strong attraction to money, which leads to her grand career in crime, to the threat of the gallows, and yet also to the prudent management of a substantial estate in Virginia. But the special poignancy of the episode is Moll's failure to understand what is at stake—not only her immortal soul but also her public status. The charming mistake of the child about the meaning of being a gentlewoman has serious consequences for the woman.

The elder brother first appeals to Moll's vanity by praising her when he is speaking to his brother and sisters. In this household she is only "Mrs. Betty," a name for any serving girl, so the praise of the elder brother, the heir to the estate, is especially thrilling, and his strategy of appearing to speak behind her back is even more flattering. Yet because he speaks as if she were not there, the elder brother's praise does not have the effect of granting her any kind of formal recognition, the necessary prelude to an honorable address. Moll does not understand the implication of the elder brother's continuing secrecy in declaring his love: his private declaration simply makes her blush with pleasure. The gold he gives her profoundly moves her, but not because she has any economic use for it. She shows no need or wish to spend it, but it "elevated" her (23). For Moll the first money functions in this episode purely as a symbol of the elder brother's esteem. She is completely ignorant of the possibility or wisdom of making any sort of special bargain with him, after he has promised to marry her when he comes into the estate:

> I seem'd wholly to have abandoned all such Thoughts as these, and was taken up Onely with the Pride of my Beauty, and of being belov'd by such a Gentleman: as for the Gold, I spent whole Hours in looking upon it; I told the Guineas over and over a thousand times a Day: Never poor vain Creature was so wrapt up with every part of the Story, as I was, not Considering what was before me, and how near my Ruin was at the Door; and indeed, I think I rather wish'd for that Ruin than studyed to avoid it. [26]

Moll is wrapped up in the story, but she does not have the power to tell it. She listens in rapture to the older brother and gazes at his gold; she shows some "cunning" when they are among the family by scarcely looking at him or speaking to him. But he tells the elaborate tale that gets her away from home, and when he proposes terms for their affair, she "could not say a word." When the younger brother, Robin, "begins a story of the same kind," it is not the same kind of thing at all, since he proposes "fairly and honorably to marry." Oddly enough, this "fair" proposal draws out her argumentative powers for the first time, as Moll tries to discourage him. His "plain" speaking to the family makes her reflect for the first time on the elder brother's secrecy.

Admirable as Robin's behavior is, it alerts the family to the danger of a marriage across status lines and therefore more seriously threatens Moll's position in the household than the elder brother's seduction. Degrees of "free" speech sensitively register differences of authority within the family. Robin, the youngest son, known by his first name in contrast to the "elder brother," whose identity is inseparable from his status, is freer in speech and behavior than his older brother, since his marriage has fewer serious implications for the status of the family. He is free to joke about loving a servant and after some family debate, free to marry her, since he has been brought up to make his own living. But the closer Robin's banter comes to an open declaration of his love, the more pressure on Moll, since the family has a right to know her reasons for refusal. Under this pressure, Moll's private conversations with the elder brother exploit most remarkably the paradoxical value of secrecy. An increasingly self-conscious, feminine reserve aids Moll's argumentative attempts to win public status.

Now Moll must be more indirect than with her nurse. Her troubled silence and signs of her tears provoke the elder brother to beg to question her about the nature of her trouble, and making him beg her to speak sets a tone of loving concern. Her mode of opening the discussion reveals her subjection. She is as good as Defoe at persuading and arguing, but as a woman and a servant she does not have a customary right to speak about her wishes, though others have a right to insist on her explaining herself. Neither her speech nor her silence are altogether a matter of her own choice. There is a reasonable expectation that the inferior will have opportunity to advise the superior, but she cannot claim a right to give advice, because that would be to command her master. Such a situation necessitates a degree of management and courteous pretense. Moll continues to put the responsibility for the conversation on the elder brother by pretending to think that the new antagonism of the family toward her comes from its discovery of their affair. The strategy also keeps subtly before him their commitment to each other. Her pretended anger at his smiles of relief and superior knowledge gives her an opportunity to reproach him with damaging her reputation. The reproach is substantial, even though her pretended ignorance of Robin's interest in her takes the sting out of it at first, since he believes that he can easily dispel her fears. The elder brother cheerfully offers her the explanation that Robin has been making the family suspicious by talking about her (he thinks it's only banter), and he argues that the family's worry about this will prevent suspicion of them.

The family's response to Robin's interest is in fact the story Moll wished to tell, and she prefixes it with tears. She asks for advice because she wants to give advice. She argues that the younger brother's public addresses will jeopardize their position, because people will seek some reason for her refusing the younger brother. She adds cleverly that they will assume "that I am Marry'd already to somebody else, or that I would never refuse a Match so much above me as this was" (35). Only when the elder brother suggests that she avoid a decisive reply does she begin to pull on the bond between them: she argues that she and the elder brother are already married, "he having all along persuaded me to call my self his Wife" (35). Moll tries to give the private name public status, but the elder brother only promises to be "as good as a Husband." He is already withdrawing from the role by avoiding sex with her.

In their next conversation Moll again suggests the cheerful solution of publicly announcing their marriage, but with a great deal of confidence and no hinted doubt of his loyalty, so that she "pleasantly" agrees to keep the secret back (37). Her trust and reliance on his advice lead him to risk advising her to marry his brother, which provokes her to a fainting fit. Moll and the elder brother then become more explicit about what they want from each other and more willing to risk an argument. When the elder brother recommends that Moll marry Robin, Moll accuses him of breaking his promise to marry her. Her appeal seems to be grounded solely on the natural obligation to keep promises,[50] but in *Serious Reflections of Robinson Crusoe* Defoe celebrated the English law that makes a promise to marry enforceable in court. Could Moll expect such a law ever to be enforced to benefit a servant at the expense of the honor of genteel people? The threat of any sort of legal compulsion would only disrupt the impression of trusting affection that Moll has so patiently designed in the previous discussions. Signs of trust are essential in her dependent position: "To believe, to trust, to rely on another, is to Honour him; signe of opinion of his vertue and power. To distrust, or not believe, is to Dishonour" (*Leviathan*, I, 10, 153).

Again and again in eighteenth-century fiction the moral authority of women in situations of familial conflict seems to require the refusal to appeal to the political institutions of the society at large. Their legal position as wards of fathers, husbands, or masters insured that women had little access to political institutions and great dependence on customary rules of behavior and on individual relations with men. Since the history of the novel developed a generic commitment to stories about women (a commitment for which Richardson is more responsible than Defoe) it should not be surprising that we expect the form to be set at a distance from political concerns. But the social orientation of the novel, like the social orientation of women, exists within a detectable legal framework. Defoe will not let us forget that feminine manners are only strategies appropriate to particular arrangements of power.

In the debate between Moll and the elder brother, each speaker appeals only to common principles of morality rather than to legal obligations. The elder brother claims that he has adhered to the terms of the promise: to provide for her, but not to marry until he comes into the estate. Moll uses his answer to reconfirm their bond of affection and mutual gratitude: "But why then, *says I*, can you perswade me to such a horrid step, as leaving you, since you have not left me? Will you allow no Affection, no Love on my Side, where there has been so much on your Side? Have I made you no Returns?" (38–39). The scene is quite passionate: both characters speak convincingly and show strong emotion, and yet the sincerity of

[50]Starr cites passages that show Defoe also considered promises of marriage morally binding, even without legal ceremony. See *Defoe and Casuistry*, pp. 118–19.

each is questionable. Moll has told the reader that she had sex out of vanity, not love, and she has suggested that the elder brother never intended to marry her; since he used money as an inducement, perhaps he never believed in her love. Each could bring forward these accusations, but neither does. Even in such privacy, the character of each in the eyes of the other is extremely important. The elder brother does not want to be seen as someone who would tell a downright lie, and Moll does not want to be seen as someone who would have sex without love. Each grants the other the fair name. But in a particularly daring move of the conversation, when the brother urges marriage to Robin, Moll gives herself the name that her lover is unwilling to pronounce:

> . . . you shall be my Dear Sister, as you are now my Dear—and there he stop'd.
> YOUR Dear whore, *says I*, you would have said, if you had gone on; and you might as well have said it; but I understand you.
> [39]

Her attempt to wring his heart reminds him of his responsibility to her and attributes honor to their relation by transforming the title of shame to a title of honor: "I had much rather, since it is come that unhappy Length, be your Whore than your Brothers Wife" (40). Though her bold expression of value moves him, neither master nor servant has the power to transform social opinion by making the legal status of their relation unimportant. The special tender meaning of "Whore" is only a meaning for their privacy, so they continue to seek a better name for Moll.

In their next conversation, Moll appeals to the horror of incest as the ground of her obstinacy, and the elder brother uses her excuse against her, as a reason to avoid living with her, though he recognizes the responsibility to support her. He now attributes formal significance to his avoidance of lovemaking. He argues that there will no longer be any physical symbol of their marriage, so Robin will be no more than minimally injured and his marriage to Moll will be free of any taint of incest. The mounting tension throws Moll into a fever, and at this point in the narrative, Moll assures the reader for the first time, "I Lov'd to Distraction," and "he Lov'd me most passionately"

(42). To her horror, Moll's long resistance to Robin finally wins the respect of his mother and sister and wipes out her last legitimate reason for refusing him. The elder brother decisively informs her that, whatever she decides about Robin, their sexual relation, the substantive token of their affection, will not continue. Though he promises to support her clandestinely, she begins to fear expulsion from the family and the helpless isolation of her situation at the opening of the book.

Is the reader supposed to accept Moll's assertions of love as true, or mere excuse, or as expressions of a corrupted sense of love, sincere but misguided? The special insight, the authenticity that the autobiographical memoir might seem to offer, is also hard to assess. How important is the reader's decision about Moll's sincerity for the interpretation of the novel? However genuine the emotions, whether hypocrisy or pathetic suffering, the evident variety of feeling is the mark of the uncertain social status. Whatever their inner opinions, the lovers are committed to the expression of love when they are close, but the elder brother's refusal of a public union drives them apart. To an extraordinary degree, *Moll Flanders* is a book that confines us to the realm of opinion and authority rather than of truth. Since in this book social situation, including legal status, determines meaning, the changing complications the characters face do not make them seem complex. At first the elder brother practices calculating lust and arouses Moll's deluded vanity; then each feels affection appropriate to the bond of a natural, if not legal, marriage that has been cemented by the elder brother's promise; finally, the brother ends the natural sexual marriage and "reasons" Moll into marrying his brother to secure prosperity and reputation. Rejected by the older brother, Moll's feeling eventually turns to jealousy of the woman he marries. Love seems to have no stable, universal meaning in this sequence. We may elucidate this situation through Hobbes's deflating list of "the Interior Beginnings of Voluntary motions; commonly called the PASSIONS. And the speeches by which they are expressed" (*Leviathan*, I, 6, 118):

> *Love* of persons for society, KINDNESS.
> *Love* of Persons for pleasing the sense onely, NATURAL LUST.
> *Love* of the same, acquired from Rumination, that is, Imagination of Pleasure past, LUXURY.

> *Love* of one singularly, with desire to be singularly beloved, THE PASSION OF LOVE. The same, with fear that the love is not mutuall, JEALOUSIE. [*Leviathan*, I, 6, 123–24]

On the model of Hobbes's definition of religion in the same chapter, we might add, "*Love*, publicly allowed, MARRIAGE; not allowed, LUST; and when truly such as we imagine, TRUE LOVE." True love for Defoe, like true religion for Hobbes, seems to be either an empty category or a belief so absolutely private and individual that it cannot win public credit except by public authority.

The first long episode has the elevated quality of a tragedy of imprudence, punished by painful inner suffering. Moll's belief that she is committing incest by her marriage to Robin has no external support in law. It is as if there were some odd economy of guilt: by failing to suffer for a commonly recognized offense (sex prior to marriage) she suffers for a personally conceived sin (incest in her thoughts). Later in the narrative, when she unintentionally marries her brother, incest is more dangerous, since public knowledge of it would dissolve her marriage and ruin her children. The repetition of the topic may be another example of Defoe's discovery of material, but it can also function thematically. The more extreme punishment follows the gradual process of spiritual hardening. But the topic is further relevant for pursuing questions of power and authority. In both cases Moll's horror of incest seems to be detached from obvious concerns about self-preservation. Few people have access to the information; those who know about it have strong motives of interest not to reveal it. In Virginia, for a long time Moll is the only one who knows about the incest, and she need not have revealed it. Instead of fearing that she'll reveal it inadvertently, she fears that she may never be able to reveal it or may never be believed.

This kind of suffering may seem to expose an ineluctable moral core of personality, truths of character and morals that are not a matter of social opinion or convenience. Yet in *Moll Flanders*, as in his essay on honesty in the *Serious Reflections of Robinson Crusoe*, Defoe shows little interest in the philosophical question: is this moral imperative the product of nature or of education? Rather, he is interested in the drama of a powerful emotion that a person feels impelled to act on that must nevertheless be hidden from the world. Even more than the conversion experiences of Crusoe or Moll, which follow patterns recognized and respected in their world and the world of their readers, Moll's incest opens up the material of the hidden world of personality and private life with which the artistic "development" of individual character has so long been associated. Secrets of sexual behavior are especially associated with the private view of character that novels are supposed to reveal, but this association holds only when sex is seen as a mark of the peculiar, individual life. Prostitution, like marriage, is presented in *Moll Flanders* typically without special detail; both appear as familiar institutions that are tools ready-made for Moll's use.

Twentieth-century readers find the lack of emotional detail puzzling. Defoe opens up the topics of sex and marriage that we recognize as novelistic subjects and then fails to sustain the interest in intimacy that we expect. Defoe does not deprive Moll of intense feelings; he merely puts them in places that surprise us, and the shock can tell us something about the political structures implicit in habits of novel reading. True revelations of the inner life, the visionary promise associated with fiction, is not the presumed goal of this novel; such information has instead a number of explicit functions. In this case, Moll's horror of incest serves to assure the reader that she has moral feelings more deeply rooted than the desire for respectability, feelings with which we can sympathize and which we can believe will be a foundation for her later experience of conversion. These episodes serve the relation of character to reader more than they do any relations within the novel.[51] Moll never finds it difficult to convince other characters of her morality; she inspires trust even as a condemned criminal. But the private suffering caused by her incest is revealed only to the reader.

The reader's belief in the truth of Moll's account of her feelings is especially important if the book is to work as a story of conversion. In

[51]John Preston discusses the importance of this section of the book, concluding that "Moll does in fact stand in closer relationship to any one of her readers than to the characters in the novel." See *The Created Self: The Reader's Role in Eighteenth-Century English Fiction* (New York: Barnes and Noble, 1970), p. 33. Starr has written that Moll's guilt about her unintended incest "matches even the most scrupulous reader in the rigor of his ethical standards" and so amounts to an assertion of moral equality with readers as well as an appeal to their fellow feeling. See *Defoe and Casuistry*, p. 123.

the editor's preface, Defoe casts a little doubt on Moll's repentance, but he does not show anyone in the novel seriously questioning her conversion; nevertheless, it surely would occur to any reader, as it has to modern critics, that the conversion is in her interest and could be insincere. The lack of strenuous questioning does not call into doubt the validity of the representation. All of those involved have good reason to accept her claims: her conversion enlarges the credit of the clergyman and provides the colonies with her labor, which is more in the interest of the government than her execution would be. As so often in *Robinson Crusoe*, self-interest and social interest are harmonized, so that there is no need for the protagonist's character to be dissected. The lack of questioning, the lack of evidence for her truthfulness, does jeopardize her credibility with the reader, who has so often seen her persuade people of falsehoods. The conventionality of her account of conversion makes it recognizable, but it also could raise doubts, especially in modern readers. The act of writing her history could itself be one more attempt to win public esteem for the rehabilitated criminal. The story of incest, however, gives the whole narrative a special status as an intimate, and therefore trustworthy, revelation. The effect on the reader's loyalty to the character and the book is the more pervasive because the intimate revelation marks a crisis in counsel and command: no authority is adequate to the peculiar needs of Moll's situation. Readers feel a sense of urgency about deliberating the facts of Moll's case, as if we were asked to supply the deficiency of counsel and command. When fiction in its intimacy veers away from representing itself as advice, it does not escape these forms so much as it seems to invest us with the authority to advise and judge at the most flattering point, where it is the most difficult. And the sense of implication in the book is increased by the numerous difficulties thrown in the way of judgment.

In earlier episodes, before her conversion, judging Moll's behavior may be difficult because she acts under the direction of a male authority. After the death of Robin, Moll understands the value of a legal marriage, and her accumulated wealth allows her to choose a mate according to her taste for a gentleman of wit and virtue. Moll's life with her second husband was a less sinful but more ruinous life of pretense. The gentleman-tradesman is not for Defoe a figure of presumption so much as a fool: he leads a way of life that he can't sustain. The literal masquerade during the comical trip to Oxford, in which they gull poor scholars by pretending to be aristocratic patrons, leads to the more criminal ruse of eluding their creditors. As she sees his fortune decline, Moll steals first from her husband, and then (at her husband's advice) from his creditors. When she goes into hiding in the Mint, she takes on the surname by which we know her, "Mrs. Flanders," so this first theft marks her identity for us in important ways.

Moll's theft from the creditors to preserve something from her husband's ruin is surely the most excusable crime in the book. The reduction of a bankrupt to starvation was something Defoe wrote against in other works and of which his readers could not entirely approve. It is an example of a legal remedy socially frowned upon. Moll's uncertain social status continues. Is she a criminal or not? The laws on debt, like many laws, were very unevenly executed, partly because prosecution was at the individual discretion of the creditor. The very existence of the Mint, a place free from arrest, and of Sunday immunity, suggests a general social leniency.[52] Moll leaves the Mint because her creditors show no intention of prosecuting her.

Many of Moll's crimes occupy areas of socially tolerated criminality. The practice of victims buying back stolen goods instead of seeking to prosecute offenders had the effect of continuously decriminalizing criminals. Moll actually makes friends with the gentleman who buys back his wig, sword, and watch. Her theft from thieves or her theft of smuggled goods especially have the quality of excusable crimes. These acts are clearly morally wrong, part of the spiritual story of hardening, and they give Moll the incentive to go on to her undoubted crimes, but they are typical of her life to the very end of the story. The frequent pardoning or transportation of criminals must have made many crimes seem less criminal, even though, or perhaps in part because, the penalties on the books were so severe. Very often in Moll's story the participation of social authorities—husbands, masters, excise officers—in her crime adds special force to the conflict in opinions about justice that we feel as readers.

Moll's abandonment by two husbands (the tradesman and the

[52] Starr collects evidence of complicated social attitudes toward debt: acceptance of the immunity of the Mint, reprobation of stealing from creditors, sympathy with the self-preservation of the debtor. See *Defoe and Casuistry*, p. 125.

highwayman) and the dissolution of her Virginia marriage relegate her to a sort of legal twilight. Is she practicing bigamy? Over time, desertion would become legally recognized as divorce, and besides, a private marriage by a priest may not have been legal, and marriage to a brother certainly is not binding. Defoe makes situations that are morally and legally unclear into creative opportunities. They bind the reader to the book in repeated efforts of judgment, and they open areas of adventurous activity to the characters. Moll learns to use her indeterminate status, the lack of a secure position as a well-known member of a community, to create identities and mold opinion at will. In this positive transformation of uncertainty, Moll usually requires at least one ally to meet threats posed by other people who seek to exploit relatively unregulated situations.

An alliance with another husband-hunting woman prompts Moll's efforts to change the bias of social conventions. Their goal is to acquire husbands of good fortune and good character, and to do this they must inquire into the situation and past of the suitor without his finding out too much about them. The low level of record keeping in their world has the advantage of enabling them to keep their fortunes a secret, but it also makes it hard to detect a suitor's fraudulence. Defoe's picture of marriage partners assumes no special intimacy, no deep knowledge of each other; their negotiation must establish the terms of trust. The Hobbesian problem of knowing character is not only complicated by the lack of a stable social setting, but also made more difficult by the conventions of courtship. Declarations of love imply that a favorable decision on the lover's character has already been made. Suspicious inquiries, requests for evidence, then become contradictory, rude offenses. For this reason, in decorous genteel society, the "friends" (that is, the family connections) of the lovers investigated the credit of the two parties. But men are usually in a better position to make these conventions work in their favor. Moll says they are more valued and more in demand and therefore can ask rude questions without answering similar ones. So Moll offers herself as an adviser when her friend (apparently not under the protection of a family) is rejected by a suitor, a captain who feels himself insulted by inquiries about him.

Moll's solution to her friend's problem is somewhat reminiscent of one of Defoe's fantasies in the *Consolidator*: in order to secure a better hearing, Dissenters take over royally chartered trading companies by dumping their shares, driving down the value further by rumor, and then buying up a majority of the shares at reduced cost and the rest when the price rises again. Moll drives down the market value of the suitor by using a network of gossiping women to circulate damaging rumors about his financial position and his reputation of morals. His material wealth cannot dictate his value in the market of opinion: "The *Value*, or WORTH of a Man, is as of all other things, his Price; that is to say, so much as would be given for the use of his Power: and therefore is not absolute; but a thing dependent on the need and judgement of another" (*Leviathan*, I, 10, 151–52).[53] Unable to make other matches, the suitor returns crestfallen to try again with Moll's friend. She now has the excuse of his bad reputation to question him, and she is almost taken in by the reality of the fiction she helped create. When she sees how confounded he is by the rumors, "she almost began to believe that all was true, by his disorder, tho' she knew that she had been the raiser of all those Reports herself" (72). The lover, now on the defensive, offers the necessary evidence of his good character and learns to feel grateful to his wife-to-be. But his protestations of love have closed him off from the chance to inquire about her fortune, so she is able to tie up part of it with trustees out of his reach and without his knowledge. In material and moral ways the wife enters her marriage less dependent than she would otherwise be. Taking a woman and equal as a counselor strengthens the position of a woman as a counselor to men, even if it cannot abolish subordination altogether.

Moll's advice to her friend proceeds to an exhortation to the women of her nation to stand their ground during courtship in order to gain what they need from marriage, not only security but also respect. The elaborate strategy, however, shows that the woman needs a pretext for questioning her suitors. Her position does not

[53]C. B. Macpherson cites this passage in evidence that Hobbes's system reflects a bourgeois market society; but one could reverse his argument. Hobbes and Defoe place economic operations within a larger political context of opinion making, to which economic markets are subject. What is at stake is the status of Macpherson's claims about Hobbes's individualism, the idea of each person's power limiting every other person's power. Hobbes is more interested in (and worried about) group power than Macpherson acknowledges. In our example from Defoe we should note that Moll is trying to make a marriage with the help of a woman friend. See C. B. Macpherson, *The Political Theory of Possessive Individualism* (London: Oxford University Press, 1962), p. 37.

give her a right to inquire. As in Defoe's *Consolidator* fantasy, Moll's strategy uses the social power of rumor and boycott to make the binding constraints of the law serve the interests of a politically subordinated class. Defoe's practices suggest that he tried to use his journalism to create the context of opinion that would get his counsel a hearing in Parliament and in secret relations with ministers of state. But Defoe's fictional analogue conveniently suppresses the ways that custom and laws could be used by the dominant group to strike back, to reinstate the abusive inequality. Slander laws that were used against Defoe's journalism have been left out of his fictional projects. Advising women to show courage and to stand their ground cannot really make men of them. When her friend uses the rumor machine to help Moll trap a husband, we see how small is the power of women and how carefully it must be concealed.

Moll's own marriage negotiation (her third) with a Virginia plantation owner is more complicated than her friend's, since she has so little money to soothe a busband after pressuring him during courtship. Deceit before marriage would risk bad treatment after marriage, when the husband could exercise the right of corporal punishment. As a result, the friend takes Moll to the country and presents her as a relative whose good circumstances are well known. Since the lie is circulated as the mistake of another person, the husband will have less reason for anger. But so crucial is the credit of a woman for her safety in marriage that Moll carries on a further negotiation to insure her future. She lures her suitor on to protestations of love and draws him into writing a rhyming love dialogue on the window with a diamond. In this context of conventional, playful male hyperbole and modest female skepticism, Moll confesses her poverty in a way that will not be believed. The suitor writes, "*I scorn your Gold, and yet I Love*" (79). Her humor conceals a confession by its very bluntness: "*I'm Poor: Let's see how kind you'll prove*." So he is forced to reiterate his disinterestedness: "*Be mine, with all your Poverty.*" This gives Moll the opportunity to probe his good faith almost dangerously deep: "*Yet secretly you hope I lie.*"[54] She cannot be later

[54]Ignoring such scenes of negotiation as this one, Robert Alter has argued that Moll thinks in capitalist, money-fixated, bookkeeping terms and "expects words to be used with neat, very definite denotations unobfuscated by any suggestion of multiple meaning or contradiction." See *Rogue's Progress* (Cambridge, Mass.: Harvard University Press, 1965), p. 45. Earlier Dorothy Van Ghent also emphasized Moll's drive to abstract all experience "into numbers, measurements, cash value." See *The*

charged with having deceived him about her wealth. Her air of "indifferency" would hardly make him suspect her of being a woman pressed hard for necessities, yet she manages to get him talking about his fortune. Her apparent reluctance to settle in Virginia makes her seem hard to win and provides her with something to grant him after his initial disappointment over her fortune.

The management of social credit helps Moll enter the marriage, but the maintenance of a good reputation within the family is necessary for Moll to hold on to a share of power. After marriage, Moll first frightens her husband by suggesting that she is utterly destitute, then pleases him by presenting her small holdings: the sum that before marriage would have looked contemptible now gives pleasure, and his gratitude is reinforced by her offer to settle in Virginia. Moll has managed to avoid any positive lies and has even managed to appear as someone eager to explain herself. Moll's strategies, which lead to a happy marriage, bring to mind Defoe's recommendation to Harley of public-spirited dissimulation: it cannot be called lying, because it is in the interest of the people fooled. But also it is not real deceit, because other people are practicing the dissimulation game and are to some extent willing to be fooled as well as willing to fool others. Writing on the window, Moll calls the bluff of hyprocrisy in courtship, but like Defoe calling the bluff of high-flying Tories, she counts on the force of conviction behind the conventional pretense of disinterestedness and unity. Moll relies on her Virginian's good humor as well as on her strategies.

All of Moll's cleverness about insuring a stable marriage turns against her when she tries to find a way of separating from her husband after she learns that the marriage is incestuous. The "careful, diligent" husband finds no sense in her appeal to his promise that she could return to England if Virginia proved unsatisfactory. The ability to make a new social identity by changing place has trapped her: to her horror, she discovers that her mother-in-law, who has also come to Virginia to make a new life, is her mother. Her goal must now be to separate without so alienating her husband as to

---

*English Novel: Form and Function* (1953; New York: Harper, 1961), p. 39. A more interesting treatment of economic topics in Defoe's fiction which could connect meaningfully to his politics would explore the social complexities of credit rather than the illusory simplicities of commodity fetishism.

leave herself or her children penniless. She is extremely fearful of revealing her secret and, as her conflict with her husband increases, fearful that he will put her away as a madwoman and that her secret could then never be explained. In a particularly savage argument the husband threatens to use violence to "reduce" Moll to duty to husband and children, and Moll frightens him by hinting at the truth. But she makes a particularly long and careful approach to the final revelation, holding back while both mother and son beg to know her secret. Once again, the emotional preparation for negotiation involves creating a larger context of opinion by bringing the mother over to her side, and then binding the husband by written promises, made this time with solemnity, not as a joke. The result of her carefully prepared revelation does indeed protect her from injury, but it has the unforeseen and dangerous result of leading him to try to kill himself. Moll speculates rather brutally about whether she should leave before their fortunes decline, or whether she should marry again in Virginia if her husband succeeds in killing himself. Rather than rely on an unstable husband, Moll chooses self-reliance and decides to emigrate, but damage to her goods in the crossing reduces her again to necessity and dependence.

The comparison of a family to a state was a moral commonplace; indeed, the bond between governor and governed was compared to the bond between father and family even by those who, like Defoe, were not patriarchalists. But Defoe's political analogy of the family in *Moll Flanders* teaches the mutability and artificiality of the political creations. Moll's first love choices were giddy affairs of impulse, but the Virginia marriage was a carefully planned arrangement, solidly based in wealth, good character, and mutual trust. Moll's skill in negotiation shows that consent to obedience is not a single gesture of submission, but a dialogue conducted under the constraints of respect to authority. There was a well-calculated slight chance of Moll's gentleman-tradesman husband turning up to cause legal complications. But prudent foresight, based on hard-earned experience, is not enough. Incalculable accidents (like the discovery of incest) upset the order and change the terms of legality and morality, feeling and discourse. Moll, her husband, and their mother slowly arrive at their now very private agreement. Though there are natural principles of morality such as keeping promises, there is no natural, inevitable social order. This is surely one meaning of Moll's abandoning her many children to the care of others. *Moll Flanders* is pervaded by an insistent concern about coming out on the right side of the law and using it to further the interests of the characters, but never in a novel has the law seemed so arbitrary, without seeming wicked or absurd. Hobbesian moral philosophy and struggles over political opinion taught Defoe the importance of coordinating human energies by shared law. But the Hobbesian teaching underlines the artificiality of every political order and the inadequacy of any narrowly legalistic code to address the variation of human needs.

The pains of uncertain status afflict Moll's next dependency, her relation with the gentleman at Bath. Their ardent friendship slips over the border into sex very readily, and the more readily because Moll thinks it is the way to secure the relation; but a sickbed repentance undoes it again.[55] The sum of money Moll gains by signing another private agreement with dubious legal status, a general release, is substantial, but not enough for a life income. Money without the knowledge of legal opportunities to invest it cannot provide the security she seeks, and this is why she so often seeks a husband.

At this point in the narrative Defoe and Moll are repeating themselves. The problem of the unhappily married clerk (who serves as her banker) resembles the situation of the gentleman at Bath, and the rumor of her fortune which tricks the Lancashire man resembles the strategy for entrapping the Virginia husband. Compared to her earlier ventures, Moll in some ways shows more prudence won from her experience, but in other ways she is more daring, ready for bold risks, including two concurrent marriage negotiations, Moll has found a reliable and agreeable banker through an attempt to learn how to invest her savings. Though she encourages his advances, Moll declines any sort of unmarried cohabitation with the clerk, as well as any other sort of binding engagement. His respect is greater security than the unlicensed bond of the flesh, and she confirms his respect by showing her trust in him, while leaving herself free to try her luck in the north. Moll's marriage to the Lancashire man was a great

[55]John Richetti's enthusiasm for Moll's mythic resilience has led him to exaggerate the impression the book gives of her powers. Of the affair with the man at Bath, Richetti writes, "in dominating marriage itself, Moll exercises power over society." See *Defoe's Narratives*, p. 114.

gamble for what each party believed was a great prize. Moll has the excuse of having her fortune misrepresented by others, this time by a confederate of the husband's, so she does not take the precautions that preceded the marriage to the Virginia husband.

The negotiation to ensure trust, so typical of Moll's engagements, occurs after the marriage to the Lancashire gentleman. The apparent willingness of each to forgive the other and treat the other with generosity creates a bond that was lacking in their original agreement. Their affection makes them consider daring schemes for making their fortunes, but since they cannot agree on which risk to take, they separate. This incident occasions the first use of Christian names in this episode, as Moll cries out to herself, "O Jemy, come back!" (153), and by a sort of second sight he comes back for a brief stay while they consider and reject both her plan of emigration to Virginia and his answering plan of emigration to Ireland. The episode has an odd, intrusive effect in a narrative that has dealt so much in names that identify social position, family status, or relationship to Moll. The Lancashire husband figures in a special way in Moll's search for power. The intimate affection that grows between them is an unexpected luxury in the story, much related to Jemy's dashing, gentlemanly ways. Although she cannot afford this luxury for a while yet, Moll is at least able to play the heroine and save him from a mob. Moll's later decision to continue the relation when she sees him in Newgate is a risk incurred more out of affection than out of need for his power, but the relation is a pleasure that it turns out she can well afford once they are transported to Virginia.

So uncertain is the creation of an entirely new estate that even this resourceful couple won't undertake it until, much later in the book, they are presented with a much worse alternative, the gallows. After they have separated, Moll finds herself with child, and she is presented with a new difficulty of her uncertain status. She has no parish settlement and no husband to protect her. Sex between consenting adults is not an entirely private matter in this society. Social pressures make her unwelcome in her lodgings, and the magistrates are entitled to inquire into the paternity of infants and to compel the father's support. Public exposure could not help her, and it would damage the engagement that she continues to rely on with the clerk.

Her solution is a private maternity hospital, an institution as elaborately detailed in the novel as any of Defoe's projects in his pamphlets. The excitement of these pages is not the bare fascination with money, but an identification with social ingenuity. Novak points out that the public provision of lying-in facilities for unwed mothers was a project that Defoe had seriously proposed to reduce abortions and maintain the population. Partly to overcome the impression of any apparent sympathy with vice, partly to insure credit for his originality of creation, Defoe assures his novel readers that the death of the governess who founded the lying-in facility has "left nothing behind her that can or will come up to it" (171). The sentence lingers in the mind a little sadly, as if the favorite project for a lying-in hospital, preserved rather oddly in a criminal biography, stood for many of Defoe's projects that "have left nothing behind it that can or will come up to it." Like the House of Orphans that Moll wished for at the beginning of the narrative, the lying-in hospital wistfully models large-scale political solutions to the worst effects of poverty and crime. But we learn later that the governess of the hospital was forced by a prosecution to turn away from this useful kind of work, and that she became a pawnbroker and fence.[56]

Marriage to the clerk satisfies Moll, since her restlessness was motivated more by fear than by greed. For five years she lived "retir'd, frugal and within our selves; I kept no Company, made no Visits, minded my Family, and oblig'd my Husband; and this kind of Life became a Pleasure to me" (189). But if the clerk avoids the faults of luxury that she suffered in the gentleman-tradesman, he is also subject to the distress of a modest livelihood, the lack of surplus. Another clerk's failure brings on his own bankruptcy, and he lacks the "courage" to begin again but instead declines and dies. Moll's advice about looking his misfortune in the face and recovering his credit can only be used by an adventurous spirit like her own. She needs a husband who will take her advice.

After her husband's death, Moll begins her life of crime. Necessity, and what is stronger, the fear of necessity, drive Moll on. The inability to distinguish avarice from a crime justified in conscience, if not in law, by self-preservation makes it difficult to find the point of

[56]Once again John Richetti finds more power in these passages than I do: "These are institutions within institutions, illegal operations which mimic and thereby undercut the legitimate operations of society" (*Defoe's Narratives*, p. 120).

culpability as Moll becomes hardened to her occupation. For a short while, after going to live at very cheap rent with her governess, Moll supports herself through sewing, though she makes clear how much work it takes her to earn her subsistence, how difficult in this job, as in any other, it is to get on without "acquaintance," without the patronage of friends (199). As in her very first job in Colchester, nearly free rent seems a necessary condition for this way of being self-supporting, and work so near the subsistence line easily slips beneath it. We might remember that the "gentlewoman" whom Moll admired as a child took in sewing but actually supported herself as a prostitute.

Stealing becomes the skilled, lucrative trade that Moll has always needed and never had. The governess who has been a "mother" to her in the lying-in hospital now sees to her education in crime, offers a safe and secret home, and makes the protection of a husband unnecessary. Her success depends on her characteristic quick-witted, imaginative responses to opportunity, the ability to feign gentility as well as other disguises, readiness of tongue, level-headed courage under threat, and most of all the manipulation of her anonymity—her greatest burden and her greatest resource throughout the book.[57] The other thieves refer to her as "Moll Flanders," but they do not know who she is.[58]

For the reader, this part of the book reads like a negative conduct book, what to avoid if you want to protect your property from thieves. Because the scenes function as practical warnings, the curiosity about society's underside, the nooks and crannies in social architecture, can be indulged without the fear of undermining respect for law and morality; Moll appears in this part as a guide to prudence and morality. Some episodes provide opportunities to attack social abuses: luxury, smuggling, drunkenness, gambling, and prostitution. Defoe teaches the lesson of the interconnection of vices and crimes. The reader's interest in Moll's criminal ingenuity is very

[57]For an admirable Marxist-feminist account of Moll which stresses her anonymity and her relations with women, see Lois A. Chaber, "Matriarchal Mirror: Women and Capitalism in *Moll Flanders*," *PMLA* 97(1982):212–26.

[58]Paul Alkon notes that the vagueness about the acquisition of this name and the use of the name in the title give the reader a strong impression of consistent criminality, even though these episodes occupy a limited portion of Moll's story. See *Defoe and Fictional Time* (Athens: University of Georgia Press, 1979), p. 141.

different from the interest taken in her marriage episodes, which provoke more reflection and debate about the laws of nature, convention, and government. Moll's career of theft is wrong in law, wrong in convention, and—in spite of initial necessity—even against Defoe's understanding of the laws of nature. Her temptation to murder a child early in the life of crime brands theft with the stigma of unnatural feeling. Once Moll becomes rich, she is driven to more theft by avarice, a sin and an obsession, the clutches of the Devil. Yet the character traits that make Moll a success in crime can be converted, under the right political arrangement, to respectability. Like Crusoe's overproduction, his fortifications, his hoarded money and gunpowder, Moll's avariciously accumulated wealth becomes personally and socially useful under the right legal circumstances.

The book moves inexorably to clear and public condemnation of Moll. The public disgrace and the fear of execution prepare for her conversion and then her public rehabilitation in America, where she can finally take on a name, a husband, a son, and legitimate property management. The moral degeneration, or "hardening," of the protagonist and the reader's increasing moral clarity about her prepare for the public sentence and its transmutation. Yet the sense of accident and the many opportunities for negotiation remind us of the contrast between the fluidity of life and the arbitrariness of justice. Moll has been seized with stolen goods by two women shop assistants. As Moll pleads poverty and then offers to pay for the merchandise, the master of the house hesitates, and his wife argues in Moll's favor. The most obstinate "wench" has already called a constable, but the justice of the peace is persuaded by Moll's arguments until the "Sawcy Jade" swears that Moll was caught leaving the shop. Moll's governess almost succeeds in persuading one maid and the master to drop the prosecution. Moll provokes tears when she addresses the court before sentencing, but the judge pronounces death. Facing death turns Moll toward religion. The minister who gives Moll spiritual guidance promises not to reveal any of her confession to the courts, but on the other hand his testimony to her conversion succeeds in obtaining for Moll a transmuted sentence. The public institutions of law have been essential in the process of Moll's rehabilitation, yet they are not aligned very clearly with the moral action of the story.

What is Defoe's attitude toward the extremely harsh judgment against a woman who is, in strict legal terms, a first offender? The readers, who know her history, can see an appropriate irony that for once Moll suffers worse than the expected consequences, but is Defoe therefore recommending the severity of the judgment? The transmutation of the judgment to transportation without more inquiry into Moll's criminal history might also raise questions about the administration of justice, though even transportation is a severe sentence for those who cannot afford to buy their freedom. Christianity teaches that the secrets of all hearts will only be known in the general resurrection, and the judicial system does not expect either Moll or her minister to reveal those secrets, but the reader is allowed to see that the fit between judicial judgment and the judgment of God is not very good.

Moll's story effects for the reader a rough correspondence between secret truth and social decisions: her unprosecuted crimes are punished by an excessively harsh judgment licensed by excessively harsh laws and biased by rumors and the personal malice of the witnesses. Moll's true repentance is rewarded by the transmutation of execution to transportation and by not having to return the booty, so that the punishment is as light as the complete pardon available only to criminals richer or more socially prominent than Moll. Defoe does not explicitly attack or defend either Moll's unpunished criminality or the abuses of criminal justice; instead he retreats to the impression of factuality and the adversarial structure of the court system. Defoe constructs an account in which he does not assume responsibility for guiding the reader's judgment.

To measure the extent of Defoe's authorial abnegation, we should consider the importance of courts throughout the later history of novelistic fiction. Often, as in Richardson's *Clarissa* or in Hardy's *Tess of the D'Urbervilles*, there is an implicit rivalry between novel and court as sources of judgment about character. The later novelist usually hints that the novel has enabled the reader to know more about the motives and the true worth of the persons in a case than a court procedure could ever reveal. But Defoe connects the moral status of his fiction to the uncertain moral status of his narrator-protagonists, and so he does not seem to offer fiction as a better alternative to any other sort of social authority. In spite of telling secrets to the reader and raising our vanity about our privileged position of judgment, Defoe does not try to create the impression of complete intimacy between reader and character. Lies, faulty memory, editor's revisions—all are invoked by Defoe to excuse inconsistencies and roughness in the narrative. They all affect the reader's respect for the authority of the novel, because Defoe has not tried very hard to win it. But if, as a result, the novel in Defoe's hands fails to "rise," it may be even more important to find that political institutions do not suffer the usual corresponding fall. The interests of novelistic fiction have not yet been set at odds with the fictions of state. The arbitrary, makeshift impression Defoe gives of all kinds of fictions does not prevent him from demonstrating their power.

Along with other happy transmutations in the ending of *Moll Flanders*, we find that Moll's persuasive storytelling, which could not save her from the legal sentence, attains new efficacy as she plans to carry her sentence out. Moll's Lancashire highwayman husband finally takes her advice about accepting transportation to America, and when he learns more about the risk he has escaped in avoiding court trial, he pledges, "*My Dear . . . Thou hast twice sav'd my Life, from hence forward it shall be all employ'd for you, and I'll always take your Advice*" (313). If, as this chapter has suggested, Moll's search for a more authoritative position as counselor bears some relation to Defoe's political self-image, it is especially interesting to see how many traditional supports he assembled in the narrative to strengthen the force of her advice.

The husband's conviction that his marriage is his salvation is backed by Moll's consolidation of a large landed estate. Part of Moll's capital derives from the earnings of her criminal career, which remains a secret from her husband, but the most dramatic scenes involve Moll's successful attempts to secure the Virginia estate left by her mother and held in trust for her by her son. Moll's only reunion with a child is celebrated and motivated by a loving exchange of legal documents, by which she wills her son her mother's estate and he contracts to manage it for her. When Moll's husband sees the first installment from this inherited estate, he lifts up his hands to heaven and becomes a true penitent. Moll has been converted into an heiress. Her "bourgeois" features are absorbed into a favorite image of the eighteenth-century elite, the proprietor who is also a good business manager.

But this is not a fable of the bourgeoisie buying into land and hence political power (an impractical model for England until the late nineteenth century).[59] Traditional power, including sex dominance, is not overturned. Even if the gentlemanly husband is kept out of the way by aristocratic toys, Moll's relation with other women, once alliances symbolic of dependents organized against a dominant class, have dwindled. The governess, once a partner in crime, is now a purchasing agent who sends female servants along with other stock for the estate. And for all of her accumulated power, Moll's return to England with her husband is penitent. Like Defoe, she still lacks the security and authority to write under her real name and tell all her secrets.[60] By giving 1683 as the fictional date of composition, Defoe has in this novel clearly located his beloved Glorious Revolution in the world that is to come after Moll's story ends; and in the book's fiction, Moll is nearly the age in 1683 that Defoe was in 1722 when the book was published, an emblem for persistent ingenuity in the long, frustrating wait for political transformation.[61] The inconclusive feeling that attends Moll's return to England suggests a hopeful as well as fearful insight: when we consider the "final" authority of the institutions of law, we may remember that their pronouncements are final, but not for ever.

[59]For a recent synthetic account of the successful preservation of political power by the small, fairly closed landed elite of England, see Lawrence Stone and Jeanne C. Fawtier Stone, *An Open Elite? England, 1540–1800*, abridged ed. (Oxford: Oxford University Press, 1986).

[60]Not all critics read Moll's pseudonym as pessimistically as I have. Nancy K. Miller follows Leo Braudy in seeing Moll's continuing adherence to a pseudonym as an assertion of autonomy, but Miller stresses the specifically female, family-connected aspect of Moll's fictional creation of identity, and she notes the fantasy of a son endowing his mother with her heritage. See Miller, *The Heroine's Text: Readings in the French and English Novel, 1722–1782* (New York: Columbia University Press, 1980), p. 20; and Leo Braudy, "Daniel Defoe and the Anxieties of Autobiography," *Genre* 6, no. 1(1973):76–97.

[61]Paul Alkon considers a different effect of the double time in *Moll Flanders*: the eighteenth-century reader followed Moll's energetic career as if the story were contemporaneous and then reached the final date 1683, which removed Moll from the reader's condemnation to death and divine judgment. See *Defoe and Fictional Time*, pp. 50–52.

CHAPTER THREE

# *Richardson: Plots of Intimate Knowledge*

For the use of Lawes, (which are but Rules Authorised) is not to bind the People from all Voluntary actions; but to direct and keep them in such a motion, as not to hurt themselves by their own impetuous desires, rashnesse, or indiscretion, as Hedges are set, not to stop Travellers, but to keep them in the way.

*Leviathan*, II, 30, 388

## Travel between the Hedges

In the 1720s Charles De la Faye, the undersecretary of state in charge of investigations for treasonous libel, may have interested himself in Richardson the printer as well as Defoe the journalist. The discovery in 1864 of five of Defoe's letters to De la Faye was the first evidence of his arrangement with the Walpole administration to appear as if he "were as before under the Displeasure of the Government" for his previous service to Harley before his fall from power in 1714; meantime he would write for Tory journals in order to enervate their criticism of Walpole's government. The active public-opinion campaign included a network of informers such as Defoe to report printers, publishers, and authors of antiministerial publications, and on the other hand, it provided funding for progovernment press. As a secret agent of the government, Defoe was nevertheless liable to be suspected for his Tory writings if they did not seem enervated enough. Anonymous authorship and the habitual destruction of original copy protected him. The discovery of these letters prompted important reassessments of Defoe and enabled the discovery of volumes of his writings, but it cannot be said to be out of keeping with what had been known about him. By contrast it comes as a shock to learn that Richardson was twice reported to the Office of the Secretary of State for his supposed Jacobite learnings.

Richardson's most recent biographers,[1] Eaves and Kimpel, pro-

[1]Biographical sources for this chapter include T. C. Duncan Eaves and Ben D. Kimpel, *Samuel Richardson: A Biography* (Oxford: Clarendon, 1971); William Merritt Sale, Jr., *Samuel Richardson: Master Printer* (Ithaca: Cornell University Press, 1950); Margaret Anne Doody, "Samuel Richardson," in *British Novelists, 1660–1800*, ed. Martin C. Battestin, in two parts that together make up volume 39 of *Dictionary of Literary Biography* (Detroit, Mich.: Gale, 1985), 2:377–409; *The Correspondence*

duce new evidence for his involvement in the printing of the *True Briton*, an opposition journal financed and chiefly written by the Duke of Wharton, later an open Jacobite. In addition, Richardson printed books and pamphlets by convicted Jacobites, Francis Atterbury among others, and he barely escaped involvement in the biggest political prosecution of the decade—in 1728 against *Mist's Weekly Journal*, one of the Tory journals Defoe secretly helped to temper.

Eaves and Kimpel are reluctant to claim Richardson as an active supporter of opposition politics, much less of treason. Since 1722–28 was the early period of Richardson's independent printing business, he was more likely to take business that others refused. Opposition to the ministry was widespread, even conventional, in the City of London, and Richardson never printed anything obviously treasonous. Printing works that attacked the ministry might not have seemed very unusual or criminal, though Richardson exercised great caution in the case of the *True Briton*. Finally, he may simply have been helping a fellow printer in publishing a number of *Mist's* when the usual printer was under arrest.[2] Margaret Doody, somewhat more sympathetic to political opposition than Eaves and Kimpel, emphasizes that Richardson never repudiated his Tory associates and that in 1737 he printed a favorable obituary of Mist. In his 1739 revision of L'Estrange's *Aesop's Fables*, Richardson removes the old Tory opinions, but he urges tolerance for the author on the grounds that his opinions were typical of the Restoration period in which he wrote.

That even a law-abiding citizen like Richardson, who observed the hedges of society so carefully, should come under suspicion shows the uncertainty of political rules at this time. The association of Tories with Jacobites after the fall of Harley and Bolingbroke in 1714 and the incidence of two major Jacobite uprisings (1715, 1728) made it possible to associate all opposition to the ministry with treason. In 1726 Richardson voted for the opposition candidate, but how deep the commitment went is hard to say. His in-laws were voting with

---

*of Samuel Richardson*, ed. Anna Laetitia Barbauld, 6 vols. (London: Phillips, 1804); *Selected Letters of Samuel Richardson*, ed. John Carroll (Oxford: Clarendon, 1964).

[2]For Richardson's Tory and Jacobite connections, see Eaves and Kimpel, *Samuel Richardson*, pp. 19–36; and Doody, "Samuel Richardson," p. 382.

the opposition, so the impression given is of Richardson following in the tracks of his family (and also professional) associates. In 1734, a period of intense national agitation against the Walpole Whigs, Richardson is already voting proadministration and enjoying very significant government patronage, the printing for the House of Commons. This reliable source of business and prestige helps make him a wealthy man, especially after 1742, when he begins to print the journal of the House and becomes more independent of the booksellers, the usual source of trade. After the fall of Walpole in 1742, it became increasingly clear that the system of political patronage he perfected was one of the rules of the game, not the special corruption of an individual villain, and the consolidation of the nation against the Jacobite uprising of 1745 silenced the revolutionary wing of the opposition. Opposition to ministers became less violent, and in turn government suppression of opposition became less frequent. England was settling down at midcentury. Richardson merely settled down a decade before many of his contemporaries. He may never have become a servile follower of Walpole, but he was content to print the *Daily Gazeteer*, the chief organ of Walpole propaganda, for nearly the whole of its existence, from about 1738 to 1746.

Richardson's career on the whole seems to exemplify the sort of channeling of powerful energies that Hobbes had in mind for life under peaceful government. In an important, long autobiographical letter, Richardson tells his Dutch translator Stinstra that he "pursued Business with an Assiduity that, perhaps, has few Examples."[3] The major events of his life seem to be recorded in the Stationers Hall, the regular course prescribed by his trade, from apprenticeship to master to major shareholder in the Stationers Company. Though he married a former master's daughter and then, after her death, the daughter of an associate, these marriages procured no sudden leap in status. Hard work in an established calling structured his life, and he continued to live near Salisbury Court, in view of his first business dealings, traveling no farther than a suburban retreat in Fulham.

The striking contrast between Richardson and Defoe reminds us

[3]William C. Slattery, ed., *The Richardson-Stinstra Correspondence and Stinstra's Prefaces to "Clarissa"* (Carbondale: Southern Illinois University Press, 1969), p. 25.

that bourgeois status includes a wide range of manners and attitudes. Richardson, whose novels raised fiction to a high place among the arts, had far less education than Defoe and came from a poorer class of tradesmen. Like Defoe's family, Richardson's family designed him for the clergy, but unlike Defoe's family, Richardson's hadn't the means to procure higher education. Lacking Defoe's Dissenting perspective, which made the operation of political coercion highly visible, Richardson was more inclined to accept his exclusion from higher education and from politics. Richardson had a little Latin, no modern European languages; his aesthetic opinions and knowledge of politics and international affairs seemed to derive from friends, such as the projector and man of letters Aaron Hill, or from works that he was printing. In fact the works of Defoe that Richardson printed, edited, and expanded—*Religious Courtship, A New Family Instructor,* and most important, Defoe's *Tour through the Whole Island of Great Britain*—must have constituted a considerable portion of Richardson's education.

There is evidence that Richardson read what he printed with studious attention. His autobiographical letter explains that booksellers often sought his trade "because of the Readiness I shewed to oblige them, with writing Indexes, Prefaces, and sometimes for their minor Authors, *honest* Dedications; abstracting, abridging, compiling, and giving my Opinion of Pieces offered them." When we consider not only his habits of careful scrutiny, but also the range of his business—which included a collection of state trials, the printing for the House of Commons, poems by David Mallet and James Thomson, the diverse works of Aaron Hill, and a project he launched himself with the help of the Society for the Encouragement of Learning, *The Negotiations of Sir Thomas Roe, in His Embassy to the Ottoman Porte, 1621 to 1628*—we must conclude that Richardson's self-education was extensive. We must imagine that he was knowledgeable about contemporary politics (the printing for Parliament made him a friend of the Speaker of the House), but he did not seem to feel that his knowledge or his wealth entitled him to a loud voice in the formal politics of his nation. Even Richardson's first writings are closely connected to his trade. The earliest published work of Richardson's own was a letter of advice to apprentices which was developed from a letter he wrote to a nephew apprenticed to him.

Yet it would be misleading to maintain an impression that Richardson's sense of himself as a novelist is as confined as his life, which was devoted to private business and family, and on which national affairs only impinged as conditions of business. For Richardson's art, however blithely it has been typed as middle class and Puritan, is set among the rulers of England, the owners of large landed estates. His first long work, *Familiar Letters,* a model letter book featuring exemplary problems, shows that Richardson's art grew out of domestic conduct books,[4] but his novelistic conduct books are addressed partly to the ruling class of England. And the ruling class paid attention, since Richardson, although the least genteelly educated of the canonized novelists of eighteenth-century England, is chiefly responsible for the rise in the prestige of prose fiction about contemporary life.

In his autobiographical letter, a loud fluttering of aristocratic wings can be heard in many paragraphs. Richardson's ancestors had been landholders originally, and his mother came "of a family not ungenteel"; somehow his father was personally beloved by the Duke of Monmouth and the Earl of Shaftesbury. Richardson's failed hopes of becoming a clergyman are followed by a mysterious "Correspondence with a Gentleman greatly my superior in Degree and of ample Fortunes, who, had he lived, intended high things for me" (*Letters to Stinstra,* 25). Finally, he enjoys not the patronage that comes to servile dedicators, but "the Honour of being esteemed by Several Persons, who by their Rank and Fortunes, as well as Merits, would be a Reputation to any Work" (29). His sense of independent standing is appropriate to the pride in his fictions as his own creations: "God and my own Diligence were ever my chief Reliance" (29). Can we reconcile the image of the industrious, obedient apprentice with the image of the independent creator of widely respected pictures of gentry life? Richardson's own hopes of social reconciliation and unification are invested in the authority of moral discourse.

When urged by Stinstra to explain the origin of his literary skills, Richardson relates an incident in early life that showed his presumptuous desire to give rules to others:

[4]See Catherine Gee Hornbeck, *Richardson's "Familiar Letters" and the Domestic Conduct Books: Richardson's "Aesop"* (Northampton, Mass.: Smith College, 1938), Smith College Studies in Modern Languages, no. 19.

> I was not Eleven Years old, when I wrote, spontaneously, a Letter to a Widow near Fifty, who pretending to a Zeal for Religion, and who was a constant Frequenter of Church Ordinances, was continually fomenting Quarrels and Disturbances, by Backbiting and Scandal, amongst all her Acquaintance. I collected from the Scripture Texts that made against her. Assuming the Style and Address of a Person of Years, I exhorted her; I expostulated with her. But my Hand-writing was known: I was challenged with it, and owned the Boldness; for she complained of it to my Mother with Tears. My Mother chid me for the Freedom taken by such a Boy with a Woman of her Years: But knowing that her Son was not of a Pert or forward Nature, but, on the contrary, shy and bashful, she commended my Principles, tho' she censured the Liberty taken. [*Letters to Stinstra*, 26]

The letter was both very "bold," a "liberty" for a child to instruct an old woman, and yet also the ideal tool of the "shy and bashful." He avoided being rude to the widow's face, since in a letter he could take on a style of character who might be an appropriate censor of her conduct, and he mustered scriptural authority for his reproof. Not the boy, but the fictional speaker and the biblical texts, reproved the lady. The act showed an extraordinary sensitivity to rules of all sorts, not only divine commandments, but also the rules of social propriety. The chief enforcement for these rules is social pressure rather than the particular pronouncements of special figures of formal authority; the boy speaks as society, and partly because of that his personal authorship is easily detected and resented. The episode is especially interesting because Richardson assumes that there is a clear difference between his act of censure and the widow's backbiting. The response of Richardson's mother shows the careful manipulation of the especially powerful tool of social pressure, parental approval and disapproval. Within the family approval can be subtly adjusted according to the special understanding of the child's character which is available to the attentive parent. Richardson's mother "commended [his] principles, tho' she censured the Liberty taken."

Not much later in his life, Richardson seems to have been a master at interpreting rules according to the circumstances, since he was entrusted by young ladies with the delicate task of answering love letters, a genre in which once again the moral rule of honesty and the social rules of propriety had to be adjusted. Richardson told Stinstra that he became acquainted with these ladies and established his wisdom as the favorite reader and literary critic to a sewing circle: "both mothers and Daughters used to be pleased with the Observations they put upon me making" (*Letters to Stinstra*, 49).

Richardson's desired authority is in the arena of society rather than of formal politics, as the interpreter of the self-regulating sort of rules or interpretations of rules that seem to emanate from everywhere and nowhere. Literature has a great deal to do with molding the understanding of such rules, and in Richardson's account he enjoyed an identification with that power from the time of his childhood. A group of his schoolfellows "delighted to single me out" to tell them stories and "often were affected by them." His anonymity as an author, unlike some of Defoe's practices, was meant to be uncovered, and the fictional status of his work seemed to be a matter of pride, yet the authority to exemplify and discuss social rules was not presented as an original authority or personal insight, but rather as the wisdom of the group.

Richardson seldom admits that at times political power must enforce social good, that the power of approval could not perform every act of regulation. One of his surviving pamphlets, for example, supports a bill for regulating the theaters, a rare instance of Richardson acting as a public advocate in the realm of formal politics.[5] Doubtless the influence of the theater, an example of the informal power of art, seemed to Richardson too strong for other kinds of social forces. In 1757 Richardson complained in a letter that there was no legal authority to regulate the press, but this sort of irritability does not indicate a commitment to a policy of repression that he would back up. On the whole, Richardson did not want to meddle with the public law that defined the balance of authority and liberty. His sympathy with wide toleration of Catholics in Ireland and of Jews in England has the same sort of detached, unmilitant quality. He regrets the public outcry against the act allowing Parliament to naturalize Jews, but he thought Jews would be well advised to ask that the law be repealed, thereby overcoming popular prejudice. Reputation rather than law was the powerful agent of happiness for Richardson, partly because he never considered himself fully quali-

[5]A *Seasonable Examination of the Pleas and Pretensions of the Proprietors of, and Subscribers to, Playhouses, Erected in Defiance of the Royal License* (London: T. Cooper, 1735).

fied to direct matters of public law: "What *aduce* has such an obscure Mortal as I am to do with Public Affairs?" (25 October 1756, Eaves and Kimpel, *Samuel Richardson*, 548).

Of the few references to national government in Richardson's works, the most important is a letter from Lord M to his nephew Lovelace, urging him to build, upon the foundation of a happy private life with Clarissa, a notable career in Parliament. Lord M's advice to Lovelace as a prospective MP is analogous to Richardson's sense of an ordinary citizen's relation to government: opposition should be reluctant, not a principle of public life. The role seems hardly active and heroic enough for Lovelace's taste, but by the time of *Clarissa*, which came out after the fall of Walpole, many people may have felt something extravagant and hypocritical in the extraordinary efforts of opposition, from the return of Bolingbroke in 1726 to the early forties. For some, like Fielding, a major disillusionment with members of the opposition who joined the government seemed to suggest that political life was inherently corrupt. Hume, in his political essays of the early 1740s, argued that some degree of government management by patronage was inevitable and useful. In any case, Lord M's recommendation of independence and the avoidance of place lacks the fervor of the political criticism of Right and Left; it carries only the sign of personal morality in public life.

The discourse on personal morality is not necessarily cut off from politics. The great opposition satires by Pope and Swift and Fielding attacked the luxurious habits that made Walpole's patronage attractive and that were promoted by it. The sense of a particular political crisis gave force to the attacks on the corruption of taste. Without this perspective, the attacks on French cookery and the Italian opera in the *Dunciad*, a work whose versions and revisions span the period of opposition politics, would seem trivial, hardly worth the status of an epic satire. In Richardson's hands, the specific political objective behind the social criticism is lost, though all his stories retain a more generalized sense of the importance of private virtue to public happiness. A healthy society would guarantee a virtuous polity without any specifically political goals. The projector is replaced by the social moralist, the pamphlet by the conduct book. The author seeks to affect the life of his nation more through manners than through laws. His tools of power are not informal access to lawmakers and administrators, or the mustering of public pressure on the political authorities, but an influence on public opinion without the necessity of formal institutional codification. The only sanctions he invokes are informal but powerful: approval and disapproval. Richardson's conception of moral power can be associated with the development of moral philosophy after Hobbes.

## Rules, Moral Language, and Vanity: Hume and Richardson

The effort of the philosophers to address Hobbes's ethical skepticism without coming to his political conclusions led them to examine the realm of shared opinion that he had so impressively argued was the origin of social reasoning. New theorists of society, especially "moral sense" philosophers such as Shaftesbury and Hutcheson, reimagined the realm of opinion as one of self-regulating stability, rather than competitive anarchy set into order by arbitrary acts of sovereign authority. Fewer philosophers claimed an entirely rational basis for morals, although the moral-sense philosophers combined rationalism and skepticism rather freely. The most skeptical of the new moralists who emphasized moral sentiment was David Hume, whose philosophical works were published in the same midcentury period as the first great period of the novel (1739–52).[6] In reworking Book Three of the *Treatise of Human Nature* to create the *Enquiry concerning the Principles of Morals,* Hume dropped the term that provided the clearest link to Hobbes, the explicit definition of the "artificial" nature of justice, a term the moral sense philosopher Hutcheson had found obnoxious in the draft of the *Treatise*.[7] Nevertheless, Hume, like Hobbes, emphasized the human rather than

[6]A short list of essential commentary on the place of Hume's moral philosophy in the context of his whole career would include J. A. Passmore, *Hume's Intentions* (Cambridge: Cambridge University Press, 1952); John B. Stewart, *The Moral and Political Philosophy of David Hume* (New York: Columbia University Press, 1963); Shirley Robin Letwin, *The Pursuit of Certainty* (Cambridge: Cambridge University Press, 1965); Duncan Forbes, *Hume's Philosophical Politics* (Cambridge: Cambridge University Press, 1975); and numerous essays by Annette C. Baier.

[7]For the political implications of the changes Hume made when he "recast" the materials of the *Treatise* into his two enquiries, see Carol Kay, "Philosophic Manners: The Writings of David Hume, 1727–1751" (Ph.D. diss., Harvard University, 1975).

divine origin of all moral rules, including the rules of justice, and he illustrated this artificiality by his large variety of examples from different cultures.

The universal principles of morality he identified—the preferences for what is useful or agreeable to ourselves or others—are so broad that they guarantee very little uniformity. The variety of moral ideas is the main subject of a work generally published with the *Enquiry concerning the Principles of Morals, A Dialogue,* which exposes the widely divergent moral attitudes—toward sex, personal violence, political allegiance, and religion—in ancient Greece and modern France and Britain. One of the most striking aspects of this account, the source of its composure, is that the morality of individual nations appears unitary; shared social life guarantees unity for belief, and shared government is only one feature of common life, important to morality as much for contributing habits and attitudes as for direct legislation of moral rules. But in turn, "The laws have, or ought to have, a constant reference to the constitution of government, the manners, the climate, the religion, the commerce, the situation of each society."[8] The creation of a shared morality is a natural-feeling historical growth, without a single, identifiable origin in acts of Hobbesian sovereign authority or Lockean social contracts.

Hume not only attacks the notion of an *original* social contract, he considers contracting too specialized an activity to serve as an adequate paradigm for social agreement. Even the obligation to observe promises—essential for Defoe and his sources in natural law, essential to Hobbes in ways that trouble his skeptical system—arises for Hume in a distinct phase of social development. Explicit promises multiply opportunities for the transfer of property. Property itself is established earlier by convention rather than by promises, and only at a later stage of property and promises do government and the obligation of allegiance arise.[9] The foundational social experience for

[8]David Hume, *Enquiry concerning the Principles of Morals,* sec. III, pt. ii, in *Enquiries concerning Human Understanding and concerning the Principles of Morals,* ed. P. H. Nidditch (Oxford: Clarendon, 1975), p. 196. Further references are given parenthetically in the text, by section, part (where applicable), and page.

[9]This account of the origin of promises is one of the excellent sections of the *Treatise of Human Nature* (bk. III, pt. II, sec. v) which was sadly abridged when Hume "recast" his philosophy in the *Enquiry concerning the Principles of Morals.* For the best and most appreciative account of this part of the *Treatise,* see Annette

Hume is not the institution of political society as it is for Hobbes. Instead, the historical origin of society, and the preparatory education for it, is found in the sympathetic relationships of the family. Although sympathy is a mechanism that enables us to feel the new moral obligations developed in society with complex property arrangements, it continues to work in a more immediate, more reliable way in the family. The "self-interested commerce," which the obligation to promises facilitates, "does not entirely abolish the more generous and noble intercourse of friendship and good offices."[10] Unlike Defoe's families, Hume's families do not often need promises.

Explicit promises are not essential for Humean morality, but shared language is. Though language for Hume, as for Hobbes, is artificial, Hume argues that its use must be social, not eccentric or individualistic, and since moral language inevitably refers to the social, it draws the user into the application of shared standards. A man who used moral terms, as Hobbes says everyone does—according to individual passions—could not be understood by others:

> When a man denominates another his *enemy*, his *rival*, his *antagonist*, his *adversary*, he is understood to speak the language of self-love, and to express sentiments, peculiar to himself and arising from his particular circumstances and situation. But when he bestows on any man the epithets of *vicious* or *odious* or *depraved*, he then speaks

---

C. Baier (University of Pittsburgh), "The Originality of Hume's Account of Social Artifice" (unpublished paper, 1986).

A careful reading of Hume on promises is at stake in an equally important article by Baier, which criticizes David Gauthier's famous argument in "David Hume, Contractarian," *Philosophical Review* 88, no. 1 (1979):3–38. Hume cannot be a contractarian, even in the expanded modern sense of such philosophers as John Rawls, because the reciprocity and mutual understanding of Humean morality, including justice, are not reduced to promising and contracting. Instead, the developed capacity for social agreement manifested in conventions such as property is the foundation for promising. So the convention of promising is not itself established by a promise; nor is any other convention agreed on in this peculiarly explicit and binding way. See Annette C. Baier, "Why Hume Is Not a Contractarian" (unpublished paper, 1986). Hume and Baier may be more realistic in their account of convention, but I am attracted by Gauthier's model of bargaining and covenanting to agree as a selection among competing and unstable conventions. He addresses a problem Hume tends to suppress, which I have identified with the Hobbesian problematic: conventions cannot always be stable, dominant, and self-regulating. See Gauthier, p. 9.

[10]David Hume, *A Treatise of Human Nature*, ed. Ernest C. Mossner (Harmondsworth: Penguin, 1969), bk. III, pt. ii, sec. v, pp. 573–74. Further references are given parenthetically in the text.

> another language, and expresses sentiments in which he expects all his audience are to concur with him. He must here, therefore, depart from his private and particular situation and must choose a point of view, common to him with others. [*Enquiry concerning . . . Morals*, sec. IX, pt. I, 272]

Even a Hobbesian sovereign would be, in Hume's understanding, subject to these rules, unable to use the language of self-love as if it were the language of morality. A hopeful element of equity seems to be built into the concept of rule observance, even when Hobbes turns to recommend prudential rules for sovereigns in Part II of *Leviathan*.

The image of moral life that emerges from Hume's description is enormously appealing: morality is learned and enforced through the use of language of approval and disapproval. Imagination of the feelings of other people, or "sympathy" as Hume called it in the *Treatise*,[11] a process of association of ideas which has in itself no moral content (by contrast to the term *humanity*), prepares for a socially organized pattern of sensitivity. Vanity or "love of fame" causes an internalization of the public standards:

> By our continual and earnest pursuit of a character, a name, a reputation in the world, we bring our own deportment and conduct frequently in review, and consider how they appear in the eyes of those who approach and regard us. This constant habit of surveying ourselves, as it were, in reflection, keeps alive all the sentiments of right and wrong, and begets, in noble natures a certain reverence for themselves as well as others, which is the surest guardian of every virtue. [*Enquiry*, sec. IX, pt. I, 276]

Hume's revaluation of vanity is one of his most striking anti-Hobbesian moves. In Hobbes "the earnest pursuit of a name" is one of the fundamental causes of dangerous competition; for Hume vanity illustrates and extends the socially beneficial functions of sympathy. It is a very good thing to care about the names people call you.

[11] For a more detailed treatment of Hume's theory of sympathy in relation to *Clarissa*, see Carol Kay, "Sex, Sympathy, and Authority in Richardson and Hume," in *Studies in Eighteenth-Century Culture*, vol. 12, ed. Harry C. Payne (Madison: University of Wisconsin Press, 1982), pp. 77–92.

So sure is Hume in his reliance upon the use of moral terms as the embodiment of shared practices and beliefs that in later editions of the *Enquiry* he emphasizes language use as the scientific basis of his argument: "The very nature of language guides us almost infallibly in forming a judgement of this nature; and as every tongue possesses one set of words which are taken in a good sense, and another in the opposite, the least acquaintance with the idiom suffices, without any reasoning, to direct us in collecting and arranging the estimable or blamable qualities of men" (I, I, 174). Language for Hume is not only the vehicle of morality, it is also an important analogy for morality. It is a social practice regulated by reliable rules that are understood without explicit articulation and obeyed without an identifiable source of authority or special sanctions. The explicitness of a law or a promise is not the proper model for much of the social activity that interests Hume. The convention of property is not a promise, but a "general sense of common interest; which sense all the members of the society express towards one another, and which induces them to regulate their conduct by certain rules" (*Treatise*, III, II, ii, 541). The gradual rise of the convention, the many experiences of disadvantage from breaking it, strengthens the common mutual assurance: "In like manner are languages gradually establish'd by human convention without any promise. In like manner do gold and silver become the common measures of exchange, and are esteem'd sufficient payment for what is of a hundred times their value" (542). Observance of mutually understood general rules, including the rules for the language of morality are practices inseparable from social life, and they make the development of political life possible.

The reason that politics can be a science in Hume's view is not, as it is for Hobbes, because the scientifically gifted can make an organization of institutions based on logical analysis and argument, but because social life has the coherence and continuity of rules: the regularities are historical and sociological, not logical. Hume indeed gave important accounts in the *Enquiry*, in the *Treatise*, and in various essays of the rise of government and its special operations, but his most important contribution to political theory is to describe the social base on which the governmental structure arises and which it partially resembles. The section of the *Enquiry* entitled "Of Political Society" is almost wholly given over to illustrating the general propensity for rule making, rather than to defining a specifically political set of rules.

Hume's arguments, powerful as they are, do not basically address Hobbes's problems. His models assume the stability and homogeneity of settled nations. Hume's *History of Great Britain* is interesting precisely for this reason. His account of the civil war points to the instability caused by fundamental disagreements about the nature of English government and society. In the face of such disagreements, Hume's arguments become Hobbesian. The preference is always to be given to allegiance when a dispute has revolutionary potential. But his account is calm and ironic, since the radical instability is past and the dangerous violence it produced has also produced more liberty, a product Hume appreciates, though he deplores the means. His political essays of the 1740s, which precede the history, bear the same lessons to his contemporaries. The public peace had been founded on a shared understanding about mixed government that necessitates a continuous but rather limited amount of conflict, mutual wear and tear. Nothing will so much contribute to the peace of postrevolutionary Britain as the recognition that such conflict, including strident disputes in the press on the one hand and a moderate amount of administration patronage on the other hand, is a regular part of British life. Even conflict can be subject to stabilizing, habitual rules. Hume's defense of British liberty is not based on general theoretical grounds, but rather on a specifically British history. Later in his life, during the Wilkes riots in London which particularly offended Scots, Hume sees with more irritable anxiety the potential instability in the lack of a single strong executive authority and the wide license for legal conflict with authority.

It seems odd to couple the notoriously skeptical Hume with the conventionally pious Samuel Richardson, but Richardson shares the fundamental strategy by which Hume answered Hobbes, the direction of attention to social rules rather than to religious revelation or the arbitrary imposition of political authority. Richardson's characters have the deep sensitivity to public opinion and the profound respect for rules which Hume describes so eloquently. Indeed, the morality of Richardson's exemplary characters is to subject themselves to the limitations of convention even when the formal law allows wider latitude for choice. But Richardson's fiction also tests the commitments it shares with Hume's philosophy. In it we see how the authority of social rules works on individuals in the process of making decisions, "writing to the moment," when the impression of regular order created by generalizations about national character cannot easily be maintained. In the setting of the family, Hume's locus of first sympathies, the order afforded by social convention can be seen as potentially uncertain and dangerous as Hobbes's imagined state of nature, a society without a clear understanding about sovereign authority. The nearly murderous conflicts in *Pamela* and *Clarissa* show the pains of this situation. The much vaunted view of the individual inner life that Richardson's novels afford shows the inadequacies of authority that is chiefly social.

While more narrowly focused, the concerns of this chapter are compatible with two recent literary histories that integrate writings of Hume in a comprehensive sketch of mid-eighteenth-century British literature. John Sitter stresses the emergence of "literary loneliness," while John Barrell finds the attempt to create and maintain "an equal, wide survey" of society. Yet both critics describe a crisis in the active, political rule exercised by the gentlemanly class and an effort to reformulate the conditions of virtuous, comprehensive social understanding in more abstract terms. For Sitter, this effort involves "a lyric flight from immediate history and an approach toward History . . . a history sufficiently generalized and abstracted to serve as the ground of a broader theodicy." For Barrell, the rise of a fundamentally economic understanding of social mechanism challenges the older understanding of aristocratic political leadership, yet also extends it, since only the polite, disinterested, and unspecialized gentleman was thought to be capable of this difficult new kind of comprehension.[12]

Fundamental to the midcentury economic and sociological analyses and to the philosophical histories written to illustrate those principles are the issues of this chapter, the understanding of social life in terms of rules systems and the revaluation of competitive vanity. I also see a connection between an abstracted, generalized

[12]John Sitter, *Literary Loneliness in Mid-Eighteenth-Century England* (Ithaca: Cornell University Press, 1982); and John Barrell, *English Literature in History, 1730–1780: An Equal, Wide Survey* (London: Hutchinson, 1983).

way of looking at society and a historical situation of political disadvantage and political disillusionment. We could compare Richardson's political disadvantages as a member of the bourgeoisie with Hume's disadvantages as a Scot whose Parliament had been abolished at the act of Union. Both Richardson and Hume matured as writers in the period of disillusionment with the Bolingbrokian opposition. Barrell's book is especially relevant to the philosophical concerns of this chapter, since he describes the codification of "correctness" in language use as a mode of social integration, a view of Johnson's *Dictionary* that is compatible with my emphasis on Hume's view of moral discourse. My detection of Hobbesian political conflict within Humean constructions of social comprehension is a more schematic way of exploring, through the example of Richardson, the tensions Sitter and Barrell find in the literary culture as a whole.

Under Richardson's close scrutiny, the attractive appearance of self-regulating social systems disappears and compulsion becomes visible. Conflicts appear in the interpretation of social rules as well as in the interpretation of public law: it proves impossible to elide questions of authority and power. Social rules may be enforced by social rather than political authority, but these forces may be more rather than less threatening. The consequences of public disapproval may amount to an execution, and, as scenes of mudslinging and stone throwing in Fielding show, public violence is not entirely excluded as a form of social sanction. The problems of conflicting interpretations and threatened punishments can be the more severe because the sovereign judge may not be available or may not be called upon to regulate the system of social opinion.

Richardson's fiction allows us to see that persistent distance from political authority signals the impairment of systematic morality. The chief characters in *Pamela* and *Clarissa* are either banned from full participation in public institutions because of sex (in Pamela's case, status as well as sex) or because of a fundamental lack of interest. The libertine hero, though qualified for public office, carries on his exploits in private and exercises the large power of acting that status and wealth afford to circumvent both public law and the social moral code. Women are confined to private authority of fathers, husbands, or guardians by law, and they are even further confined by moral beliefs and social practices that make it disgraceful to challenge family authority. Yet Richardson's suspicion of independent marriage settlements and self-sufficiency for wives and daughters seems more like the notions of conjugal unity appropriate to postwar America, than to eighteenth-century England. The situation of intimate trust seemed to him essential for family life, and the appeal to outside authorities, which we may conclude to be necessary, nevertheless seemed to him destructive or irrelevant. The tremendous investment in learning about one another that Richardson pictures in his characters and that he requires of us operates as a compensation for the public, political judgments he underrates. Intimate, mutual knowledge of character will be the anchor and the safety net for a mutual understanding of rules.

Although Richardson wishes to present this state of intimate trust as normal, the extreme difficulty of attaining it and of maintaining it are among the chief lessons of his plots, an important reason his books are so long. Unlike Moll Flanders, for whom promises are reliable guarantees, Squire B. and Lovelace, even Clarissa, experience great difficulty in bringing themselves to decide on marriage. The degree of trust necessary to marriage—mutual understanding of rules, belief in each other's honesty, extensive sympathy—is not merely a difficulty for cynics. Instead, the suspicious libertine provokes Richardson to explore the difficulties and necessities of trust. The fear that haunts these narratives is not merely the "Puritan" dread of sex, but something we all can feel when we seek some kind of secure grounding for confidence in others. The unprecedented detail of individual characterization in Richardson's novels seems to offer opportunities of knowing character which can provide that secure basis of trust for the decisions of characters and the judgments of readers. However, continuing debates among readers about the morality of Pamela, Clarissa, and Lovelace show that Richardson has not succeeded in portraying methods of attaining certain knowledge of character. Instead, he has shown the impossibility of such certainty and the dangers of seeking it.

The isolation of the lovers, who conduct this massive scrutiny of character, is not in Richardson an inevitable, unconscious outgrowth of bourgeois culture—urbanization and privatization and the conjugal family—as Ian Watt pictures it. In *Pamela* and *Clarissa* the isolation of characters is extraordinary and dangerous, even if it also provides extraordinary opportunities for intimate knowledge. In each book the heroine is not merely confined to home, which with its large number of servants and family relations is not, after all, a very intimate place in the eighteenth century. There is a further removal, an abduction, which more radically limits the number of friendships and makes dependence on a single intimacy more crucial. Knowledge of individual character in such a setting is both more accessible and more necessary.

Richardson's epistolary mode seems to provide a rare access to this isolated, remarkably intense and protracted scrutiny of lovers, yet by its very premise the letter form, however detailed or believable, cannot be a direct view of an entirely individual psychology, since letters are addressed to another person. And as Richardson constructs his novels, the reader is especially made to feel the social nature of the correspondence. The intimate friends and relations addressed are not just repositories of confidence, not merely a medium in which private personality crystallizes. The correspondents are addressed as representative social authorities, have a right to pronounce judgment on the behavior of the letter writer and join in the interpretation of other characters. Pamela writes her parents, who direct her conduct, but even Clarissa writes to measure her behavior by rule, because Anna Howe demands an account for those young ladies who have taken Clarissa as their example.

Nonetheless, few of the epistolary exchanges conform to the clearcut assumptions embodied in Hobbesian definitions of counsel, even when advice is given or received. The authority that shapes Richardson's fictional correspondence seems to be the ubiquitous authority of moral discourse itself, as Hume has described it. The act of writing represents the willing subjection of conduct to social rules; the active internalization of those rules becomes even clearer when the writing may never be seen or answered by the intended correspondent—for example, when Pamela's writing turns into a journal in Lincolnshire, or when Clarissa writes her fragments after the rape. Yet the act of correspondence opens up the isolation of intimate relationships in a number of ways, besides bringing social rules to bear on the relationship, and the opening to society also entails the opening to Hobbesian perceptions of the potential for conflict caused by moral discourse. Letters can be used to muster public opinion, and they thereby become not only an internalized authority but also a power that can be used to influence another person. The tremendous importance of letters for the lives represented in Richardson's narratives measures the social importance Richardson may claim for his art, and his Hobbesian sensitivity to potential conflict enables him to reveal the dangers in even this, his most cherished form of power.

## *Pamela*: Love and the Love of Fame

At the opening of *Pamela* the reader learns, in the same way that Mr. B. makes the discovery, the most important trait of the heroine: Pamela is, as she signs herself, "dutiful." She writes home regularly: "You are a good Girl, *Pamela,* to be kind to your aged Father and Mother,"[13] says Mr. B. in his first approach to intimacy with her. Is he drawn to this trait, or does he know what sort of praise will most easily win her heart? Unlike Moll Flanders, Pamela knows who her parents are and what they wish her to be. She has been well brought up, by both family and employer, and has been nourished with the constant approval fed to dutiful daughters and servants. The concern with duty and the stream of praise for his paragon have frequently been thought blights on Richardson's art, primitive traits of didactic art which blemish his peculiarly vivid pictures of the repressions, contradictions, and perversities of the inner life. But the psychological interest of his novels is inseparable from their morality; the registration of the ambition to be dutiful has conflicts, contradictions, and perversities enough to satisfy the modern taste for complexity.[14]

Pamela's first letter reveals in a number of ways how difficult it is to know how to maintain the character of being dutiful. If rules are unclear, the character may be so too. So good a servant was Pamela

[13]Samuel Richardson, *Pamela, or Virtue Rewarded*, ed. T. C. Duncan Eaves and Ben D. Kimpel (Boston: Houghton Mifflin, 1971), p. 26. All further references to this edition in this chapter will be given parenthetically.

[14]Even favorable critics of Richardson tend to picture a conflict between his morality and his art, his precepts and his dramatic imagination. See, e.g., Carol Houlihan Flynn, *Samuel Richardson: A Man of Letters* (Princeton: Princeton University Press, 1982), p. x: "Ostensibly promoting principles of absolute morality, Richardson creates a world of infinite complexity and ambiguity where commonplace maxims have little effect on real situations."

to her "good Lady" that "my Lady's Goodness had put me to write and cast Accompts, and made me a little expert at my Needle, and other Qualifications above my Degree" (25). Out of careful training rather than destitution, Pamela finds herself in young Moll's ambiguous position, with traits inappropriate for her station. We should remember that for this reason alone a quarrel with her new master would be dangerous, since "it would have been no easy Matter to find a Place that your poor *Pamela* was fit for." Her letter writing is the most massive evidence of qualification above her degree. It attracts Squire B.'s attention in the first letter and throughout the book, but his response to it is ambivalent. Letter writing is good; it shows duty to parents and duty to her former mistress's training. But reading and writing are not servants' work. Mr. B.'s interest in Pamela's writing and his permission for her to read the family books are acts of unusual kindness that make Pamela's parents suspicious (27). In Pamela's account, she was "scared out of my Senses" by her master catching her at writing. Does she fear the charge of wasting time? Richardson boasted that as an apprentice he never made his master suffer for his love of reading and correspondence: "I took care that even my Candle was of my own Purchasing." When Mr. B. is angry at Pamela, he complains, "This Girl is always scribbling; I think she may be better employ'd" (34).

In revision, Richardson added to the first letter a broader hint, in keeping with the development of the story, to explain why masters might be angry at servants' writing and why a servant might hide a letter from the master: "I am not angry with you for writing such innocent matters as these: though you ought to be wary what tales you send out of a family." The ability to write well gives the servant access to public opinion outside the household; the power to affect the reputation of the master is important for people who otherwise have few formal powers; and the power to read and write also makes it more likely that the servants will know how to enforce more formal protections against unlimited household authority. Pamela has threatening powers as well as charming allurements with which she can bargain. The danger of tale bearing is serious enough for Fielding, the presumed author of *Shamela*, to reprove the author of *Pamela* for teaching servants to betray the secrets of families. The point is made with more humor in *Joseph Andrews* when Joseph protests repeatedly to his sister, "I never loved to tell the secrets of my master's family" and then proceeds to report that his mistress never loved his master.[15] When we have been sensitized by Fielding, the full indiscretion of Richardson's book appears shocking, especially if we consider that the premise of factuality in *Pamela* was a matter of literal belief for many of the first readers: the whole narrative, not just the scenes of sexual abuse, continues the presumptuous offense of telling the secrets of families. But as the book progresses, Pamela gains the license to narrate the family history. Her master's early approval then appears as a happy prefiguration, not the mark of uncertain status.

The uncertainty of rules is not just a result of Pamela's special gifts. The great change of authorities, from old mistress to young master, reported in her first letter puts the rules into doubt. Even though Pamela may understand the general rules governing servants, the personal character of household authority means that a change of masters may make a great change in the rules. *Shamela's* author complains that in *Pamela* "all chamber maids are strictly enjoined to look out after their masters," to learn things they should not learn.[16] Yet it is a duty to pay close attention to the master's peculiarities. A servant who has no special acquaintance with the new master may be dismissed in spite of previous dutiful behavior. And as we have seen, not every master allows the special privileges and honorable duties that Pamela has had. The change from mistress to master is of the greatest consequence. The highly personal service in which Pamela has excelled may have a different meaning. Signs of favor, such as gifts of clothing and money, may also change their meanings. Pamela's parents try to puzzle the matters out in their reply: a neighbor has told them that, after all, the gift of the deceased lady's garments and the money in her pockets was not so very unusual or suspicious. But they decide to leave the meaning of the money in suspense, to put it away until they know whether to spend it as the appropriate wages of duty or to return it as an attempted bribe of shame. Afterward, they are hard pressed and use some of it, but the narrative redeems their implicit interpretation: it turns out to be an

[15]Martin C. Battestin, ed., *"Joseph Andrews" and "Shamela"* (Boston: Houghton Mifflin, 1961), p. 24.

[16]Ibid., p. 338.

honest gift. Pamela likewise puts the clothing into escrow and withdraws it when the plot has presented a clear meaning.[17]

Pamela and Squire B., it turns out, have not been utterly unacquainted before his mother's death. Later in the book, he complains of Pamela's distrust, reminding her that they had known each other as children. But the relationship has not been continuous. Some early impressions and habits may have changed; their distance in rank has certainly become more important. The greatest change made by age is the change in the rules of behavior that comes with sexual maturity. For fifteen-year-old Pamela the change has been recent, and if we keep in mind the uncertain borderline between child and woman, a great deal of the book becomes more interesting.[18] The parents' early warning about the master becomes more understandable and acceptable. Pamela's womanliness may have come about very recently indeed: "Every body talks how you have come on, and what a genteel Girl you are, and some say, you are very pretty; and indeed, Six Months since, when I saw you last, I should have thought so too, if you was not our Child" (27). Will Pamela be able to tell the difference between the loving encouragements she has enjoyed as a child and the praise of would-be lovers? "You seem so full of Joy at his Goodness, so taken with his kind Expressions" (27). Pamela at first resists seeing a difference between kinds of attention: "My master continues to be very affable to me. As yet I see no Cause to fear anything. Mrs. *Jervis* the House-Keeper too is very civil to me, and I have the Love of every body. Sure they can't *all* have Designs against me because they are civil. I hope I shall always behave so as to be respected by every one; and hope nobody would do me more hurt, than I am sure I would do them" (28).

Pamela's open display of her love of praise seems appropriate to her time of life.[19] Some of her letters to her parents sound like

[17]See Carey McIntosh, "Pamela's Clothes," in *Twentieth-Century Interpretations of "Pamela,"* ed. Rosemary Cowler (Englewood Cliffs, N.J.: Prentice-Hall, 1969), pp. 89–96.

[18]For an account of *Pamela* as an instance of the long affiliation between the novel and adolescence, see Patricia Meyer Spacks, *The Adolescent Idea: Myths of Youth and the Adult Imagination* (New York, Basic Books, 1981), pp. 24–30.

[19]Mark Kinkead-Weekes has written one of the most spirited defenses of *Pamela* and addresses with great tact the love of praise Richardson shows in his character:

excited tales of childhood triumphs: "You must know then, that my Lady *Davers*, who, you know, is my Master's Sister, has been a whole Month at our House, and has taken great Notice of me, and given me good Advice to keep myself to myself; she told me I was a very pretty Wench, and that every body gave me a very good Character, and lov'd me; and bid me take care to keep the Fellows at a distance; and said, *that* I might do, and be more valu'd for it, even by themselves" (29). Pamela eagerly partakes of the wisdom about keeping the fellows at a distance, repeating the lesson with proud precocity and the assurance that following the rules is not only right, but will always make everyone love her, as Lady Davers guarantees. Losing the gratification of immediate approval is the most painful of Pamela's trials. After Pamela begins to put her rule into practice and learns that it doesn't immediately make the fellows value her more, she gets her satisfaction for a while from the approval of Mrs. Jervis. It is a scene of childish wisdom and parental pride:

> And must it not be look'd upon as a sort of Warrant for such Actions, if I stay after this? for I think, when one of our Sex finds she is attempted, it is an Encouragement to a Person to proceed, if one puts one's self in the Way of it, when one can help it; and it shows one can forgive what in short ought not to be forgiven. Which is no small Countenance to foul Actions, I'll assure you.
>
> She hugg'd me to her, and said, *I'll assure you!* Pretty-face, where gottest thou all thy Knowledge, and thy good Notions, at these Years? Thou art a Miracle for thy Age, and I shall always love thee! [48]

Pamela's rigidity is partly a youthful design for clear and straight paths to approval. Her tendency to extreme language seems entirely in keeping with an ardor for rectitude. In Letter VI, she thinks that Mr. B. "look'd like an Angel" (31); in Letter X, "to me, Nothing appears so black and so frightful" (34). It is worth taking seriously Mr. B.'s complaint that Pamela is romantic, at least in her first responses. The extreme language does not represent her settled convictions. Letters tend to prolong the life of temporary responses,

---

"He seems unworried by the possibilities of smugness in his idea of moral pleasure. Morality for him was always public; but he doesn't seem to question the open angling for approval." Perhaps Kinkead-Weekes questions this problem too much. See his *Samuel Richardson: Dramatic Novelist* (London: Methuen, 1973), p. 18.

a reason why correspondence can be such a dangerous and misleading evidence of character. Pamela worries about the effect that her bold expressions of resentment will have on Mr. B. when he reads her writing later in the story. Similar liberties of expression in the letters between Clarissa and Anna Howe infuriate Lovelace. But how far from true judgments are these negative comments? Once again, the outcome determines meaning: in retrospect Pamela's anger seems exaggerated; Anna Howe's abuse of Lovelace turns out to be pale prefiguration. But the matter of exaggerated name calling is even more complicated. Both Mr. B. and Lovelace warn the suspicious heroines against pronouncing self-fulfilling prophecies.

Sometimes exaggerated sensitivity about being touched, a readiness to give it crucial significance, characterizes Pamela's new womanliness. As a servant, decorum pronounces her not so untouchable as Clarissa. Her master's first touch seems to her an exciting sign of honor, when he "took me by the Hand; yes, he took me by the Hand before them all" (25). Some of the scenes suggest how easy it is for people to offer her physical affection as if to a pretty child. As ominous as Mr. B.'s rough grasp becomes, Mr. Jonathan the butler offers Pamela physical comfort without constraint and without offense: "He took hold of my Hands, in a gentler manner, tho', than my Master, with both of his; and he said, Ah! sweet, sweet Mrs. *Pamela!*" (56). The contrast in this scene is poignant, but in another even Mr. B.'s embrace seems hard to interpret. When Pamela has dressed herself in her pretty new peasant costume and turns to Mrs. Jervis for the expected praise, Mrs. Jervis is so enchanted that she insists on bringing her to Mr. B. Though Pamela describes Mr. B.'s behavior as "cunning as Lucifer," the scene reads like a typical game between a dressed-up child and an affectionate adult.[20] Since Mrs. Jervis is looking on as chaperone, there is a built-in protection:

> He came up to me, and took me by the Hand, and said, Whose pretty Maiden are you?—I dare say you are *Pamela's* sister, you are so like her. So neat, so clean, so pretty! Why, Child, you far surpass your Sister *Pamela*.

[20]Margaret Anne Doody gives an excellent account of the literary history of country clothes and their association with rustic innocence. See her treatment of *Pamela* as "pastoral comedy" in *A Natural Passion: A Study of the Novels of Samuel Richardson* (Oxford: Clarendon, 1974), pp. 35–70, esp. 40–42. The charming effect of the dress may prepare for the redemption of Mr. B.'s lust as a "natural passion."

> I was all Confusion, and would have spoken; but he took me about the Neck; Why, said he, you are very pretty, Child; I would not be so free with your Sister, you may believe me; but I must kiss *you*.
> O Sir, said I, I am *Pamela*, indeed I am: Indeed I am *Pamela, her own self!*
> He kissed me for all I could do; and said, Impossible! you are a lovelier Girl by half than *Pamela;* and sure I may be innocently free with you, tho' I would not do her so much Favour.
> This was a sad Bite upon me indeed, and what I could not expect; and Mrs. *Jervis* look'd like a Fool as much as I, for her Officiousness.—At last I got away, and ran out of the Parlour, most sadly vex'd, as you may well think. [61–62]

Mr. B.'s pretense lacks the threatening intent of base designs. However, after a pause, what follows is the bitter resentment of an adult attraction. His praise is replaced by complaints: "and so you must disguise yourself to attract me" (62). With the change in mood, Mr. B. reinterprets the scene. The dress she intended to please because it showed her as clever housewife who knows her station instead turned out to have the erotic appeal of novelty. Mr. B.'s physical gestures change: "He then took me in his Arms, and presently push'd me from him" (62). Frustration with his own confusion turns to anger: "He stept after me, and took hold of my Arm, and brought me in again: I am sure he made my arm black and blue; for the Marks are upon it still" (62). Pamela can only interpret this contradictory behavior as "silly." Her attention is directed toward putting herself in the right by answering his objections, and she cries when Mrs. Jervis scolds her for impertinence. Pamela quite misunderstands his romantic hyperbole, "Robbed me!" (63). When he has been thinking of their sexual relationship, she has been thinking of their relation as master and servant: "why then you are Justice of Peace, and may send me to Gaol, if you please, and bring me to Tryal for my Life!" (63). But when Mr. B. returns to the mode of master and reminds her that he has promised his mother to take care of her, she reminds him of their sexual relationship: "Why, then, if your Honour must know, I said, That my good Lady did not desire your Care to extend to the Summer-House and her Dressing-Room" (63).

The shifts in tone in this letter are extraordinary, as each character tries to establish the nature of the scene, what their respective roles are, and the decorum appropriate to these roles. Pamela's flippant last words sound like slightly spiteful family teasing, like coquettish flirtation, like the retort of a servant who hopes to be dismissed. But the episode ends with what seem to be clear roles and a clearly intended plot. Pamela receives a warning that Mr. B. has been overheard to say to Mrs. Jervis: "By G—— I will have her!" Mr. B.'s physical approaches have moved from affectionate, teasing embraces, to sad, reluctant ones, to angry pinching, to perhaps a merely irritated slap if Pamela had not run for it. The sexual violence threatened in the overheard remark seems an effort to find a single set of roles to resolve these differences. The staginess of Mr. B.'s remark and Pamela's willingness to accept it at face value should not be taken as reliable clues to the nature of their relations; it is the purpose of the book not to allow the melodramatic tone to predominate.

Pamela's serious attention to Mr. B.'s remark, even though it was uttered privately in a state of exasperation, cannot be seen as simply deluded. In a situation of such confusion, authoritative voices are most likely to provide definition, even if only according to uncharacteristic moods. We could call this perception the Hobbesian political component, which is a necessary, though somewhat disguised, part of the Humean social picture. Systems of social rules are never entirely harmonious or perspicuous. When conflicts and confusions appear, the importance of the political settlement of authority emerges. Repeatedly Mr. B. will try to establish his authority to make definitions of Pamela's character, of his own and of their past history, of the rules governing their relations.

The first effort of sovereign definition is, in accord with Hobbesian theory, the attempt to define moral words and terms of honor: "I will make a Gentlewoman out of you, if you be obliging" (35). But unlike Moll Flanders, Pamela clearly understands the significance of her master's secrecy. He does not have the power to change public definitions; he cannot protect her from the shame to which she would be exposed. Indeed, Mr. B. is more likely to share the general scorn for fallen women than to abide by his personal terms, since he shows himself extremely concerned about his own reputation. By contrast, indifference to reputation is an ominous feature of Lovelace. Mr. B. has the authority of a landowner and household master, authority enforced by economics, law, and morality. In addition, though he is not politically sovereign, as justice of the peace he is the most immediate representative of the sovereign. Nevertheless, in a way typical of Richardson, the most important limit on his authority is social, not political. A curious struggle takes place betwen Pamela and Mr. B. to win the approval of the household staff. When Mrs. Jervis defends Pamela for trying to protect her reputation, Mr. B. objects that she is injuring his good name: "She has told you all, and perhaps more than all; nay, I make no doubt of it; and she has written Letters; for I find she is a mighty Letter-writer! to her Father and Mother, and others, as far as I know; in which she makes herself an Angel of Light, and me, her kind Master and Benefactor, a Devil incarnate!" (45). Mrs. Jervis represents community opinion; she moderates their debates until Mr. B.'s open assault on Pamela in her bedroom makes it impossible to maintain the saving fiction of Pamela's forgivable if groundless apprehensions: "Mrs. *Jervis*, said he, since I know you, and you know me so well, I don't know how we shall live together for the future" (68). Pamela had confided Mr. B.'s first attempt to Mrs. Jervis, against her master's orders, and he continues to be nervous about the letters she sends her parents. Will she draw on the full force of her popularity in the household and her power to tell people outside the house about him?

The regard for reputation might seem to put Pamela and Mr. B. on more equal footing, but their incentives to act on this motivation differ greatly, since the social enforcement of the rule of chastity differs greatly according to sex and status. For Pamela, the rule is a religious rule backed not only by eternal sanctions, but also by social sanctions that could be extremely severe. No one except her lover would be eager to employ his mistress, and even her parents might not receive her. The awesome risks of childbirth would make physical and psychological suffering highly probable and make the prospects of eternal punishment seem much nearer. Without his protection, she might even be imprisoned for her sins, or for the vagrancy to which they might lead her.

Not only were there no equivalent sanctions for Mr. B.'s intended offense, there was even a considerable degree of social encouragement, as Pamela gradually recognizes. She first shows a pathetic confidence in the influence of consistent, shared moral opinion: "I am sure that my Master would not demean himself so, as to think upon such a poor Girl as I, for my Harm. For such a Thing would ruin his Credit as well as mine, you know" (30). Later she comments more realistically to Mrs. Jervis, "Those Things don't disgrace Men, that ruin poor Women, as the World goes" (49), but Pamela is nonetheless shocked when even the fine ladies laugh about her possible seduction, as a matter of course: "O you little Rogue, says she, and tapt me on the Cheek, you seem born to undo or be undone!" (58). After Squire B.'s rudeness in Mrs. Jervis's bedroom, when he has agreed to let Pamela leave, she writes her parents in a "grave and serious mood" about the bad influences on Mr. B.:

> Sure the World must be near an End! for all the Gentlemen about are as bad as he almost, as far as I can hear!—And see the Fruits of such bad Examples: There is 'Squire *Martin* in the Grove, has had three Lyings-in, it seems, in his House, in three Months past, one by himself; and one by his Coachman; and one by his Woodman; and yet he has turn'd none of them away. Indeed, how can he, when they but follow his own vile Example. There is he, and two or three more such as he, within ten Miles of us; who keep Company and hunt with our fine Master, truly; and I suppose he's never the better for their Examples. [72–73]

Do the differences among these quotations represent a growth in worldly wisdom on Pamela's part, or rather a continuing conflict in Mr. B. between different social codes? In the scene that preceded the reflections on bad influences, Mr. B. has been "civil" and showed his rakish opinions only in jokes; because he now expects her outraged responses, he takes her pertness with good humor, rather than as outrages against his will. He urges Pamela to show more cheerfulness, to keep up her own reputation in the household, and shows pleasure when Pamela accepts his advice and assures him that she will protect his honor. He gets the last dig in this scene, and one wonders whether Pamela's determination to interpret his jokes as signs that he has become a rake does not show mere irritability at his verbal triumph.

The next letter gives a dramatic example of Pamela's loyalty and her willingness to protect Mr. B. Mr. Longman, the steward, has successfully interceded for Mrs. Jervis and saved her job, and now he tries to do the same for Pamela, without knowing the cause of the trouble. In this more public situation, Mr. B. uses the humiliating terms that in the past have provoked Pamela's hard words in reply.

But in this context Pamela, deeply affected, only blesses him and uses his hard words on herself:

> I have been a very faulty, and very ingrateful Creature to the *best* of Masters! I have been very perverse, and sawcy; and have deserv'd nothing at your Hands, but to be turn'd out of your Family with Shame and Disgrace. I, therefore, have nothing to say for myself, but that I am not worthy to stay, and so cannot wish to stay, and will not stay: And so God Almighty bless you, Sir, and you, Mr. *Longman*, and good Mrs. *Jervis*, and every living Soul of the Family! and I will pray for you all as long as I live. [75]

This speech moves Mr. B. more than anything else Pamela has said or done, including her frightening fits. The honor she pays him is not extorted by self-interest, since she is leaving anyway. She is repaid by the gratification of behaving in a visibly dutiful manner, which helps to salvage the reputation he is trying to damage, but at the cost of some pain, whether her statement is considered a white lie or true admission of an error.

Richardson's heroines never gain so much as when they give up their power: a scene such as this makes the reader realize that there is some power to give up, but at the same time it limits any developing interest in the power that subordinates can or should have. Exercising her power to sacrifice her interest continues to be Pamela's favored form of self-determination in the next letter, when she consults Mrs. Jervis about what of her possessions to leave behind, "a Point of Equity and Conscience" (79). As Mrs. Jervis points out, leaving anything that she has been given as a mark of the master's favor "will be the highest Affront that can be offer'd" (80). The supposed privacy of the conversation takes away the sense of presumption that there would have been in speaking her mind directly to her master, so that Mr. B., who has been hidden in the closet by Mrs. Jervis, is as touched by the scene as she had hoped. One of the things that makes Pamela so likable, however, is her inability to interpret duty as perpetual self-sacrifice. If Mrs. Jervis had not sent her out of the room, she would have spoiled the touching effect by taking a private revenge for her respectful silence during the scene with Mr. Longman. She is cut off in the windup, "Now Mrs. Jervis . . ." (81).

The emotion created by Pamela's willingness to refrain from using her power to damage Mr. B.'s reputation has been matched by Mr. B.'s restraint in using his power to damage her. The Humean realization of mutual satisfaction in limiting the full play of power has preceded the marriage bargain, and it is the necessary precondition of it. Mr. B. shows himself surprisingly willing to praise Pamela in public, even after she has refused him. At the party with the ladies of the neighborhood, Mr. B. replies to their teasing comments about Pamela's prettiness: "She is well enough, as I said; but I think her greatest Excellence is, that she is humble, and courteous, and faithful, and makes all her Fellow-servants love her; my House-keeper in particular doats upon her, and you know, Ladies, she is a Woman of Discernment" (57).

The mutual accommodation that seems to be leading to trust and affection takes place in a kind of limbo between the time Pamela first decides to leave and the time she does leave. Her delays figure in readers' interpretations that see Pamela as the archcontriver, but at this point in the story ordinary prudence about the means of transportation and Mr. B.'s legal power as master combine to explain why she waits for his permission. Her position in the house becomes less like that of a servant, since their quarrels interrupt her duties; and after the bed scene, he assures her that she stays as Mrs. Jervis's guest. The result of their increasing intimacy is the admission from Mr. B. that he loves Pamela and the ambiguous proposal that she stay on as a guest, for a week or two while he struggles with his pride. This confession of love is so affecting and moving because Mr. B. has avoided any such inducement up to this point; the perception of his struggle confirms Mrs. Jervis's earlier insight, the belief that Mr. B. has true feeling for Pamela, which led her to advise Pamela to stay. But once again, Pamela's sensitivity to the difference between public and private honors makes her refuse this promising offer.

When Mr. B. tries to move Pamela to stay by assuring her of financial and social security, we begin to address the intractable problem in their situation. The rakish encouragement to seduce maids is only a minority code, in competition with the general codes of honor. But the prohibition against gentlemen marrying servants is much more serious. Insofar as Pamela attracts Mr. B. for good, moral reasons and he is moved to work out an honorable relation that protects her, the sense of duty that her virtue activates in him works against their marriage. Indeed, one of the major charges against Richardson's book in *Shamela* is that it teaches the lesson of unequal marriages. Mr. B. clearly thinks that a formal settlement to protect Pamela's interest without sullying his family name is a reasonable solution to his dilemma, and he seems genuinely surprised that Pamela does not agree. In the following explanation of his love, Mr. B. finds the clue to the solution that enables him to marry Pamela, and it also excuses Richardson for telling such a tale: Pamela's extraordinary superiority deserves unprecedented recognition:

> I am awaken'd to see more Worthiness in you than I ever saw in any Lady in the World. All the Servants, from the highest to the lowest, doat upon you, instead of envying you; and look upon you in so superior a Light, as speaks what you ought to be. I have seen more of your Letters than you imagine, (This surpriz'd me!) and am quite overcome with your charming manner of Writing, so free, so easy, and so much above your Sex; and all put together, makes me, as I tell you, love you to Extravagance. [83]

It is reasonable to ask at this point why the novel should not have ended here with a proposal of marriage. The rather simple lesson of virtue rewarded has been well exemplified, and at the same time the growing respect of each party has been detailed with unprecedented skill. In some ways the episodes in Lincolnshire only replay the earlier events in Bedfordshire, but in grimmer tones, without the excitements of surprise and with the disadvantage so many readers have felt of showing a marriage after an attempted rape. Sadly, Richardson's extravagant complication of distress was clearly intended to obviate the possible view of the story as a low bargain, but instead the stubborn resistance of each person makes the final marriage harder to like, rather than more attractive, as he wished. The problem springs from the extraordinarily high idealism about marriage that Richardson promulgates and that his critics find easy to take to even greater heights. As Mr. B. explains to Pamela later in the story, his pride has made it difficult for him to marry anyone; Pamela's superiority to every other woman flatters his pride, but the more testing, the more superiority. A common solution to a common confusion will not establish the absolute confidence in his choice which he seeks.

At the midway point in the book, Squire B. briefly becomes a letter writer himself, contriving a story to placate Pamela's parents and a plot to get Pamela to Lincolnshire. In an unwitting preparation for the romantic marriage choice, his imagination becomes as romantic as he has charged hers with being. The most threatening aspect of the next test is the strangeness of the environment and the bad company he has chosen. He has arranged social pressures to encourage himself to be loyal to his rakish moods, rather than to his respectable side, just as Lovelace does when he takes Clarissa to Mrs. Sinclair's house. Once again, the ambiguity of exaggerated language maintains suspense. Mrs. Jewkes's foul speech may be worse than her heart or her employer's intentions. Even the susceptible Pamela finds some of it no more than "horrid romancing." Richardson has displaced the most violent threats onto Mrs. Jewkes so that the relation of Pamela and Mr. B. could be protected from undue stress. Similarly, Pamela leaves her efforts to gain power over Mr. B. to an agent, Mr. Williams, who decides on his own authority to appeal outside the family. The chief purpose of the abduction to Lincolnshire is not to prepare a scene of violence but to stage a series of tests of Pamela's affection and respect, and of her noble adherence to duty rather than to interest.

The first test is Mr. B.'s letter urging Pamela to protect his reputation and not complain of him to the innkeeper and his wife; however, he put nothing at risk since he had sent a letter denouncing her, so that they would not believe any story she told against him. The next test has more appearance of trust; Mr. B. promises not to come down to Lincolnshire unless Pamela invites him. Though she might be induced to invite him, in the hope of shortening her imprisonment, the risk of seeing him in such an unprotected condition more than outweighs the hope. Her invitation, he assures her, will put him under obligation, and he adds the additional allurement of the opportunity to fire the servants in Lincolnshire who have oppressed her. The next test is the offer of marrying Pamela to Parson Williams. Pamela's responses to these tests are unsatisfactory; she is prompted to counterstrategies that fail to give Mr. B. the information he seeks: that she is truly dutiful and truly loves him.[21] Her strategies escalate

[21]Kinkead-Weekes (*Samuel Richardson*, p. 44) debates the implications of this sequence for the morality of Pamela and Richardson: "There is always the possibility that Pamela's suspicious prudence and delight in subterfuge simply reflect her

in romantic inventiveness as his do. The most extravagant episode is her attempted escape, an attempt modeled on the hero of a book, "a great Captain, who being in Danger, leaped over-board, into the Sea; and his enemies shooting at him with Bows and Arrows, he got off his upper Garment, and swam away, while they stuck that full of their Darts and Arrows; and he escaped, and triumphed over them all" (149). After her failure, the temptation to suicide strikes the adolescent note again. The danger to her health brings Mr. B. to Lincolnshire. His anger toward her in their first meeting may have something to do with his fears for her safety. In any case, in spite of his anger, he formally offers her an enormous settlement to induce her to become his mistress.

An attempted rape is Mr. B.'s final effort to make these terms attractive on purely prudential grounds: "I must say one Word to you, *Pamela;* it is this: You see, now you are in my Power!—You cannot get from me, nor help yourself: Yet have I not offer'd any thing amiss to you. But if you resolve not to comply with my Proposals, I will not lose this Opportunity: If you do, I will yet leave you" (176). This test of threatened rape is perhaps more important for Pamela than for Mr. B., since he pulls back when he sees her in fits. This episode assures her that his real concern for her acts as a natural limit to his sexual desires. Richardson intends this to be the last use of sexual threat, as if it were a definitive experiment, but Richardson's readers are even more suspicious than his characters. The next test of her affection Pamela passes by agreeing to stay with Mr. B. and to forgive Mrs. Jewkes because he asks her to do it. The language they use to each other improves. She is once more his "good girl," and they discuss frankly the reasons for using extreme language. To his complaint that being called "Lucifer" makes him act the part, she replies: "How, then, Sir, can I act, but by shewing my Abhorrence of every Step that makes towards my Undoing? And what is left me but Words? And can these Words be other than such strong ones, as shall shew the Detestation, which, from the Bottom of my Heart, I have for every Attempt upon my Virtue? Judge for me, Sir, and

---

creator, as indeed they must in some way." As in the case of the love of fame, so with prudence, Kinkead-Weekes seems at war with the main lines of Richardson's morality. I would say that Pamela does not transcend those principles, but she carries them into more favorable circumstances.

pardon me" (182). As he explains his reluctance to marry beneath his station, she shows sympathy, as he has shown sympathy with her fits over her honor; their physical gestures change. She is less resistant to his embrace and takes the initiative in touching. Their personal trust seems complete. But as Mr. B. cries out in the last paragraphs of Volume 1, "What must we do about the World and the World's censure?" (188).

The decisive event turns out to be not the threat of rape, but the discovery of Pamela's letters, which—because they were not written to impress him—give very convincing confirmation of her love of piety and her secret love of Mr. B. Mr. B. learns not only more respect for Pamela and sympathy for her pain, but he also learns to identify with her story as a glorification of both of them. The struggle to have control over defining words that escalates into full-fledged plots is replaced by the fascination with their story as Pamela has told it: "There is such a pretty Air of Romance, as you relate them, in your Plots, and my Plots, that I shall be better directed what manner to wind up the Catastrophe of the pretty Novel" (201).[22] Mr. B.'s fascination with Pamela's version of their story has begun even earlier with Pamela's artless narrative of her tale to Mrs. Jewkes, before the threatened rape.[23] In asking for more of her letters, Mr. B. even accepts her impertinence, which angered him before, as the license of an effective stylist: "I'll allow you to be a little witty upon me; because it is *in you*, and you cannot help it" (201).

Another amazing transformation takes place: they both begin to use the language of power in joking ways. He embarrasses her by asking if she has hidden the journal in her clothes, and he teases, "I can do as they do abroad, when the Criminals won't confess; torture them till they do" (203). She pertly reminds him that "Torture is not

[22]For Richardson's use of fairy tale and romance, see Flynn, *Samuel Richardson*, pp. 145–95. When we consider elements of pastoral (Doody) and fairy tale in this story, it is worth noting this passage in which Mr. B. begins to work out with Pamela the authorized version of their story. They decide on their romantic plot, and this decision makes them Hobbesian political persons as well as romantic characters.

[23]Lennard Davis describes Mr. B.'s eroticized interest in Pamela's letters (as if they were private parts) as an index of the news-novel discourse, which operates to reduce the cognitive distance between reader and text and to "textualize" experience. See *Factual Fictions: The Origins of the English Novel* (New York: Columbia University Press, 1983), pp. 173–92, esp. 185–86.

used in *England*," and he continues the teasing with a mock threat to "press" her to death. An aesthetic appreciation for the account of the struggle has replaced the struggle. They have attained a pleasure in joint creativity which allows for debate and disagreement, but debate that is contained and controlled. The newfound balance is precarious; Pamela still gets tears in her eyes at the sound of the mock threats and the mock rebukes. With a strange nostalgia they revisit the landmarks of her trials, embracing. But Pamela's suspicions of a sham marriage, a game with sinister intent, cause her to cool his ardor and lead him to send her away. Yet once again reading the rest of the journal makes him beg to have her back. The achievement of the new sense of mutuality represents the benign version of Mr. B.'s earlier threat to give Pamela something worth writing home about. Pamela's artistry allows Mr. B. to see their relation in a heroic, not a demeaning, light, and most important, the letters serve to convert the rest of society to their point of view. The threats are reworked as blessings. The tales Mr. B. feared now become the foundation of their happiness.

In a way similar to the transformation of verbal power, Pamela's watchfulness and cautious detection become the foundation of the ideal marriage. Mr. B.'s ideal wife "must have watch'd and study'd my Temper" (367). This sort of habitual detection makes the open use of authority unnecessary: "She should not have given Cause for any Part of my Conduct to her, to wear the least Aspect of Compulsion or Force. The Word *Command,* on my side, or *Obedience,* on hers, I would have blotted from my Vocabulary" (367). In keeping with this solution to the power struggle, in which mutual knowledge is so complete that commands are unnecessary, Pamela draws up her own private list of rules extrapolated from Mr. B.'s conversation. In the same way she takes out her irritability and love of answering back, appending smart comments and complaints to the list. Their debate has been entirely internalized on the one hand, or, in its explicit form, it has been turned into a text about the past. The last rule, the generosity of husbands, appears as a description, hardly visible as a rule at all. Like Hobbes's sovereign, who observes natural law and the customary privileges of subjects, the husband is not bound by rules, but he gives his wife her due out of a prudential love of peace: "that a Husband who expects all this, is to be incapable of returning Insult for Obligation, or Evil for Good; and ought not to abridge her of any Priviledge of her Sex" (372).

The duty to analyze her husband's wishes extends to the last dramatic part of the narrative, Pamela's jealous curiosity about Sally Godfrey, which she is able to turn into the gracious reception of Mr. B.'s illegitimate child. After such a prolonged avoidance of contact with the formal institutions of power, the final confirmation of the private creativity of Pamela and Mr. B. occurs in Mr. B.'s account of his will, which assures Pamela's "independence" after his death. The sort of arrangement that might in an ordinary gentleman's life have preceded the marriage, the arrangement usually made by the suspicious "friends" of the prospective bride, here appears once more as a mere adjunct of personal morality, entirely private and voluntary, as if it were the natural expression of an esteem that does not have to be extorted.

The testing action of the plot and the mode of private letter seem to offer what Hobbes denied, a privileged view into character, one that will guarantee a firm basis of trust for other characters in the book and for the reader. But the many readers who continue unconvinced suggests that not even testimony offers absolute guarantees about the essence of a character. The most persuasive aspect of the narrative is the gradual adjustment of each character which is made possible by the quest for an ultimate test of character, but which is not a direct product of it. The adoption of a joint fiction, their story as told by Pamela, and the legal fiction of married union as represented by the husband, formalize their mutual willingness to continue the process of accommodation, even though the purity of their motives can never be entirely verified. The power that Richardson attributes to Pamela's writing tends to suggest that her fiction produces his; that is, that social morality, crystallized in Pamela's writing, inevitably brings about the institutional protections (marriage, the will) necessary to preserve and promulgate the moral voice.

It is helpful to recall Hume's optimistic account of the moral education that accompanies participation in ubiquitous moral discourse. The arts in his view are a constant part of this process, and indeed, he took the capacity of an audience to make similar judgments about characters they read about or see on the stage as proof of the social orientation of moral feeling. But when we consider how cautiously the moral voice of Pamela has been presented to Mr. B., most efficaciously as writing directed to someone else, not as rules, judgments, interpretations, arguments delivered to him, we are led to recognize the Hobbesian limitations on moral speech. Like the Hobbesian sovereign seeking counsel, Squire B. requests Pamela's letters, she does not offer them to him; and he reads them in private, for his own good. In the action of the book, the letters reach a larger audience only because Mr. B. has authorized them, as a result of his decision to marry Pamela, and because the sayings of the gentry, even when they are not speaking as magistrates, have special impact on moral discourse.

In Hume's more detailed accounts of the operation of moral feelings and moral language, especially in Books II and III of the *Treatise*, the differentials of sex and class emerge as important qualifications to his general picture. But these exceptions operate in a systematic manner in the societies he knows, so they help to provide more evidence for his account of our social capacities, since even unjustifiable preferences (for example, for a family name derived from dull men rather than from witty women) or unnecessary restrictions (for example, chastity for women past the age of childbearing) can be seen as part of a coherent system of rules and can be transmitted by the mechanisms of sympathy and love of fame.[24] Hume leaves unexamined the contribution that positive law makes to the perpetuation of this sort of moral rule. The progress of *Pamela* depends on the Humean capacity to understand complicated and varying situations in terms of rules sensitively applied, even the less useful and justifiable ones. The reliable operation of these principles, though far from machinelike regularity, smooths some of the conflict and pain in Pamela's social transition, but also removes from it some of its magic, its idealism, and its revolutionary implications.

## *Clarissa*: Trying Moral Discourse

The happy success of Pamela's letters, the power of the letters to help the writer enact her ideals, to enchant her lover with the image

[24]For Hume's use of the double standard to illustrate the artificial, systematic qualities of moral rules, see Kay, "Sex, Sympathy, and Authority."

of an ideal moral life, and to win the hearts of the otherwise more callous observers, also won Richardson's audience. Whatever immodesty in Richardson's arranging for characters in his book to praise his art, it could not detract from the strength of his claim. The convincing account of learning morality—the mixture of the desire for moral approval with other kinds of desire, the odd ways people affect one another, the uncertain birth of a new form of social life—is a more moving, more interesting account than Richardson was ever able to summarize. The list of lessons at the end of *Pamela,* like so many of Richardson's efforts to define his achievement, wretchedly betrays it. There is no better evidence of the gap between the summary and the narrative than the absence of any final mention of the virtues of writing and reading. The continuing preference of Richardson for the fictional identification of editor, even after the anonymous work proves popular and the author becomes well known, shows his persistent difficulty with the authority his art won for him.

Richardson was the first writer in England to win literary fame through novel writing alone. However much previous writing may have contributed to his ability to compose *Pamela,* the novel made him an author. Until he had written it, he did not preserve his letters. Of course, because of his novels, Richardson's correspondence must have changed character: he acquired interesting new friends and had more important topics to share with the people he had known before *Pamela,* such as Aaron Hill and Edward Young. In his autobiographical letter to Stinstra, Richardson offers to show Stinstra, as if they constituted one of his masterpieces, "Volumes of Epistolary Correspondence with Ladies," the only work he intends to continue after *Sir Charles Grandison* is published. The chief allurements of these letters he mentions are the "charming contentions, on different Parts of what I have written."

Richardson's love of praise should not be seen merely as an embarrassing personal blemish that he somehow failed to evaluate properly and so passed on naively to his favorite characters. An awareness of the desire for approval and self-approbation is an invaluable aspect of his social vision. We could compare Hume's consistent defense of vanity from the *Treatise* and his first essays to his deathbed conversation with Boswell and the open admission in his posthumously published autobiography of his own "love of literary fame." Nevertheless, when we consider Richardson's collection of flattering letters to preface *Pamela* and his love of hearing people talk about his books, we should think about the peculiar defensiveness, the special need for reassurance, which must attend an ungentlemanly author who claimed to be writing crucially important works in a new form. We should also remember that Richardson's books were his chief connection to a world outside business and family, the basis of a broader social life. Boswell, indulging his usual sense of competition with Johnson's other friends, reports a sharp-tongued comment about Richardson's society: "Richardson had little conversation, except about his own works, of which Sir Joshua Reynolds said he was always willing to talk, and glad to have them introduced."[25] Without this insight, one might wonder about Richardson's many appeals for help with the manuscript of *Clarissa*, when he showed so little ability or desire to take advice. His story about blackening the character of Lovelace, after a young lady auditor showed too much sympathy with him, should reveal not so much anxiety about his characterization as pleasure in provoking the debate. Richardson's exciting interchange with Lady Bradshaigh is initiated by debate over Lovelace's character, which must have been conceived to provoke debate (*Selected Letters*, 103–22).

Richardson had difficulties with this contentious mode of social distinction. He was ultimately not at ease with debate; as he said, he was a bashful man; he sought reassurance and was unwilling to push a debate to the point of unresolvable difference. In addition, he could not build a new social sense of himself on these drastically limited, private relationships. The topic of his books could wear thin, at least for other people. Richardson's difficulty shows up painfully in a letter to Stinstra, in which he shows panic when he discovers that Stinstra has included in a preface a remark Richardson made about

[25]Boswell's source is Bennet Langton. Johnson had promised Langton to draw Richardson out into conversation, but "he failed, for in that interview Richardson said little else than that there lay in the room a translation of his *Clarissa* into German." In a footnote Boswell mentions another, more humiliating, instance of Richardson's vanity, when he tried to get a guest to repeat the flattering news that in Paris he had seen *Clarissa* lying on the table of the king's brother. The guest squelched the appeal for a repetition, and Richardson was so mortified that "he did not speak ten words more the whole day." See *Life of Johnson*, ed. R. W. Chapman, rev. J. D. Fleeman (London: Oxford University Press, 1970), p. 1086.

five bishops who were his friends, one of whom had read *Clarissa* eleven times. This private credit must not become public credit directly, but only through rumor. Richardson must not seem to claim it. For similar reasons, Lady Bradshaigh bought a portrait of Richardson to adorn her dressing room, but she disguised the name on the frame.[26] The letters that Richardson appended to *Pamela* had caused much criticism and parody. How could he have developed his new relationships? He did not want patronage in the form of money or employment, and his art could not redeem his lack of qualification for aristocratic society. No wonder he did not dedicate his novels.

The best use of encouragement Richardson took from the success of *Pamela* was his astonishing commitment to *Clarissa*. The continuation of *Pamela* was against his own judgment, an attempt to protect the integrity of his creation by his own violation of it. It was used to answer some of the objections to the first part through direct argument, and also through forgetfulness, the displacement of crucial contention by problems of adjustment. But it seems that almost immediately after *Pamela* II and the extensive changes in Defoe's *Tour*, Richardson may have been hard at work on *Clarissa*. In 1744 Aaron Hill seems to have received a very long draft.[27] The rise in the social status of the characters, the enormous length of the book, unified by a single action in which tension is sustained, the three-year period of revision—all show the great seriousness and confidence Richardson brought to writing this novel. The courage to dig more deeply into his great subject, the psychology of approval, seems more an important effect of the success of *Pamela* than it is an example of learning from mistakes.

Pamela was dutiful: her novel makes a model, an example; Clarissa is a model character within the action of the story, and part of her duty is the additional responsibility and risk of being exemplary. Richardson has given the heroine the favorite attributes of his fiction, including the power of moral discourse, and he has tested the power of moral example and moral discourse in exceptionally trying circumstances, that is, in trials that may have no possible end except in death. For in addition to the special responsibility Clarissa bears to

[26]For Richardson's relationship with Lady Bradshaigh, see Eaves and Kimpel, *Samuel Richardson*, pp. 220–34.

[27]On the composition of *Clarissa*, see ibid., pp. 205–20.

seem as well as to be virtuous, she is thrust into a situation of fundamental disagreement about interpreting rules of behavior. Mr. B.'s attempts to change the terms of duty were weak even in his own eyes. The power of his position and the prevalence of bad social habits in his class could not override his own respect for the rules of chastity that Pamela followed. Clarissa shares less common ground with her antagonists—both her family and her suitor.

The contrast between the two books is disguised by the appearance in *Pamela* of more open conflict between classes and the more obvious possibility of violent oppression as an outcome to the conflict. Though people in *Clarissa* agree to use very similar words and rules in their debates, though they belong to a part of society in which violence (except for dueling) is not an approved solution of conflict and access to the protection of the law is easier, *Clarissa* is a more violent book. On the face of it, a rape is a more likely event in *Pamela* than in *Clarissa*. Accounting for the great apparent improbability of a rape among genteel people motivates the enormous length of *Clarissa*. The rape itself takes up little of the space of the book and seems almost as much a surprise to the perpetrator as to the victim, but the threat of violence pervades the whole, from the very beginning. As Hobbes knew, it is not violence, but the presumption of violence, that dissolves order. Instead of harmonizing society as in *Pamela*, in *Clarissa* moral language and the concern for reputation add fuel to competitions in power.

The greater violence of *Clarissa* is due partly to the greater savagery of ideological disputes, rather than competition over material possessions. Though in form Clarissa and her family agree on the binding force of the Fifth Commandment ("Honor thy father and thy mother"), they disagree profoundly on the interpretation of the law, and, Hobbes emphasized, no law interprets itself.[28] Since there are

[28]Recent criticism of *Clarissa* has fruitfully cultivated the hermeneutical problem in terms of a new literary theory, which begins with the dictum, common to Hobbes and to modern semiotics, that there is no natural meaning of the sign. For William Warner, Terry Eagleton, and Terry Castle, Clarissa adheres to a naive view that language has natural meanings and reveals moral truths about actions and characters, while Lovelace appears as a libertine deconstructor who reveals the multivalence of words and the ambivalence of actions and characters. For Castle the semiotic inequality results in the victimization, ultimately the silencing, of Clarissa, except when she learns to exploit multiple meanings at the very end of her life. For Warner, Clarissa's discourse on nature is a powerful, even tyrannical, humanism that secures

other commandments, this one cannot be thought to give parents absolute authority, for example, to command murder or idolatry. These limits on parental authority did not rest only on moral principles. The laws of eighteenth-century England interfered with parental power: for example, to prevent Catholic parents from disinheriting an heir who turned Protestant, or to bar the inheritance of an heir who converted from Protestantism to Catholicism.

In a similar way, Clarissa's grandfather attempted to use the public law to give Clarissa's judgments an independent base of economic power through his will. One reason that Clarissa's family is so reluctant to accept her offer of signing over her grandfather's estate is that they might be suspected of, could even be prosecuted for, compelling her to resign her legal title. For reasons of this sort, married women were protected by law from being induced to change the terms of their marriage settlements after the wedding. The state sought to limit family authority, and through the constructive power of the law private persons could further affect the power of fathers and husbands. But as is typical in Richardson, Clarissa tries always to rely on personal trust and the influence of social opinion rather than on the compulsory powers of the state. She turns over the management of her estate to her father, and though she clearly understands how futile are the chances of the family to win their threatened litigation to obtain full rights over it, she holds fast to the determination never to litigate with her father and makes this a condition of her

---

her enduring reputation even while it closes her off from enjoying Lovelace's playful interruptions. Eagleton, who adapts from Bakhtin a dialogic view of discourse, finds Clarissa's hermeneutic faith the powerful ideological tool of an emerging class but finds that at the same time it implicates her in the web of Lovelace's (also powerful) meanings. Patricia McKee has appropriately turned the deconstruction of Clarissa inside out by making her the superior to Lovelace in the practice of linguistic openness and indeterminacy. My own account in this chapter assumes that the theoretical interest of *Clarissa* lies not in its exposure of the inherent indeterminacy of language, but in its exploration of the means by which we (may) agree on determinations.

See William Beatty Warner, *Reading "Clarissa": The Struggles of Interpretation* (New Haven: Yale University Press, 1979); Terry Eagleton, *The Rape of Clarissa* (Minneapolis: University of Minnesota Press, 1982); Terry Castle, *Clarissa's Cyphers: Meaning and Disruption in Richardson's "Clarissa"* (Ithaca: Cornell University Press, 1982); Patricia McKee, *Heroic Commitment in Richardson, Eliot, and James* (Princeton: Princeton University Press, 1986), chap. 3. I have further discussed these matters in "On the Verge of Politics: Border Tactics for Eighteenth-Century English Studies," *boundary 2* 12, no. 2 (1984):197–215.

marriage contract with Lovelace. She holds the right to this property but renounces the power to enforce the right.

Nevertheless, she does not see her position as inevitably weak, partly because of her high reputation in the smaller society of her family and in the larger social world. But the novel begins with a threat to her standing: the duel over her between her brother and Lovelace. Anna Howe begins the book by writing to Clarissa of her onerous responsibility as an example to be judged by every respectable woman: "Every eye, in short, is upon you with the expectation of an example" (1, 4; 1, 3).[29] This special responsibility is also a power: the public is ready to believe Clarissa in the right, and Anna urges Clarissa to write in great detail, so that her letters can be used to move public opinion: "And pray write in so full a manner as may satisfy those who know not so much of your affairs as I do. If any-thing unhappy should fall out from the violence of such spirits as you have to deal with, your account of all things *previous* to it will be your best justification" (1, 3–4; 1, 2).

It is, however, never clear how this general social opinion of rules and the widespread good opinion of Clarissa's character can act to regulate paternal authority, which was so very much supported by law and social opinion, except by shoring up Clarissa's confidence and thereby intensifying conflict within the family. For this reason, the family tries to cut Clarissa off from the support of public opinion, first by shutting her up in the house and then by trying to prevent her from corresponding with people outside the house. Barring Clarissa from attending church, the guardian of the commandment they seek to enforce, has the appearance of a contradiction, but it reveals the dilemma created by resting on social means of enforcement. Even the family clergyman, Dr. Lewen, a social authority licensed by the state church, is unwilling on principle to interfere in Clarissa's duel with her parents, for which principle no one, not even Clarissa, condemns him.

[29]Samuel Richardson, *Clarissa, or the History of a Young Lady*. All page references are given parenthetically in the text, citing two editions: first the better text, from *The Shakespeare Head Edition of the Novels of Samuel Richardson*, of which *Clarissa* constitutes eight volumes; second, the more readily available Everyman edition, ed. John Butt (London: Dent, 1962), 4 vols. The recent Penguin edition gives the text of the first edition, which is not preferable to these.

Clarissa assumes that honoring parents in the marriage choice means accepting their veto, but retaining a veto over their choices. The family argues that honoring parents means complying with their choice. As against the seduction of servants, the authority of parents over marriage is an issue about which even morally rigorous people disagree, and there is no court or sovereign authority to decide the question. Though we may assume that Richardson gives his exemplary heroine the better side of the argument, the course of his story is designed to prevent the wholehearted defense of her debatable principle. Instead she uses the conventional tactic for criticizing the sovereign respectfully; she claims that he has been misled by his counselor: "This is not my father's original will." Citing the precedent of her right of refusal previously acknowledged by the family, she argues that her brother, who has no parental right, has urged the Solmes marriage, not her parents. She also points, rather dangerously, to an important element of the commandment, that parents include the mother. As Hobbes warned, divided rule offers dangerous possibilities for conflict.

The political resonance of the family debate about paternal authority is loud, but the significance is unclear. As a strategy against Filmer and other patriarchalists who argued a derivation of monarchical government from God-given father right, Locke brought up Clarissa's point, the duty to obey mother as well as father enjoined by the Fifth Commandment; and both Hobbes and Locke stressed the role of the mother in the generation and care of the child. But they shared with the patriarchalists and most other members of their society assumptions about the dominance of men in families, so that the mother's authority slips out of their accounts, and the presence of patriarchal authority in a state of nature slips back in.[30] Scrupulous

[30]To sort out the different strands of the patriarchalist tradition, see Gordon Schochet, *Patriarchalism in Political Thought* (New York: Basic Books, 1975). The common resolution of the apparent conflict in the accounts of Hobbes and Locke has been to discriminate between the historical account of the origin of government and the logical analysis of the grounds for political obligation. Nevertheless, since Hobbes argued that even children consent to obey their parents (and the father often has power over the mother, so the children obey him), his historical account of the familial origin of society as a compact among fathers is compatible with the more abstract and individualistic picture in Part I, Chapter 13, of *Leviathan*. For Locke the distinction between paternal authority and political authority became extremely important, even though he admitted that the historical evidence points to an origin of govern-

philosophic modifications of the traditional analogy of family and state did not necessarily characterize the political consciousness of Richardson or his readers, who had been exposed to the Anglican catechism, which taught that the Fifth Commandment applied to all authorities, including the magistrate. Nevertheless, the association of patriarchalism with Stuart "tyranny" was there for Richardson to rely on when he wanted to call into question extreme forms of paternal authority within the family. By naming the overweening older brother "James," Richardson suggests that extreme patriarchalism is the principle of a usurper.

Officially, Clarissa's mother takes a consistent position that the father is the sovereign of the family. But at times she acts independently, in a very ambiguous way authorizing Clarissa's attempt to cool Lovelace down by writing to him and so prevent another duel. Once again, Richardson is not willing to push the point of principle. Anna criticizes Clarissa's mother for her lack of effort, but in another context she criticizes women who run their family affairs. The exact degree of maternal authority is never defined. Sometimes Clarissa suggests that it is not a right to authority so much as the fine talents or will of the individual that make power within the family: "Yet, would she but exert that authority which the superiority of her fine talents gives her, all these family-feuds might perhaps be extinguished in their but-yet beginnings. . . . Upon my word I am sometimes tempted to think that we may make the world allow for and respect us as we please, if we can but be sturdy in our wills, and set out accordingly" (I, 32–33; I, 22). As Solmes's character becomes better known, and his threats of future punishment for a contemptuous wife are reported, Clarissa's resistance to marrying him comes under the rule of self-preservation, obedience to the law against self-murder. This change of emphasis moves attention away from the debatable rights of wives in family decision, while at the same time it tends to discredit the more socially approved forms of paternal authority asserted by the Harlowes, as it associates them with the wife abuse Solmes threatens.

---

ment in the fatherly rule of families. Yet at each point in his historical narrative, he stressed that political authority, even the very extensive prerogative of early monarchs, was held in trust for the public good.

Clarissa's family also hesitates to rest their authority exclusively on the controversial right of determining the marriage choice, and instead they stress other kinds of authority: the right to make prudential judgments, the right to assess Clarissa's character, the right to set the terms of their discourse with her and to determine the rules of family government. Clarissa's offers never to marry without her parents' consent are disbelieved, and declared in any case irrelevant, since Lovelace will not give up until she is beyond his reach. Her past signs of honoring the family are reinterpreted, so that resigning management of her grandfather's estate is seen as calculating self-interest rather than family piety.

What lies behind this strife? The story of her grandfather's will seems to Clarissa to be the beginning of the enmity of her brother and sister, of their fear of seeing her gain the majority inheritance, because she has a better chance of the sort of marriage that will raise the family status. "You are all too rich to be happy," Anna Howe complains (I, 60; I, 41). This aspect of the plot by itself reveals the violent passions that fuel even peaceful pursuits. But the competition for wealth and status is set off by another, more frightening motive, which reverses Richardson's favorite moral mechanism, the influence of good examples: James and Arabella envy the praise of Clarissa. Clarissa's sister, Arabella, complains: "How often . . . have I and my Brother been talking upon a subject, and had every-body's attention, till *you* came in, with your bewitching *meek* pride, and *humble* significance? And then we have either been stopped by references to Miss Clary's opinion, forsooth; or been forced to stop ourselves, or must have talked on unattended to by everybody" (I, 316; I, 216). Credit is a kind of power, at times more important than material wealth, since it is a blank check upon the future, and it is Clarissa's credit that her brother and sister wish to impair. When Clarissa complains that she resigned the income to her estate, her sister replies that the act "left you with such distinctions, as gave you a reputation of greater value than the Estate itself" (I, 317; I, 216).

There is an irrational, nonutilitarian element in the family situation that enables the brother and sister to mask their obvious interests: hatred and suspicion of excellence and the independent status excellence confers. The resentment is heard clearly in Uncle Anthony's letters. In situations of conflict, the use of universal moral terms is not the subtle agent and reflection of social life, but political weaponry, dangerous eloquence. The love of fame, rather than sympathetically binding people to one another, raises the stakes of any particular competition. History is not the reassuring record of the growth of stabilizing rules, but a charged field of debatable precedents, susceptible to coercive interpretation. Richardson shows that Hume cannot argue away Hobbes.

Instead of picturing the reverential confinement to home as a scene of retreat from the contentions, plots, exaggerated name calling, and selfishness that Richardson associated with politics and law, *Clarissa* shows that the family is also an arena of conflict: "Who will wonder at the intrigues and plots carried on by undermining Courtiers against one another, when a private family, but three of which can possibly have clashing interests, and one of them (as she presumes to think) above such low motives, cannot be free from them?" (1, 89; 1, 61).[31] The political scene in the home is the more dangerous because the theory of absolute obedience of child or wife has not yet been discredited, as the theory of passive obedience had been in public politics. Richardson's analogies give his domestic story dignity and perhaps lead him to uncomfortable ground. Clarissa's father denies any right in the child which is not merely a temporary grant from the father, no right of participation in decision, nor even a right to speak: "No protestation, girl! No words! I will not be prated to! I will be obeyed! I have no child, I *will* have no child, but an obedient one" (1, 53; 1, 36). Richardson is not ready to say that the child has the last say over her marriage, nor is he ready to define how much say she ought to have. But to silence speech is un-English, and like a king's refusal to listen to counsel, it argues a tyrannical tendency.

In the way that Defoe sometimes argued that the Church of England's doctrine of passive obedience encouraged James II in his tyranny, so Clarissa and Anna argue that Mrs. Harlowe's passivity has encouraged belief in the doctrine of paternal despotism. Anna claims that even Clarissa's compliances have led the family to assume that oppressing her would be easy. Within the family, this observa-

[31]For lists of references to historical leaders, campaigns, and court political issues, see Irwin Gopnik, *A Theory of Style and Richardson's "Clarissa"* (The Hague: Mouton, 1970), appendix E, pp. 133–34.

tion becomes an article of blame. Clarissa's usual obedience has misled the Harlowes so far into marriage negotiations with Solmes that it would be dishonorable to recede. As the tensions escalate, Clarissa's resistance is called rebellion by her father and brother, and she accuses her brother, an illegitimate authority, of attempting to enslave her:

> I have contented myself till now to take *second-hand* messengers, and *first-hand* insults: You are but my Sister: my Brother is not my Sovereign. And while I have a Father and Mother living, I will not be thus treated by a Brother and Sister, and their servants, all setting upon me, as it should seem, to make me desperate, and to do a rash thing. —I will know, in short Sister Bella, *why* I am to be constrained thus?—What is intended by it?—And whether I am to be considered as a *child* or a *slave?* [1, 332; 1, 227]

The attack on a sovereign through his ministers was the primary convention of opposition politics in England. This tactic saves the principle of paternal (or monarchic) authority while criticizing it, though, as many people keep telling Clarissa, she must recognize that however it came about, her brother's will is now her father's will. Indeed, she never does openly rebel. Her correspondence has been halfheartedly approved by her mother, and her desertion of the house was a mistake.

Clarissa's own solution to the uncertain boundary of parental authority and child right is that neither side should push the point of principle. As she explains to Anna about refusing the opportunity to be independent which was offered by her grandfather's legacy: "We should not aim at *all* that we have power to do" (1, 134; 1, 92). One critic has counted over one hundred uses of some form of the word *generous*.[32] Family relations cannot be governed by the jealous structures of contracting, but with no formal rules abuse becomes easier. A situation requiring judgment and negotiation requires intelligence and goodwill in all parties. As Anna complains, "I wish to heaven you were at liberty to pursue your own methods" (1, 4; 1, 3). Even in a situation of confinement and distance from her parents, Clarissa tries the effects of persuasion, and an immense battle for public opinion within the family is waged. Each side tries to muster a

[32]Ibid., appendix B, pp. 122–25.

majority, though some voices (like those of her father and his eldest son) have more weight. Yet there is a continuous suggestion that Colonel Morden, one of Clarissa's trustees, would tip the balance of family opinion in favor of Clarissa, or if he could not do that, he was legally empowered to put her in possession of her grandfather's estate. Paternal authority, like regal authority, rests on opinion, and the opinion of paternal despotism is divided. In this situation, the Harlowes simply try to choke off discussion, showing a positive fear of Clarissa's eloquence. There are signs that she never accepts this silencing as legitimate. Her most shocking, most rebellious act is to plead against Solmes to her mother while Solmes is in the room, after private time to speak to her mother was denied.

The shapelessness of letters, the way dramatic scenes never dominate whole letters, illustrates the problem of a structure lacking a final court of appeal. No conversation, however extreme; no argument, however decisive; no scene of judgment, however solemn—not one of these really decides the question. After she has left home, Clarissa's family torment her by claiming that the scene of confronting her with the marriage settlements was to have been the last test, but the many threats about being abandoned to Solmes, her brother, and her violent Uncle Antony had suggested no possible end but violence to the many scenes. In this atmosphere, the moral person who loves peace and shrinks from aggression longs to be the victim instead: Clarissa's comments become shocking. When she refuses her mother's promised "act of Oblivion," a clean slate if she will marry Solmes, her father pronounces her a rebel, and when she refuses Solmes, "he would have come up in his wrath," Clarissa continues, "I wish he had!—And, were it not for his own sake, that he had killed me!" (1, 310; 1, 212).

Clarissa's horrifying wish is a reaction to the Hobbesian nightmare. Only death can end conflicts that have no natural limit. But in Hobbes's theory the possibility of choosing self-extinction as a path to peace seems to be excluded. The war of all against all cannot be deduced unless self-defense is an axiom of the passions. The power of law in Hobbes's view always comes under threat when it conflicts unmistakably with self-preservation. For this reason he writes an escape clause into the duty of military service and cannot imagine criminals who cooperate in their own executions. By contrast, the analyst who stresses the penetrating influence on the passions of cohesive social opinion ponders different insights. Even the healthy-minded Hume can imagine a place for "malice against ourselves," though he seems to assume that only a justly self-condemning criminal would feel it, rather than a persistently accused innocent person. In a similar spirit Hume defended the moral status of suicides who can no longer give themselves or anyone else pleasure. The basis for this way of thinking, the sympathetic susceptibility to social education, is close enough to Richardson's morality that suicide becomes for his heroines a serious, if fleeting, temptation. Even Hobbes seems to admit at times the far-reaching power of education. On the one hand, he insists that individual motivations cannot be known and that a sovereign should not seek to punish sins of thought. On the other hand, he argues that the sovereign should authorize teachers not merely to condemn crimes, but to condemn criminal intentions, to teach obedience that is "sincerely from the heart" (*Leviathan*, II, 30, 383). In another passage he ponders whether those who maintain that even the "first notions of the mind towards crime (though checked with the fear of God) be Sinnes" may be too severe, even if they err on the safe side (II, 27, 336). He seems to admit the possibility of learning self-defeating guilt.

Influenced by Hume, Adam Smith developed in his theory of sympathy a distinction—between the love of praise and the love of praiseworthiness—which can illuminate Clarissa's situation. She wishes to please the "impartial spectator," as Smith would say. Unfortunately, as Richardson shows and Smith acknowledges, actual representatives of the impartial view may be very difficult to find, and the virtuous person, deeply attuned to social feeling, may suffer severely from the immediate judgments of other people. The tedious, exhausting effort to accommodate to others or to persuade them, even when differences are fundamental, characterizes the morality of Richardson's heroines. The dilemma leads Smith as well as Richardson to invoke the hope of a life to come, "where exact justice will be done to every man, where every man will be ranked with those who, in the moral and intellectual qualities, are really his equals."[33]

[33]Adam Smith, *The Theory of Moral Sentiments*, ed. D. D. Raphael and A. L. Macfie (Oxford: Clarendon, 1976), III, 2, 132.

Nevertheless, Smith ends his discussion of the conflict between social approval and morality with a renewed assertion of the harmony of religion with the persistent themes of social sentiment. In a similar way, Richardson closes the gap in his social vision when Clarissa experiences some of the social approval she deserves from Belford and the Smiths, before going to her heavenly reward.

The Harlowes seek to weaken Clarissa by the techniques of approval and shame that had reared her and by the appeal to the reputation that she values. One by one she is stripped of her marks of honor, denied the right to pour tea, denied the keeping of the house, denied her loyal personal servant, denied the title of child, or even of her name. It is inevitable, as she says, that she is increasingly allured by the prospects of another family that would pay her respect and allow her more liberty to follow her own judgment. She is drawn to Lovelace when he seems to eschew any great insistence on paternal authority: "Nor is it a very bad indication, that he has such moderate notions of that very high Prerogative in Husbands, of which we in our family have been accustomed to hear so much" (I, 263; I, 130). But later, when Clarissa is resentful of Lovelace's pressure, Anna once again urges her to show firmness in order to protect the place she values:

> The suiting of the tempers of two persons who are to come together, is a great matter: And yet there should be boundaries fixed between them, by consent as it were, beyond which neither should go: And each should hold the other to it; or there would probably be encroachments in both. To illustrate my assertion by a very high, and by a more manly (as some would think it) than womanly instance—If the boundaries of the Three Estates that constitute our Political Union were not known, and occasionally asserted, what would become of the Prerogatives and Priviledges of each? The two branches of the Legislature would encroach upon each other; and the Executive power would swallow up both. [II, 149; I, 340–41]

Anna argues much as Hume does that a certain level of conflict is necessary and legitimate, even stabilizing, in a mixed constitution. Lovelace, however, is no respecter of boundaries, but is a hedge jumper, a rule breaker. It takes only one restless Hobbesian man to destabilize a balance of power. His encroaching imagination takes him far beyond the commandments of Clarissa's family, partly because he lacks any formal basis for his authority. He is attracted to the jealous tyranny traditionally associated with usurpers. Even his images of monarchical power are extreme. After telling Belford of his stratagems to get Clarissa away with him, Lovelace summarizes, "and so I became her Emperor" (III, 30; I, 513).

Lovelace's sense of limitless power comes not from the open claims of authority but from the lack of clear boundaries in the situation he contrives after the elopement. The only salve for Clarissa's reputation is marriage, which he has proposed. But he takes advantage of her sense of decorum, her previous reservation and continuous arguments, to prevent the establishment of firm plans. Clarissa has already noticed how Lovelace manipulated the conventions of womanly modesty to extract a refusal from her sister. The conventions of courtship encourage insincerity, which (as Anna keeps arguing) is inappropriate to the situation of a woman run away from home. But Clarissa, in defending her sister, has argued the ultimate prudence of "punctilio," nicety of manners: "For what can any young creature in the like circumstances say, when she is not sure but a too ready consent may subject her to the slights of a Sex that generally values a blessing either more or less as it is obtained with difficulty or ease?" (I, 11; I, 8).

The great power of men in marriage means that their loyalty to the marriage must be ascertained beforehand. Clarissa's lack of "friends" to do her negotiating and cross-examining for her is a great embarrassment, since courtship also requires signs of trust and respect. We could wish for Clarissa some of Moll's resourcefulness in negotiation, but Clarissa's higher moral, and social, position forbids the dissimulation that Moll practiced, and it makes marriage a less urgent but more risky commitment than it was for Moll. Clarissa's embarrassing circumstances and her genteel standards prevent her from forming fully helpful alliances with other women. She does not avail herself of Anna's canny, practical advice, and she prides herself on not contaminating Anna's reputation by accepting her offers of companionship. Essential structures of the book keep Clarissa separated from Anna, as they have also pried her away from her mother and the motherly Mrs. Norton. Instead, Clarissa is surrounded by women of Lovelace's choice.[34]

[34]For one of the best treatments of the friendship between Anna and Clarissa, see Janet Todd, "Sentimental Friendship: Samuel Richardson's *Clarissa*," in *Women's*

Signs of honor are now under debate with Lovelace, as they were before with Clarissa's parents, and once again, correspondence outside the relation, especially with Anna Howe, comes under suspicion. The signs of honor for a husband-to-be, as Lovelace predicts to Belford, will include the sort of physical affection that could be a prelude to seduction. The seduction never materializes, though physical signs of love are the source of crucial arguments between them. Lovelace further clouds the situation by getting Clarissa to appear as his wife, to prevent her family from trying to reclaim her with violence. As a result, the ordinary social pressure to keep up decorum is removed not only at Mrs. Sinclair's house, but even among the respectable ladies in Hampstead. Clarissa has accepted Lovelace's arrangements as a sign of compliance that is an appropriate prelude to marriage, "as I have actually received his addresses" (III, 324; II, 198).

It is odd to think of the disparity between Lovelace's letters to Belford and his conversations with Clarissa, in which he never hints at seduction, only at courtship. The courtship is real enough for Lovelace to have marriage settlements drawn up and letters of approval from his family solicited, and for him to attempt to attain a license. He would never have been able to defend himself against a breach of promise suit, but his sense of liberty rests on assumptions about Clarissa: that she will never choose the public exposure of a law court nor the dangerous indignity of compelling him to marriage. On the other hand, he assumes that her regard for reputation will always make her agree to marry him, if he should choose it: "Marriage will always be in my power," is his refrain. What does he intend? The notes, index, and new pages Richardson added to the third edition tend to lay the blame for everything on Lovelace and suggest his bad character from the beginning. The letters alone suggest the sort of openness of fantasy, a resistance to making up his mind. Even the plotting letters to Belford could be interpreted as

---

*Friendship in Literature* (New York: Columbia University Press, 1980), pp. 9–68. We may suspect that the opposition to female friendship effected by the structure of *Clarissa* reveals a latent misogyny in Richardson. A daring article puts forward the modest proposal that Mrs. Sinclair's women were the real agents of Clarissa's rape and that the feminine aspects of Lovelace are what destroy him. See Judith Wilt, "He Could Go No Farther: A Modest Proposal about Lovelace and Clarissa," *PMLA* 92 (1977):19–32.

the extravagance of wit rather the signs of an irreparably perverted heart.

In conversation with Clarissa, Lovelace deliberately exposes an unstable nature, although not as various and outrageously fanciful as in his letters to Belford. Clarissa writes, "There is an *apparent*, even an *acknowledged* unfixedness in his temper" (III, 124; II, 62); he is a "Proteus" or "chameleon" (III, 154; II, 82). Lovelace presents himself to Clarissa as a suitor who is always on the road to reform. So he gains wide latitude to hang back from commitments; to unleash anger, resentment, and sexual aggression; and to manage information—as long as he apologizes, acknowledges his imperfect reformation, and continually involves her in his repentance. Richardson's objection to the notion that reformed rakes make the best husbands becomes plausible as he shows the manipulative scope and the self-delusions of the moral amphibian. The game could extend through the life of a marriage, complete with "stratagems," abject apologies petty resentments, and fits of generosity. Richardson gives a small glimpse of this possibility in the letter Lovelace writes to Belford when he misunderstands Clarissa's allegory of meeting him at her "father's house" and thinks she has agreed to marry him. After a transport of happiness and grateful appreciation for exalting them both, Lovelace's imaginary address to Clarissa takes a familiar detour to prolong the suspense:

> And if, my beloved creature, you will but connive at the imperfections of your adorer, and not play the *Wife* upon me: If, while the charms of Novelty have their force with me, I should happen to be drawn aside by the love of intrigue, and of plots that my Soul delights to form and pursue; and if thou wilt not be open-eyed to the follies of my youth [a transitory state!], every excursion shall serve but the more to endear thee to me, till in time, and in a very little time too, I shall get above Sense; and then, charmed by thy soul-attracting converse; and brought to despise my former courses; what I now, at a distance, consider as a painful duty, will be my joyful choice, and all my delight will centre in thee! [VII, 193; IV, 159–60]

If this is an attempt to blacken Lovelace's sexual character, Richardson abysmally fails. Nothing is less convincing than that Lovelace should have irresistibly promiscuous appetites, since he has performed at most one act of sexual intercourse during the action of the book, and he shows no attraction to any other woman. This flight is a deliberately lame version of Lovelace's earlier pictures of sexual utopia, like his projected history of their "life of honour," a life of unwedded bliss punctuated by infidelities "in order to bring him back with greater delight to his charming Clarissa" (IV, 383; II, 496–97). The later passage admits the importance to him of "soul-attracting converse" but dully repeats the fantasy of his impulsive "sense" and her forgiving tolerance, in a way that could only have perpetuated their conflict in the less heroic mode of an unhappy marriage.

Some of the most attentive and appreciative of Richardson's critics, especially those who wish to rescue the first edition of *Clarissa* from what they take as Richardson's defensive, rigidifying revisions, prefer to see in Lovelace and in the early course of his relationship with Clarissa the open possibility of love, which both characters gradually close down in their self-protectiveness and polarizing arguments. Lovelace's puzzling indecisiveness, rather than his calculating manipulation, must be the focus of such an interpretation. These readers seek the point at which the love story could have taken place, for example, the proposal scene in which Lovelace makes a "most clear and explicit" offer (III, 235; II, 138); according to Clarissa, one that Lovelace himself called "quite destitute of reserve" (III, 241; II, 141).[35] The moment passes, however, as each observes the reluctance of the other, rather than the vulnerable readiness. Although Clarissa seems to have mistaken Lovelace's feeling of being "overwhelmed" for one of his usual strategic retreats, she is not (like a literary critic) seeking to sort out the authentic from inauthentic moments of feeling in order to find the minimal potential for love. She wants to identify stable and stabilizing commitments. She watches him so closely not because she wants to chart the ebb and flow of his emotions, but because she must examine the evidence of his intentions.

The detection we make when we see that Clarissa's consistent moral character is a deliberate construction would not have dismayed Richardson nor unmasked his morality. Conscious effort, imitation of

[35]On this scene, see William Beatty Warner, "Proposal and Habitation: Temporality and Authority in a Scene of Richardson's *Clarissa*," *boundary 2* 7, no. 2 (1979).

others, modeling behavior on good books are good indications, when they are persistent; they are not signs of inauthenticity. Anna Howe criticizes Arabella for being "unimitating" (VIII, 228; IV, 497). Moral effort offends when it fails to be moral, not because it is effort. The most ominous thing about Lovelace is his lack of desire to appear in a consistent character that would prompt trust and respect. In Richardson's art not being able to distinguish a person's character signals that the observer is confronted with a bad character; in Clarissa's words, "This Impenetrableness, my dear, is to be put among the shades in his character" (I, 295; I, 201).[36] Good characters make themselves legible. Impenetrability for this reason connects to impenetrable feelings, the incapacity to experience normal feelings about others. The man who enjoys keeping others in uncertainties lacks a heart. Lovelace's "teasing" connects to his cruelty.

In spite of his attacks on hypocrisy, Lovelace does not claim for himself the expression of an authentic, inner self any more than Clarissa does. He loves contrivance, but he wishes to make himself without social pressure; he prides himself on the personally asserted rather than the socially enforced role. Although Richardson continually exposes the libertine's subjections to the pressures of his parochial society (the women at Mrs. Sinclair's continually humiliate Lovelace), Lovelace takes inventive liberties; he is no ordinary rakish user of drink, blasphemy, or prostitutes. He sees his stratagems in terms of sovereignty. He creates characters for others, like "Captain Mennell," whom he introduces to Clarissa, boasting to Belford: "And I have changed his name by virtue of my own single authority. Knowst thou not, that I am a great Name-father? Preferments I bestow, both military and civil. I give Estates, and take them away, at my pleasure. Quality too I create. And by a still more valuable prerogative, I *degrade* by virtue of my own imperial will, without any other act of forfeiture than for my own convenience. What a poor thing is a monarch to me!" (IV, 44; II, 267). Creating captains and bestowing preferments are the sorts of things aristocrats ordinarily do when they pull on the web of family patronage and power. Besides

[36]For an argument that both Clarissa and Lovelace wish to be impenetrable as well as to penetrate the other, see Leo Braudy, "Penetrability and Impenetrability in *Clarissa*," in *New Approaches to the Eighteenth Century*, ed. Philip Harth (New York: Columbia University Press, 1974), p. 186.

autonomy, an essential feature of Lovelace's fantasy power is its reversibility. Creations that have long life, that multiply the power of others along with his own, have no appeal for Lovelace. He can never understand that the distrust, the impression of mobility that he loves to create, extends an influence on Clarissa beyond his ability to control.

Casting himself as the reforming student of Clarissa's virtue is especially frustrating to Lovelace's sovereign imagination since it authorizes her as his teacher, irritating whether she teaches by precept or example: "To be *excelled by a* WIFE too, in every part of praiseworthy kowldege!—to *take lessons*, to *take instructions*, from a WIFE!" (IV, 240; II, 399–400). The situation is the more humiliating because he can become the willing pupil he pretends to be. Her mere presence "half-assimilates me to her own virtue" (IV, 241; II, 400). Lovelace's irritable remarks have been prompted partly by reading the stolen copies of Anna Howe's letters, which abound with criticisms of him, advice to Clarissa about how to manage him, and even plots to help Clarissa escape from him. The escalation in self-protective anticipation makes every gesture and word seem an attempt at manipulation. Lovelace opens the letter I have quoted with an enclosed letter from Clarissa to him about his proposed marriage settlement. In this context her moral teaching is compatible with the assurance that she is thinking of their mutual interest and their mutual honor, as she begs him to agree not to litigate with her family or fight her brother. Her letter tries to detach them from the situation of recurrent debate in which her regrets about her family and her anger at his criticism of them seem to show that she underrates him. This time she makes clear criticism of her brother and shows that she can look forward to being a wife: "For it is my earnest hope, that in time you may see each other without exciting the fears of a Wife and a Sister for the consequence. Not that I should wish you to yield in points that truly concerned your honour: No, Sir; I would be as delicate in such, as you yourself: *More* delicate, I will venture to say, because more *uniformly* so" (IV, 233; II, 395).

By arguing with her, Lovelace has made Clarissa hesitate about taking this tone toward him, so she has torn the letter and thrown it in a drawer. The copy he reads is a stolen one, and he reflects that perhaps she thinks it "too *good* for me" (IV, 237; II, 398). His stratagems to read Clarissa's private thoughts through Anna's letters reveal to him temporary doubts, anxieties, and contingency plans that do not express her firm intentions, and then his anger deprives him of her most explicit efforts to create mutual trust. Her decision not to send him the letter about the marriage settlement could be read as a sign that it expresses genuine commitment, too serious to send without absolute conviction. But with his heightened suspicion (or with resentment that makes the excuse of suspicion) Lovelace speculates that she may have deliberately leaked it to impress him and to test the loyalty of the maid. This overelaborate, even self-parodic, doubt about Clarissa's intentions is redundant, since his undisguised bad temper has already modified them. His prying, ever-dissatisfied curiosity can only discover, not a secret inner truth about Clarissa, but the results of his own activity. It is as though Richardson were reworking the story of Mr. B.'s successful search for a definitive test of Pamela and withdrawing his approval from it.

Lovelace's proclaimed search for a final test of Clarissa is indistinguishable from the desire to find his own influence on her, to educate her rather than to be educated by her. Lovelace's teaching cannot be the subtle, gentle activity of moral discourse or the compelling admiration of grand examples that have already worked on her another way: "Her LOVE OF VIRTUE seems to be *Principle*, native Principle, or if *not* native, so deeply rooted, that its fibres have struck into her heart, and, as she grew up, so blended and twisted themselves with the strings of life, that I doubt there is no separating of the one without cutting the others asunder" (IV, 238–39; II, 398). Lovelace is curious to take Clarissa apart, to separate her heart and her virtue, which could easily combine in a marriage to him. But then he would not have been able to distinguish his influence from the influence of morality.

Even when he is to be the immediate beneficiary of Clarissa's goodness, Lovelace is jealous of her adherence to morality as if it were his rival in her affections. By showing her encouraging letters from his family, by depositing the marriage settlement with a lawyer, and by making other plans, Lovelace has sweetened his conversations with Clarissa, so that she does after all send her half-torn letter to him, and it affects him deeply, as if it were new to him. He offers her better terms than she will accept, and her insistence on moderation in providing for Mrs. Norton oddly mortifies his pride:

> I cannot bear this. I would have the woman I honour with my name, if ever I confer this honour upon any, forego even her *superior duties* for me. I would have her look after me when I go out, as far as she can see me, as my Rosebud after her Johnny; and meet me at my return with rapture. I would be the subject of her dreams, as well as of her waking thoughts. I would have her think every moment lost, that is not passed with me: Sing to me, read to me, play to me when I pleased; no joy so great as in obeying me. When I should be inclined to Love, overwhelm me with it; when to be serious or solitary, if apprehensive of intrusion, retireing at a nod; approaching me only if I smiled encouragement: Steal into my presence with silence; out of it, if not noticed, on tiptoe. Be a *Lady Easy* to all my pleasures, and valuing those most who most contributed to them; only sighing in private, that it was not *herself* at the time. Thus of old did the contending wives of the honest patriarchs; each recommending her handmaid to her Lord, as she thought it would oblige him, and looking upon the genial product as her own. [IV, 264–65; II, 416]

Lovelace expands his fantasy of her romantic idolatry into a vision of an alternative moral order with its own biblical precedents. While Lovelace exalts in fantasies of rakish patriarchalism, he has actually politely come to terms with Clarissa. A brief, moderately hopeful letter from Clarissa to Anna appears incongruously before Lovelace's most extended fantasy in the book, an imagined abduction and rape of Anna Howe and her mother, followed by a mock heroic criminal trial. The weather and the moral sentiments of the court alike move at his command.

Clarissa then passes the test that so influenced Mr. B. in Pamela's favor. She shows inadvertent concern for Lovelace's self-induced illness, a sign necessary to show that her interest in the marriage settlement is not just a calculation about survival but the desire for happiness with a lover. The warmth between the two seems to grow as Lovelace introduces a new actor, the fake "Captain Tomlinson," who apparently offers hope of reconciliation with Clarissa's family. Clarissa accepts Lovelace's kisses with modesty, but not revulsion. When he breaks the mood of trust by kissing her breasts, the test receives the expected anger, though new happiness helps her subdue her resentment. Lovelace tries again: surprise and fear in a nocturnal fire scene. Although he claims that this episode has given him "full proof" of her excellence, he obviously feels it has proved nothing but his own weakness. This test has, however, satisfied Clarissa's uncertainty about Lovelace. The most infuriating part of the scene is Lovelace's coercion of Clarissa's forgiveness, since it is a revealing parody of his previous suit:

> I do, I *do* forgive you.
> Heartily?
> Yes, heartily!
> And freely?
> Freely!
> And will you look upon me tomorrow as if nothing has passed?
> Yes, yes!
> I cannot take these peevish affirmatives, so much like intentional negatives!—Say you will upon your honour.
> Upon my honour, then.—O now, be gone! Begone!—And never-never—
> What, never, my angel!—Is this forgiveness!
> Never, said she, let what has passed be remembered more!
> [IV, 396–97; II, 505–6]

For the moment he can dictate her lines, constrain her morality. Even though Clarissa may not believe, with Hobbes, that promises oblige even when made under compulsion, Lovelace seems to enjoy the thought of putting her technically in the wrong. The cooperative enterprise that has seemed so promising in the last few days has been rejected by Lovelace in favor of what he can do more on his own authority: create grief. At the same time that Clarissa recognizes this fact about Lovelace's character, Anna Howe writes her (in a letter that she does not receive until much later) the shocking news that the house to which Lovelace has brought her is a house of ill fame. Anna pronounces the doom of Hobbesian man on Lovelace: "He prefers his Pride to his Interest" (V, 39; III, 7).

In the frantic escalation of stratagems we see why the transforming power of reading letters and identifying with a shared image of mutual life cannot work for Lovelace as it had for Mr. B.: he must be the only artificer. In a particularly frightening twist of plot, Lovelace intercepts Anna Howe's letter and begins to replace the letters between Clarissa and Anna with letters of his own. He has been yearning after the correspondence for a long time. Stealing a letter of Anna's caused one of his most violent arguments with Clarissa. He has used stolen copies of Anna's letters to infuriate himself against Clarissa, whenever his affections are moved toward her. Now he remakes the women according to his wish. His version of Clarissa empties out her will: she is "broken spirited" and "really ill—Very ill"; "My *heart is too weak* to bear up against such a stroke as this" (V, 47; III, 13). Lovelace sends the forgery for Belford to appreciate, but he does not send it to Anna. Perhaps he knew that the debility he portrayed, and wished for, was too much out of Clarissa's character.[37]

Lovelace increasingly replaces the voice of morality with his own. In Hampstead, where Clarissa has taken refuge, Lovelace details for the ladies of the house a version of his relation with Clarissa maddeningly close to the facts, so that he can win sympathy and approval from them even when he confesses his "liberties" during the fire. Once the ladies believe in the story of a clandestine and unconsummated marriage, Clarissa cannot effectively deny that they are married. Lovelace's enjoyment of confident, moral speech must be at the cost of any dialogue with Clarissa. He cannot persuade her by these tactics, but he can, and increasingly does, silence her: "You have heard *his* story. Mine, as I told you before, is too long and too melancholy; my disorder on seeing the wretch is too great; and my time here is too short, for me to enter upon it. And if he has any end to serve by his own vindication, in which I shall not be a *personal* sufferer, let him make himself appear as white as an angel; with all my heart" (V, 127; III, 67).

Five hundred pages of the Shakespeare Head edition—from the fire through the rape and Clarissa's second escape—are narrated almost exclusively by Lovelace. In Hampstead Lovelace tries to draw Clarissa back into negotiation with him by calling on Tomlinson, the

[37]John Preston's chapters on *Clarissa* anticipate the emphasis on textuality in recent criticism. Preston takes this forgery as an example of the way the book foils the belief of readers that the letter is a privileged medium of consciousness: "The book seems to be about the literary evidence itself, letters rather than people." See *The Created Self: The Reader's Role in Eighteenth-Century English Fiction* (New York: Barnes and Noble, 1970), p. 66.

pretended agent of her uncle, to mediate between them. Once again, Clarissa pulls back from telling her story or from listening to Tomlinson's judgment about Lovelace's version: "I am and ought to be, the sole judge of insults offered to my person" (v, 196; III, 115). Even in conversation alone with Lovelace she tries to break off any recapitulation and shows no interest in justifying herself to the ladies of his family, new impostors of morality he will soon introduce: "Call me to *them* over-nice, petulant, prudish; what you please, call me to them. Nobody but Miss Howe, to whom, next to the Almighty, and my own Mother, I wish to stand acquitted of wilful error, shall know the whole of what has passed" (v, 251; III, 153). It seems that she has not energy enough for even reflecting on her conduct for her own satisfaction.

At this point in the novel what has gone before begins to assume a new aspect of privacy, the privacy of unusual, highly complicated experiences. The contrast between the hundreds of pages we have read with the prevaricating versions of Lovelace or the halting, broken references by Clarissa makes their story seem untellable, in a way symbolized by the privacy of sexual offense. Even when Clarissa escapes from Lovelace a second time, after she has been raped, and resumes writing, she feels unequal to the task of telling her full story. The contrast with the use of letters in *Pamela* is immense. Pamela could make a song out of her plight or a lesson for children, and she could feel that her letters easily bore out the briefer recapitulation. She and Mr. B. read and reread her letters to themselves and to others. But neither Clarissa nor Lovelace reads the whole collection of their correspondence, although each gains access to particular letters of the other in the course of the book; neither of them even rereads his or her own sequence of letters. Only if Belford and Anna decide to show the complete compilation will anyone see it. Belford's conclusion pictures Clarissa's family deepening their remorse by reading "large extracts from some of the Letters" (VIII, 278; IV, 532) which particularly relate to them, but no one in the novel is pictured reading and responding to the archive in its immensity.

We readers have no model for our own activity. No one in the novel is converted by letter reading as Mr. B. and other gentry are in *Pamela*. Clarissa's family was already made remorseful by her religious death, even without reading the details of Lovelace's machinations. Indeed, Clarissa began to refer to her death as the "answer" to any questions they might have about her. Belford did not need to see Clarissa's letters. Moved by the picture of her that Lovelace drew in his letters, deeply impressed by her preparations to die and her trust of him, he could hardly be more convinced by any further evidence of her excellence. The monstrous size of the collection suggests to us that since we read more, and more consecutively, than the characters do, we should be able to come to an understanding in some way superior to theirs. As always in Richardson's fiction, the superabundance of evidence and explanation rouses the suspicions he had hoped to allay.

Clarissa's direction for the collection of letters was first prompted by Mrs. Howe. Anna reports that Mrs. Howe believed Clarissa's report of the imposture and drugging that led to her rape, but that she was still dissatisfied without a more public and complete account. At first she demands that Clarissa launch a criminal prosecution of Lovelace, not merely to protect other women from him and see justice done, but also to defend her own character: "Will it be thought, Nancy, said she, that Miss Clarissa Harlowe can be in earnest, when she says, she is not solicitous to have her disgraces concealed from the world, if she be afraid or ashamed to appear in Court, to do justice to herself and her Sex against him? Will it not be rather surmised, that she may be apprehensive that some Weakness, or lurking Love, will appear upon the Tryal of the strange Cause?" (VI, 201; III, 378–79). Later Mrs. Howe seems satisfied with the prospect of a different form of self-defense, a detailed "tragical story" to be "published under feigned names" (VII, 25; IV, 46). Too exhausted even for this task, Clarissa arranges for Belford as her executor to gather the letters that would serve to tell her story. The letters then function as an alternative to a public prosecution, a sort of public testimony that gives enough evidence for a firm moral judgment, and so shows that Clarissa is willing to subject herself as well as Lovelace to social judgment. It becomes clear that a law case and the collection of letters are mutually exclusive alternatives when we remember that Clarissa has promised Belford that the collection of Lovelace's letters she wishes to have made will be used at Belford's discretion: "I give you my honour that no use shall be made of it to his prejudice, in Law, or otherwise" (VII, 68; IV, 75).

The novel provides an opportunity for judgment that rivals a court.

How does Richardson make the novel seem a preferable opportunity? The letters seem to offer more believable testimony because they are not testimony; they were written for another purpose. Clarissa ascertains from Belford that Lovelace's letters "do her justice," and that they would make her case even without her own letters. Nevertheless, the continuous defensiveness of each correspondent throughout the novel tends to break down this distinction. Clarissa and Lovelace have been on the witness stand every day; each has had reasons all along to prefer something or other to the truth.

Clarissa's letters to her beloved Dr. Lewen explaining why she does not want to prosecute can reveal more about what Richardson thought to be the superiority of his form. Setting aside reasons of health, she first argues that evidence of her compliance could be brought up in court, for instance that she agreed to a clandestine meeting and lived under the same roof with Lovelace for several months. For some reason she thinks that his "infamous methods" would have little weight in court, compared to their effect "*out of Court*, and to a *private* and *serious* audience" (VII, 230; IV, 184). In the wrong kind of audience "it would, no doubt, have been a ready retort from *every* mouth, that I ought not to have thrown myself into the power of such a man, and that I ought to take for my pains what had befallen me" (VII, 230; IV, 184–85).

Clarissa seems to imagine not so much the evidentiary procedures of lawyers and judges, but the effect of the court case on the callous and anonymous public. A private and serious audience, like the audience for the collection of letters, assumes the attitude of sympathy as it follows every detail, but in court the pleas may be "bandied about, and jested profligately with." Her further arguments develop the assumption that underlies her fears, that without the careful preparation of a private audience, the public at large is ready to pardon this crime "thought too lightly of," and so Lovelace could easily escape even a sentence of death by a pardon. She adds that the criminal prosecution, whether it succeed or fail, exasperates bad passions, making an acquittal or pardon even more dangerous. She guesses that Lovelace would actually enjoy the confrontation of a trial, a pleasure he has displayed to us in his fantasy trial for the fantasy rapes of the Howes. Only by giving up the prosecution can she show forgiveness, give his conscience a chance to work, and protect herself from the censure of "pursuing with sanguinary means a man who offered me early all the reparation in his power to make." Once again Clarissa offers the collection of her letters in place of a prosecution.

Inscribed within the self-definition of his novel we can find Richardson's deep preference for social means of enforcing morality over legal and political means. Masculine sexual cruelty is certainly a good case for his position. Because social opinion about sexual standards is divided and deeply contradictory, laws against rape and seduction do not prevent these abuses, and prosecutions often further injure the victim and harden the public. Nevertheless, Richardson's novel has shown that it is equally difficult to find social means of unifying and enforcing moral opinion in such cases. Anna Howe and her group of young ladies are not able to shame Lovelace at Colonel Ambrose's ball. Because the rake is a recognized character of fashion, attempts to chastise him for his faults are hard to distinguish from playful banter:

> *Little Sins!* replied Miss D'Oily: Mr. Lovelace's character is so well known that nobody believes he can commit *little* sins.
>
> You are very good to me, Miss D'Oily.
>
> Indeed I am not.
>
> Then I am the only person to whom you are *not* very good: And so I am the less obliged to you.
>
> [VI, 445; IV, 19]

Anna's anger becomes merely part of the amusing spectacle, and her account of it ends with the agreement of the whole set of ladies that Clarissa should marry Lovelace. Lovelace makes a delightful comedy out of his own family's attempt to bring him to "trial." Before exonerating Clarissa, admitting his faults, and promising to marry, Lovelace takes his family through a scene of mock defense so impudent that he makes them purse up their mouths to avoid smiling. They cannot sustain a punitive disapproval, and their solution of marriage would further remove any reason for it. Clarissa may get a better hearing in a private group out of court, but so does Lovelace.

The intractable nature of the problem has inspired feminists in our own day to combine an enormously varied group of strategies against rape. Feminists have sought to change the laws that define the crime, to change the legal rules of evidence, to reeducate and expand the personnel of the police and the court. But Richardson's preferred social, and especially literary, means—prudential education of women, the education of the public in sympathy for victims, and sweeping analysis of the distortions in the ordinary conduct of sexual life—have also been pursued very vigorously. But as we debate the possible influence of pornography on rape, and as we debate the appropriate means of suppressing pornography, we encounter, as in a negative, a version of Richardson's dubious hopes for the reformative power of art.

As Richardson delves deeply into the grounds for his belief in the reformative power of his art, he loosens the foundation of his confidence by digging up innumerable small obstructions to Clarissa's authority as a moral example and a moral teacher. Rarely does he try the easy solution of defining the effectiveness of her letters by contrasting them with failed moral voices, probably because he is unwilling to weaken any echo of social morality, no matter how faint. The Reverend Brand's letters define the outward boundary of Richardson's tolerance. Brand shows that bad moral teaching is not merely interested, but mercenary, teaching for pay to please the moods, not the abiding interests of the client. Brand is bookish (an especially bad sign is his idolatry of the classics) rather than a patient student of human actions in human circumstances. He even intends to quote Clarissa to herself as if her previous life were only a text. Worst of all, he prides himself on the studied quality of his letters. His week-long revision costs Clarissa's family their chance of comforting her before she dies. His mechanical list of "pleadings" and "comfortings" (not unlike Richardson's lessons at the end of *Pamela*) makes his letter a monstrous hybrid, "*a Letter*, and *not a Letter*, as I may say; but a kind of *short* and *pithy* Discourse" (VII, 433; IV, 321). In spite of the secondhand character of his wisdom, he fatuously yearns for personal credit, a hamper of wine for each Latin tag and the glory of publication. By contrast with Brand, Clarissa's teachings are disinterested, unselfconscious, applied to herself and others in the context of life drama. But the aura of presumption and calculating will cannot always be dismissed so easily from Clarissa's teaching.

Like Richardson, Clarissa takes up ventriloquism as a humble mode of moral instruction. Anna reminds Clarissa of two occasions in which she attributed important wisdom to other authorities. In advising a gentleman designed for the gown to keep his countenance before "free" company, Clarissa attributed her insights to Dr. Lewen, "as she uses to do, when she has a mind not to be thought what she is at so early an age; and that it may give more weight to any-thing *she hit upon, that might appear tolerable,* was her modest manner of speech" (II, 18; I, 251). The second example is more elaborate. Clarissa has already, before the action of the novel, pronounced the complex moral Richardson wants to assign to it. In a letter of advice to Miss Drayton's mother about the mistaken severity of parents that makes children desperate in disputes about marriage, Clarissa wrote "personating an anonymous elderly Lady" (II, 82; I, 295). Anna shows the letter to her mother, who says that "it *deserved* to have the success it met with" (II, 83; I, 296). Clarissa then reminds Anna that Mrs. Norton had helped her with the letter.

Whether consulting with them or not, Clarissa embodies the wisdom of her elders; she does not speak merely for herself or for young women. By contrast with Richardson's childish letter, young and old are equally pleased by her observations, and in a normal situation of this kind her advice has "success." But Mrs. Howe dolefully threatens, "What excuse could be offered for a young Lady capable of making such reflections (and who at her time of life could so well assume the character of one of riper years) if she should rush into any fatal mistake herself?" (II, 83; I, 296). Clarissa's efforts to speak morally, at a distance from a merely personal voice, result in a double load of personal responsibility. In her reply to Anna, Clarissa quivers under the burden of the judgment, but accepts it as "just" (II, 88; I, 299).

In Anna's long memorial portrait of Clarissa, she pictures other devices Clarissa had for teaching the group of young ladies without appearing to do so. Clarissa would address her disagreement with the other ladies to Anna and so create the impression of an intimate, trusting, reciprocally free exchange: "We had agreed to take each other to task when either thought the other gave occasion for it; and when by blaming each other we intended a *general* reprehension, which, as she used to say, it would appear arrogant or assuming to level *more properly*" (VIII, 221; IV, 492). The whole of their correspondence is intended to be this sort of unassuming teaching. At times Richardson seems to make their acts of censoring each other or themselves, their acts of detection, hypothetical examples of what would be faults in others who might not have the excuse of their special circumstances and their self-correcting awareness. Richardson was exasperated when his audience read these criticisms purely as characterization and accused Clarissa of a secret weakness for Lovelace or disobeying her parents' injunction against corresponding with him. With her young ladies Clarissa plays the victim of scandal who successfully defends herself to her friends (VIII, 221; IV, 493), an elaborate image of the disinterested self-defense Richardson was struggling to create in Clarissa's correspondence.

Belford is crucially important for establishing and verifying Clarissa as a social authority who claims no social authority. Clarissa cannot be suspected of a calculated assault on Belford's heart because he has been drawn to her through Lovelace's account of their relations. By acting as the intermediary through whom Lovelace learns about the consequences of his actions—Clarissa's mild reproaches of him, and her religious preparations—Belford is intended to filter out any appearance in Clarissa of manipulating Lovelace's feelings; rather, Belford uses her out of his friendship for Lovelace. The conviction of Clarissa's disinterestedness made possible by this division of labor, by her resignation and Belford's use of her resignation, becomes strained when Lovelace asserts his intention of maintaining the debate directly with her and seeks her out at the Smiths'. She evades him but leaves behind her newly discovered forms of selfless speech, religious meditations gleaned from the Bible. She has already silently answered letters from her family with meditations of this kind, going so far as to stitch one to the bottom of a cruel letter from her Uncle John Harlowe. Nothing is more typical of Richardson, however, than that he gives her space to make a pointed response in letters addressed to them as well as in the silent, undirected meditations. He could not bear to leave the impression that she lost a debate. Clarissa's meditation on (we cannot say that it is "to") Lovelace, "On being hunted by the enemy of my soul," has been copied for her own edification by Mrs. Lovick, who then shows it to Lovelace and joins with Mrs. Smith in trying to bring the lesson home to him.

In more ways than one Lovelace is incapable of replying to Clarissa. He cannot effectively criticize what would be grossly exaggerated speech if it had been directed to him. When he takes exception to certain phrases, it seems to be a mistake of literalism: he cannot recognize that it is the Bible speaking, not Clarissa. He is punishing himself by forcing her private meditation into the form of a dialogue. His foolish, somewhat self-parodic literalism is underlined when he interprets the pathetic phrase "a lonely sparrow on the housetop" as a clue to Clarissa's hiding place (VII, 166; IV, 141). Richardson cannot bring himself to disarm the personal assertiveness of Clarissa's religious speech. Her allegorical letter to Lovelace about seeing him at her father's house, for all its mildness, makes a strategic use of her meditative preparation for death. With a masterful touch Richardson has Belford register the confusion about whose voice speaks this joyful hope by having him suspect Lovelace of forging the letter to further his purposes (VII, 210; IV, 171). Lovelace had already appropriated the first of Clarissa's meditations to his own use by reading it aloud dramatically to his relatives as if it were his own contrite response to his illness (VII, 127; IV, 114). Religious speech is potent, and it cannot restrict its users to religious ends.

The entry of Belford into the story marks the limits of a purely noncoercive moral education in another sense. Belford brings the power of a rich, well-born, and legally skilled male to shelter Clarissa's morality. His presence coincides with the political structure necessary for morality. From the beginning Belford was drawn into his relation with Clarissa because her dilemma had finally come to the attention of the authorities. Only at moments of extremity, theatened by a second rape, will Clarissa invoke "the LAW" (VI, 67–68; III, 289), and then only because she believes that the people she addresses are devoid of any moral emotions other than fear. Typically for Richardson, it is fallen women who use the law as their tool, by having Clarissa arrested for debt to secure her for Lovelace. Whatever the motives, the arrest immediately protects her from them and draws Belford to her side. Although Clarissa is never forced into the impropriety of living at Belford's expense, he is a good protector, not simply because he has Lovelace's trust, but because he is Lovelace's equal. It will no longer be possible for Lovelace to bully, patronize, or flatter the people around Clarissa, as he did at Hampstead, because a man of equal standing will refute him. A scorner of the ordinary activities of his class, Lovelace nevertheless unhesitatingly relies on his status to get his way. Even at the Smiths', when he can expect to gain very little from any imposture or persuasion, his first impulse is to insist, "I must and will see her. I have authority for it. I am a justice of the peace. I have a Search warrant" (VII, 144; IV, 126). After threatening them, he makes them laugh at the enchanting game of a highborn gentleman playing shopkeeper. He never leaves the advantages of his birth behind.

Under Belford's protection, Clarissa's ruin allows her the greatest freedom of action she can enjoy in the story. She chooses her own household, gathers a body of friends entirely her own, not friends of the family, and makes all the arrangements for her death. Her evident enjoyment of this creativity should not be passed off as ordinary funerary art:[38] the new friends are shocked deeply when her coffin appears and overwhelmed by her heroism: "With an intrepidity of a piece with the preparation, having directed them to carry it into her bed-chamber, she returned to us: They were not to have brought it in till after dark, said she—Pray excuse me, Mr. Belford: And don't you, Mrs. Lovick, be concerned: Nor you, Mrs. Smith—Why should you? There is nothing more in it than the unusualness of the thing" (VII, 335; IV, 255). With Belford as executor, Clarissa's final enlargement of power is her will, as she at last resorts to the compulsory power of the law and resumes her right over her grandfather's estate. The most important act of the will is to do what she claimed she always wanted to do, to resign her independent property to her father's control. Like her grandfather, however, she obviously believes that her will can have no efficacy without family respect. She urges Belford not to litigate with her father to enforce it, and in fact the terms of the will win the respect required for its observance. Only the brother and sister quibble about it. The odd course of Richardson's story has created a moving image of paternal dominion by consent (*Leviathan*, II, 20). Clarissa uses the dignity and publicity rather than the power of the law in order to symbolize the noncoercive relationships of sympathy and generosity which she prefers to contractual relationships but which have been denied her.

[38]It is, however, helpful to understand religious elements of this part of the novel. See Doody, *Natural Passion*, pp. 174–79.

We have come to understand how unremitting a meticulous filial consent can be. The moral traveler spends a great deal of energy maintaining the hedgerow laws of society, tending all the offshoots and even filling in gaps by creating new rules (for example, "Thou shalt not litigate with thy father") in order to win heroic stature. Clarissa has secured a posthumous right to powerful moral speech, but at the cost of having anything very challenging to say. One change her will effects gives a tiny glimpse of a suppressed and rejected alternative to the plot. Clarissa's will leaves Mrs. Norton financially independent of the Harlowes and, with the permission of Mr. Harlowe, installs her on the grandfather's estate as manager of Clarissa's fund for the poor. What Clarissa's elaborated filial duty will not accept from her grandfather's legacy she leaves to Mrs. Norton: the single life. If she had independence—the wealth and political power of the male gentry—then the prying curiosity, the testing, the exhausting debates, and the elaborate validation of the moral authority of a subordinate would be as unnecessary for Clarissa as they are for Sir Charles Grandison. The conventions relevant to a man's marriage decisions would be more stable and harmonious, or, if not, his more authoritative position at least would allow more voice in the selection among competing conventions. Clarissa would then figure, as Grandison does, in a story of conspicuous illustration rather than in a plot of intimate knowledge.

# CHAPTER FOUR

# *Sterne: Scenes of Play*

Speciall uses of Speech are these: First, to Register, what by cogitation, wee find to be the cause of any thing, present or past; and what we find things present or past may produce, or effect: which in summe, is acquiring of Arts. Secondly, to shew to others that knowledge which we have attained; which is, to Counsell, and Teach one another. Thirdly, to make known to others our wills, and purposes, that we may have the mutuall help of one another. Fourthly, to please and delight our selves and others by playing with our words, for pleasure or ornament, innocently.

*Leviathan*, I, 4, 101–2

A fifth Law of Nature is COMPLEASANCE, that is to say, *That every man strive to accommodate himself to the rest*. For the understanding whereof, we may consider, that there is in mens aptnesse to Society; a diversity of Nature, rising from their diversity of Affections; not unlike to what we see in stones brought together for building of an Aedifice. For as that stone which by the asperity, and irregularity of Figure, takes more from others, than it selfe fills; and for the hardnesse, cannot be easily made plain, and thereby hindereth the building, is by the builders cast away as unprofitable, and troublesome: so also, a man that by asperity of Nature, will strive to retain those things which to himselfe are superfluous, and to others necessary; and for the stubbornness of his Passions, cannot be corrected, is to be left, or cast out of Society, as combersome thereunto. For seeing every man, not onely by Right, but also by necessity of Nature, is supposed to endeavour all he can, to obtain that which is necessary for his conservation; He that shall oppose himselfe against it, for things superfluous is guilty of the warre that thereupon is to follow; and therefore doth that which is contrary to the fundamentall Law of Nature, which commandeth *to seek Peace*. The observers of this Law may be called SOCIABLE, (the Latines call them *Commodi*;) The contrary, *Stubborn, Insociable, Froward, Intractable.*

*Leviathan*, I, 15, 209–10

In cases where the Soveraign has prescribed no rule, there the Subject hath the liberty to do, or forbeare, according to his own discretion, and therefore such Liberty is in some places more, and in some lesse; and in some times more, in other times lesse, according as they that have the Soveraignty shall think most convenient.

*Leviathan*, II, 21, 271

**Compleasance**

Hobbes's fifth law of nature dictates sociable manners, the art of fitting (or being fitted) smoothly into place in the edifice of state. The passage is abstract; it does not picture any preferred means of accommodation. In spite of (perhaps because of) his years among the English nobility and at the French court, Hobbes does not idealize court life as the best way of knocking off rough edges. The dangerous striving to retain things superfluous could be the vice of great city merchants, but it could also be the vice of the monopolist courtier or the arrogant aristocrat. How smooth and regular the pieces need to be depends on what sort of social building is at stake. With his eccentric gentry family at ease in their country homes and his clergyman out for whimsical encounters on holiday, Sterne suggests that Englishmen have room for some roughness of character. This English liberty is orderly because everyone can enjoy it or identify with it, and everyone can accommodate to it. To a modern political theorist, Hobbes's understanding of consent needs to be expanded to embrace the cohesive practices of a political culture. But once again we may find that Hobbes is correct about the structural requirements of sovereignty to which political culture will be subordinate.

Fitting into place was not an easy process of accommodation for Sterne.[1] Like the other major eighteenth-century novelists, Sterne only began writing novels after he had established himself in another

[1]This section is indebted to Arthur H. Cash, *Laurence Sterne: The Early and Middle Years* (London: Methuen, 1975); Wilbur Cross, *The Life and Times of Laurence Sterne*, 2 vols. (New Haven: Yale University Press, 1925); Lewis Perry Curtis, *The Politicks of Laurence Sterne* (London: Oxford University Press, 1929); and Lewis Perry Curtis, ed., *The Letters of Laurence Sterne* (Oxford: Clarendon, 1935).

career. As the son of a gentleman soldier who had married down (though not so far down as Sterne often complained), fallen on hard times, and died young, Sterne had a difficult way to make in the world. The church was one of the few routes of genteel social mobility, especially if you were reasonably well connected, as Sterne was. One relation paid for Sterne's education at Cambridge, where he made a number of useful friends. After graduation and his first small curacy, Sterne's Uncle Jaques Sterne (an important figure in the church at York) obtained for him several positions in the York diocese, the most important of which was the vicarage of Sutton and the prebendary of Givendale. On the strength of his £75 a year, Sterne married an heiress of £40 a year and set up a gentleman's household in 1741.

In a letter of angry self-defense addressed to his Uncle Jaques in 1751, Sterne details the terrible pressures of his struggle for gentility, "that long train of Difficulties & Drawbacks with Which (you know) I began the World":

> (as namely) the whole Debt of My School Education, Cloathing &c for nine Years together, which came upon me, the Moment I was able to pay it,—To this, a great Part of the Expense of my Education at the University, too Scantily defray'd by my Cosin Sterne wth only 30 pds a Year & the last Year not pay'd, but with the Money I borrow'd—The Expences of coming into my Preferments—The great Repairs of a large ruinous House upon my Living—The entire furnishing of it, when I had done—the want of good Health for many Years—perhaps with it, the Want of all that good Management in beginning the World with wch I hope to end it. [*Letters*, 39–40]

In this letter Sterne attempts, without hope of success, a reconciliation with his uncle, who had been antagonistic toward him since Sterne ended a political alliance that had been established between them in 1741–42. Sterne complains that Jaques has unfairly encouraged his mother to harass him for funds and has ruined his reputation by lodging her in the local jail as if she were an indigent, abandoned by her son. When she and his sister had heard rumors of his marrying an heiress (back in 1741), they began their campaign to share in Sterne's already scanty fortune. His mother, Sterne asserts, had unreasonably given up her embroidery school, and his sister refused to work in a shop or to enter in service to a noble family, saying that "she was the Daughter of a Gentleman" (38). Sterne claims that he did his best to help them, but he was also determined to keep them away, and he clearly regarded their ambitions of gentility as offensive. Near the end of this letter, Sterne asks in outrage whether he has the right to deprive his wife in order to support his mother, considering that his wife brought money into the family and his mother brought none, and that his wife was raised a gentlewoman not used to struggling in the world, while his mother was only the daughter of a poor sutler who followed the corps in Flanders (an exaggeration of her low status). Sterne never made it up with his uncle and never again enjoyed preferment or financial help from him.

All the pressures on Sterne in 1741—a new wife, a vicarage to repair, a mother to buy off—must have made him especially eager to cooperate with his uncle in the political schemes that had advanced him so far in the church. Jaques had helped break the political power of the strong local "country" interest in the late 1720s, and many of his offices had come to him in reward for his service to the Walpole ministry in the bitterly fought campaign of 1734, when Walpole was facing down the excise crisis. In that campaign was launched the long enmity between the Sternes and Dr. John Burton, the Tory scholar, male midwife, and hospital founder, some of whose traits appear in Dr. Slop of *Tristram Shandy*. Political contests, although reduced to a minimum by the Septennial Bill (and often by common informal agreements about representatives among local magistrates), were nonetheless very rough in York in 1734 and again in 1741, when Walpole was fighting his last fight for control of Parliament. Burton was said to use his influence with poor patients to extort their votes. He accused Jaques Sterne of stealing the sacrament money for party purposes, of pressing debtors to change their votes, and of blacklisting antiministerial tradesmen. Burton had bought a large share of the *York Courant*, so Jaques Sterne, with the help of his nephew, launched the *York Gazeteer*. Laurence Sterne's contributions were effective, and he saw to it that several of them were republished in London, where people watched the York contest with lively interest. But Jaques seems to have betrayed him into an embarrassing imbroglio, from which Laurence never quite recovered.

Caught in an exchange of anonymous letters to the editor with a writer who signed himself J. S., Sterne suggested (probably on the authority of his uncle) an identification of J. S. with James Scott, a local clergyman; more dangerous, Sterne suggested that he was a Jacobite. Outraged denials were accompanied with galling literary attacks. Especially galling perhaps was the attack that identified Sterne (Lorry, as he was called locally) with Lord Hervey, as attacked by Pope in the "Epistle to Dr. Arbuthnot":

> Let L——y scribble—What? that Thing of Silk
> L——y that mere white Curd of Ass's Milk?
> Satire or Sense, alas! can L——y feel?
> Who breaks a *Butterfly* up on a Wheel?
> [Curtis, *The Politics of Lawrence Sterne*, 63]

Curtis is surely right in finding that this characterization fits well with some of Sterne's own later language about his alter ego, Yorick, and the light, charming lack of seriousness that was part of his reputation (62). It must, of course, have been maddening to be taken as a social butterfly when one has been trying for deadly blows against an adversary. Eventually Sterne tried his own hand at unbutterflyish, devastating Scriblerian satire against J. S., likening him to an impotent animal of Egypt that "lets fly backward full against his Adversary, and thereby covers his Retreat with the Fumes of his own Filth and Excrement" (Curtis, 70). By this time J. S. had more reason than Sterne to think that his opponent had let fly backward. Yorick in *Tristram Shandy* was among other things an overhasty name caller.

The outcome of the election was a rapid revolution of political ironies. The Sternes returned their candidate, but Walpole fell nonetheless. A short time later another Court Whig MP died, and the man the Sternes had defeated in the county election (George Fox) was returned in the city without opposition. Sterne resigned from the *Gazette* and wrote to the editor of the *Courant* a letter that Sterne's biographers read as a revenge against his uncle, but that outshandys even Tristram Shandy for self-parody: "Sir, I find by some late Preferments, that it may not be improper to change Sides; therefore I beg the Favour of you to inform the Publick that I sincerely beg pardon for the abusive Gazettes I wrote during the late contested election for the County of York, and that I heartily wishe Mr. Fox Joy of his Election for the City" (Curtis, 114).

In later years, choosing a more disgruntled tone and blaming his uncle for his mistakes, Sterne drew the line on politics just at this point, when he stopped writing paragraphs in the newspapers. The following account was included in a solemn autobiographical letter to his daughter, composed in 1767: "My uncle and myself were then upon very good terms, for he soon got me the Prebendary of York —but he quarreled with me afterwards, because I would not write paragraphs in the newspapers—though he was a party-man, I was not, and detested such dirty work: thinking it beneath me—from that period, he became my bitterest enemy" (*Letters*, 41).

Curtis titled his book *The Politicks of Laurence Sterne*, as if to suggest by this old-fashioned spelling that Sterne's politics was a rather embarrassing and comic episode of his youth, of real but limited interest to lovers of his fiction. But is it true that in ending his newspaper career Sterne ended his politics or even stopped being a party man? Sterne was rewarded for his political service, even if the reward was modestly arranged without the cooperation of his uncle. With the fall of Walpole, there was a shift of coalitions and party strategies; but the Whig connections Sterne had solidified in 1741 continued to stand him in good stead, and the politics he supported—anti-Jacobite, anti-Catholic, pro–standing army, pro–Septennial Act—got new life in the tumult of the 1745 Jacobite rebellion.

In the aftermath of the rebellion, Sterne even effected some rapprochement with his uncle over the prosecution of John Burton for treason in 1745–46. Although accusations of Jacobitism were part of the repressive politics of the Court Whigs, these accusations still had enough truth part of the time to give credit to the whole machinery of political constraint. Identifying J. S. without certain evidence may have caused Sterne lasting embarrassment, but he never expressed opposition to the whole system of political control. Getting up close to Walpole's methods for achieving "political stability" reveals the violence implicit in Hobbes's metaphor of planing down excrescences and casting out misfits. Yet the rule of compleasance suggests that there are also milder and more agreeable ways of attaining social unity.

In preserving the Sterne family enmity against Burton by caricaturing him as Dr. Slop in *Tristram Shandy*, Sterne can hardly be said to repudiate entirely the politics of his uncle and the Whig church establishment. Although Sterne holds back from making Burton a Jacobite (except for some hints about pistols), making him a Catholic suggests the rest of the charges, but perhaps only for those in the know. The teasing in *Tristram Shandy* is certainly a gentler way of dealing with Burton than incarceration on charges of treason. Sterne's milder politics of the 1750s tends to be less readily visible than his activities of 1741–42, but conciliation was very much the policy of the Pelhamite coalition that succeeded in the Walpole heritage of Court Whiggery. In 1747 an old Cambridge friend of Sterne's, John Fontayne, became dean of York and pulled Sterne into the magistracy and into the Peculiar Courts of Pickering and Pocklington. Fontayne was strongly marked as a latitudinarian and a Pelhamite who moved in the direction of Rockinghamite reform, in contrast to Jaques Sterne, who had antagonized the ministry by such activities as overzealous persecution of a Catholic girls' school from 1747 to 1751. It is an interesting sign of the more peaceable times that local pressure on Jaques Sterne halted him in his tracks. Apparently more people sympathized with the view of the *Courant*, against "a certain little Doctor, that left unattempted no methods of Persecution in his Power, to banish the Roman Catholic Gentry, who, by spending the winter here, circulated amongst us many thousand Pounds yearly" (17 January 1748–49, quoted in *Letters*, 42).

Laurence Sterne may have stopped short of campaigning for candidates after his embittering experience of 1741–42, but he hurled himself into diocesan politics, engaging in controversies that culminated in his satire *A Political Romance* (1759). The fate of this explosive little book was death by fire at the request of the archbishop, who was on the side of Fontayne and Sterne but wished also to make peace in the diocese. Sterne therefore suffered a second disappointment as a political controversialist, and he seems once again to have felt betrayed by his chief ally. In 1759, while working on *Tristram Shandy*, Sterne explained to a correspondent his reasons for "turning author": "Why truly I am tired of employing my brains for other peoples advantage.—'Tis a foolish sacrifice I have made for some years to an ungrateful person.—I depend upon the candour of the publick, but I shall not pick out a jury to try the merit of my book amongst *******" (*Letters*, 84).

Sterne certainly turned away from certain provincial political controversies. In his progress from *A Political Romance*, to the Rabelaisian fragment from the earliest version of *Tristram Shandy*, to the first volumes of the published novel and beyond, Sterne decreased his literary reliance on local controversy.[2] But I shall argue that in making a trial of the "candour of the publick," he contrived an alternative, nonsatiric, political aesthetic, a politics of play that made differences of opinion fun and offered models of national comprehension.

Even *A Political Romance* hints at Sterne's later transformation of satire. Sterne's own self-portraiture as "Lorry Slim" is quite different from the indignant *vir bonus* who speaks out in traditional satire. He is set a little to one side of the main controversy, a figure who is a bit woebegone and tattered, but who has a "light Heart."[3] He is not above a certain rueful enjoyment of the frustration of his opponent, even though the preferment in contention between them is very slim pickings, not much to exult over. Although it provides some brief, helpful clues, the appended "key" wanders wonderfully away from the satire into a mock debate among members of a political club, whose grandiose interpretations of the preceding romance further dwarf the small tempests in the churchyard, but even more important, add a friendly, humorous charm that the main text lacked. In the text, controversy was initiated by competitive greed; in the key, competitive interpretation of the satire is part of the order of the club. All this talk seems as harmless and delightful as reading for pleasure:, "Thus every Man turn'd the Story to what was swimming uppermost in his own Brain; so that, before all was over, there were full as many Satyres spun out of it,—and as great a Variety of Personages, Opinions, Transactions, and Truths, found to lay hid under the dark Veil of its Allegory, as ever were discovered in the thrice-renowned History of the Acts of *Gargantua and Pantagruel*" (221–22).

The reading tastes prominent in the club are for political news and political history. Although the excitement of the speeches seems

[2]For the early fragment, see Melvyn New, "Sterne's Rabelaisian Fragment: A Text from the Holograph Manuscript," *PMLA* 87 (1972):1083–92.

[3]Laurence Sterne, *A Sentimental Journey, . . . "The Journal to Eliza," and "A Political Romance"*, ed. Ian Jack (London: Oxford University Press, 1972), p. 207.

ridiculously overdone and self-important, their patriotic fervor survives the silliness. The reprobation of the king of France "by whose shifting and intriguing Behaviour, all *Europe* was set Together by the Ears" (214) could well have roused in the audience a feeling of cheerful solidarity with the popular war (later known as the Seven Years War) which was being conducted by one of Sterne's heroes, William Pitt. And we think of Toby Shandy when we read about the club member who "had come piping-hot from reading the History of King William's and Queen Anne's Wars" (216), which indeed served as explanation for and parallel to the Seven Years War as it was understood in its time. Making fun of these patriotic enthusiasms makes fun out of them. It helps put them over and seems to offer a way of transcending the partisan conflicts of the satire. The gentleman who claims that the satire portrays the French king moves that it be printed, "For, continues he, if we can but once turn the Laugh against him, and make him asham'd of what he has done, it may be a good Means, with the Blessing of God upon our Fleets and armies, to save the Liberties of *Europe*" (222). As is so often the case in *Tristram Shandy*, such a grandiose notion of the transformative power of art is subtly mocked and rejected. Yet as an official record of all the opinions that have been so freely aired in the rambling course of discussion, Sterne's text preserves a feeling for "Liberties," a political arrangement sufficiently secure to allow more space for irregularities.

### *Tristram Shandy*: Playful Purposes

Sterne presents a teasing challenge for an investigation of political interpretation. If, with Hobbes, we can say that any matter of human activity might be political, must every matter therefore be considered political? The distinction between the two positions helps maintain a distinction between a theory of absolutism and a theory of totalitarianism. Perhaps not so much is at stake in the related question for literary studies: when we investigate the politics of the novel, must we read everything politically? It is interesting to find that even Hobbes has a place for play that he calls "innocent." It appears as the fourth item in the list, quoted above, of the uses of words: "to please and delight ourselves and others by playing with our words for pleasure or ornament, innocently." Since moral words like *innocent* are for Hobbes "words of inconstant signification," judgments of what is or is not innocent will be debatable and can be grounds for political conflict and political regulation.

Nevertheless, it seems worth trying out the proposition that *Tristram Shandy* plays with words for pleasure or ornament, innocently, and that with this work we reach the framing limit of our subject. *Tristram Shandy* may be the point at which the ambitions of the novel seek the status of play, not politics. We recognize a kind of modernity in Sterne when we take his art as antididactic. He does not offer counsel or exemplify the natural law of contracts, as does Defoe. He does not define his book as a source of sustaining and transformative moral discourse, as does Richardson. He seems to approach a notion of the literary as a practice or realm that is autonomous, free from social intent or social influence. So foreign is this idea of the literary to Sterne's culture that it takes his massive ingenuity to create an art that seems autonomous, or at least an art that is gratuitous, noninstrumental. We could say that this effort is the occasion, if not the goal, of Sterne's originality.

Viktor Shklovsky took Sterne's practice as paradigmatic of his formalist credo: "His typical method is to proceed by laying bare the literary device; form exists for itself and has no ulterior motivation. The difference between Sterne's novel and an ordinary novel is like the difference between a poem of typical sound orchestration and a futuristic poem in extra-rational language."[4] But the concept of an antididactic aesthetic need not be entirely formalist. Its most important critical heritage is of course romantic, and the popularity of Sterne among German romantic poets and critics suggests that his art represented for them the creative freedom of play that Schiller identified with art in *On the Aesthetic Education of Man*.

In Goethe's aphorisms, Sterne both illustrates and inspires creative freedom:

> Yorick-Sterne was the most beautiful spirit that ever lived; who reads him feels free and beautiful; his humor is inimitable, and not all humor frees the soul. . . .

[4]Viktor Shklovsky, "A Parody Novel: Sterne's *Tristram Shandy*" (1929), trans. W. Georg Isaak, in *Laurence Sterne: A Collection of Critical Essays*, ed. John Traugott (Englewood Cliffs, N.J.: Prentice-Hall, 1968), p. 66.

> Even now at this moment every educated person should take Sterne's works in hand so that the nineteenth century may also learn what we owe him and recognize what we can still borrow from him. . . .
>
> He felt a definite hatred for seriousness because it is didactic and dogmatic and very easily becomes pedantic, qualities which he despised.
>
> He is a model in nothing and a guide and stimulator in everything.[5]

In his delightful essay of 1909, "Richness, Chaos and Form: A Dialogue Concerning Laurence Sterne, " Georg Lukács took these aphorisms of Goethe as a starting point for a vigorous debate on the aesthetics and ethical value of Sterne's "playful gesture of sovereignty" (condemned by the opposing speaker as "his impotence").[6] Perhaps Sterne would have appropriated these elevated conceptions of his art, if they had been available to him, but modern revolution and mass culture had not yet given the "playful gesture of sovereignty" the political and metaphysical significance that it would assume after the French Revolution. Yet the mistaken recognition of aesthetic modernity in Sterne is interesting. His gestures of play may show us something about the relationship of art and sovereignty even if Sterne and his contemporaries were not ready to imagine play as sovereignty.

Our heritage of romantic art and philosophy leads us into another common mistaken recognition of Sterne: that the "world" of his book is the isolated, sovereign self. Sterne's epistemological heritage from Locke is supposed to drive headlong into a blind alley of solipsism with no access to morals or politics except by some kind of deus ex machina.[7] But our gathering familiarity with the eccentric family identity that we learn to call "Shandyean" does not suggest a very high epistemological fence between individuals. We accept Tristram's querulous narration of the scene of his engendering and then

[5]From *Wilhelm Meisters Wanderjahre* (1828), in Alan B. Howes, *Sterne: The Critical Heritage* (London: Routledge & Kegan Paul, 1974), pp. 433–34 (taken from translation by W.R.R. Pinger, *Laurence Sterne and Goethe* [1918]).

[6]Georg Lukács, *Soul and Form* (1910), trans. Anna Bostock (Cambridge: MIT Press, 1974), p. 136.

[7]For the most attractive argument of this kind, see A. D. Nuttall, *A Common Sky* (Berkeley: University of California Press, 1974). For Nuttall the escape hatch from solipsism must be language (rather than sentiment, as it is for so many commentators on Sterne).

learn that his source is Uncle Toby, who has heard Tristram's father frequently lament it. This initial account of family exchanges has to float much of Tristram's account of his prenatal knowledge throughout the novel. Tristram's occasional elaborate documentation only underlines his inadequacy as a witness or scholarly historian. Rather, his information and opinions are signs of his participation in his family, a participation rarely dramatized but always assumed. Even Lockean philosophy may be offered more as a family parlor game than as the philosophical framework of the book. The play in this novel is irremediably social: we need to ask what sort of society produces it.

The Hogarth illustration that Sterne solicited as a frontispiece for the second edition of Volumes One and Two helps identify the primary setting and structure of the novel as a scene of domestic retirement and leisure. Sterne pleads with a friend of Hogarth's, "the loosest Sketch in Nature, of Trim's reading the Sermon to my Father &c, wd do the Business—& it wd mutually illustrate his System & mine."[8] Sterne had already solicited a connection to Hogarth by including in his original description of the scene two references to Hogarth's *Analysis of Beauty* (1753), the first of which reads like unsolicited puffery in search of a gratuitous reward: "If you have read Hogarth's analysis of beauty, and if you have not, I wish you would" (II, 9, 104–5).[9] In the print the two pipe-smoking brothers Shandy sit comfortably close, even if their gazes go in different directions. Walter we have learned is a retired merchant, a person of great eloquence who now has nothing to sell but his many oddball ideas.

[8]See Sterne's letter to Richard Berenger in *Letters of Laurence Sterne*, ed. Lewis Perry Curtis (Oxford: Clarendon, 1935), pp. 99–101. With typical allusiveness, Sterne quotes Swift making a similar request of Pope in the language of Cicero.

[9]Parenthetical reference here and throughout the chapter is made to Laurence Sterne, *The Life and Opinions of Tristram Shandy, Gentleman*, ed. James Aiken Work (New York: Odyssey Press, 1940; copyright © 1940 by Macmillan Publishing Company), by volume, chapter, and page. Quotations appear by permission of Macmillan Publishing Company.

William V. Holtz considers that in these passages Sterne implicitly criticizes Hogarth's *Analysis*, marking a difference between caricature and comic art in the figures of Slop and Trim that Hogarth comes to adopt under the influence of Fielding's distinction in the preface to *Joseph Andrews*. See *Image and Immortality: A Study of "Tristram Shandy"* (Providence: Brown University Press, 1970), pp. 21–38. See also Frederick Antal, *Hogarth and His Place in European Art* (New York: Basic, 1962), p. 164.

His brother Toby, wounded in the battle of Namur in 1695, has retired to the country to conduct imitative battles on his bowling green, attended by Corporal Trim, who stands with his back to us reading the sermon.

This scene of retirement is not like Pope's retirement at Twickenham in the poems of the 1730s; it is not a place close to London and peopled by the leaders of the opposition to Sir Robert Walpole. The Yorkshire of *Tristram Shandy* is a long way from London. Walter's stock country gentleman's abhorrence of the growth of the metropolis and the court (I, 18, 46–47) makes him unwilling to return to London. The consequences of Walter's political views are domestic. His marriage contract guarantees his wife a conjugal trip to London for her lying-in, but her mistaken (or faked) pregnancy has released him from that stipulation, and they have arrived at terms for a lying-in at home. Dr. Slop, the short, squat character sleeping or sulking in the foreground of the print, is a "man-midwife" whom Walter hopes to foist upon his wife—only if, as she has insisted, her midwife, a more experienced if less technologically advanced female attendant, should happen to fail. As the men wait, they entertain themselves listening to Corporal Trim read a sermon in the parlor while the women (wife, maid, midwife) scurry about upstairs trying to give birth to the narrator and eponymous hero Tristram Shandy.

Sterne's wonderfully long-sustained joke, that it takes four volumes (published over two years) to get Tristram born, helps keep the central characters in a state of suspension. They bring nothing forth. This situation of bringing nothing forth is, as the print shows, a situation of reading, and it is also the situation Sterne chooses for his innovative writing. For Tristram Shandy, our narrator, who purports in the title of the book to offer the reader his life, cannot produce it. Not only does he have great trouble bringing himself to birth in the first four volumes, his story and opinions keep being displaced by stories about his father and uncle, so that the last volume (number nine), published eight years after Volumes One and Two, concludes with the story of Uncle Toby's courtship of Widow Wadman, which was conducted five years before Tristram's birth. The book runs backward to unbirth. The structural importance of the much promised, much delayed episode of Toby's failed courtship is part of Wayne Booth's argument that Sterne really finished *Tristram*

*Shandy*.[10] Otherwise one might think that it merely ended without being properly finished when Sterne died.

In spite of boasting to the reader about his digressive-progressive method, Tristram likes to give the impression of a writer who cannot get his business done, even though he can keep at it "these forty years." The activity of composition puts him farther and farther behind:

> I am this month one whole year older than I was this time twelve-month; and having got, as you perceive, almost into the middle of my fourth volume—and no farther than to my first day's life—'tis demonstrative that I have three hundred and sixty-four days more life to write just now, than when I first set out; so that instead of advancing, as a common writer, in my work with what I have been doing at it—on the contrary, I am just thrown so many volumes back—was every day of my life to be as busy a day as this—and why not?—and the transactions and opinions of it to take up as much description—and for what reason should they be cut short? as at this rate I should just live 364 times faster than I should write—It must follow, an' please your worships that the more I write, the more I shall have to write—and consequently, the more your worships read, the more your worships will have to read. [IV, 13, 285–86]

Sterne's planned ending (if indeed he planned it) and Tristram's endlessness suggest the same thing about the novel. Reading and writing are adventures without attainable goals; they never catch up to life and so cannot affect it except to produce more reading and writing. Although the passage starts with the disproportionate size of life to writing, writing and reading at the end threaten to engulf all of life.

Many critics have written about "impotence" in *Tristram Shandy*, but we usually find ambiguous situations of impaired or dubious potency which suggest the pointlessness, the lack of directed purpose, for writing or reading or speaking in the novel. Walter Shandy performs his conjugal duties reluctantly once a month when he winds

[10]Wayne Booth, "Did Sterne Complete *Tristram Shandy?*" *Modern Philology* 48 (1951):172–83. For different views, see Marcia Allentuck, "In Defense of an Unfinished *Tristram Shandy*," in *The Winged Skull*, ed. Arthur H. Cash and John M. Stedmond (London: Methuen, 1971), pp. 145–55; and in the same volume, R. F. Brissenden, "Trusting to Almighty God: Another Look at the Composition of *Tristram Shandy*," pp. 258–69.

the grandfather's clock. Colonel Toby's retirement, his modesty, and the failure of his courtship are all caused by a mysteriously located wound on the groin. The Shandy noses are small, which puts the men at a disadvantage in marriage contracts. Tristram's nose is mashed when Dr. Slop gets sloppy with his forceps, and later in his childhood he suffers some sort of circumcision by a window sash. Not knowing for sure about these men, we keep reading without being able to pass judgment. Even the family bull is rumored to be ineffective with the local cows. This final anecdote allows the clergyman Yorick to pronounce the last words of the novel, which tell us of its indifference to didacticism. Mrs. Shandy asks, "L--d! . . . what is all this story about?—A COCK and a BULL, said *Yorick*—And one of the best of its kind, I ever heard" (IX, 33, 647). Even as jokes go, the cock-and-bull story is pointless. It gets an effect by its unjustifiable protraction. Mrs. Shandy's "interrogation" of Walter does not prevent the conception of Tristram; it only sets Tristram's animal spirits "cluttering like hey-go-mad" (I, 1, 5).

Sterne's daring in beginning the novel in the beginning shows the narrator and the author of the novel as anti-Horatian artists, since Horace had advised authors to begin in the middle, not *ab ovo*. (A strong hint of the relevance of this advice to Tristram's method can be found at IV, 13, 286.) This violation allows the more challenging violation of Horace's other precept, quoted by Samuel Johnson in *Rambler* 4: that art should join both profit and delight. The acts of men who bring nothing forth cannot serve as either good or bad examples. But the manipulation of the narrative time scheme cannot by itself guarantee Sterne a sense of play. He must actively make his writing "innocent" by invoking forms of writing that usually function as authoritative social acts and converting them to play. Of these conversions, the novelization of the sermon on conscience is the most important.

The sermon, intended to be delivered by a member of the state church entrusted with the education of the nation, is here delivered by a servant in a parlor. The clergyman Yorick, author of the sermon, is missing from the scene. His is the first death Tristram recounts, so that in the unchronological order of the book he is "already" dead in the reader's eyes at the time his sermon is read. Yorick's marginal status in the other sections of the book helps define the novel as a scene of play rather than of authoritative instruction. The sermon has drifted into the hands of Toby, Trim, and Walter. It falls out of a copy of Stevinus, one of Toby's favorite books on military fortification, and Walter asks to have Trim read it to them in the same slapdash, spontaneous spirit that Tristram often tells us characterizes his narrative. Walter says, "I have ever a strong propensity . . . to look into things which cross my way, by such strange fatalities as these" (II, 15, 119). And the sermon got into Stevinus, we are told later, because Parson Yorick has been peering into Stevinus in the same spirit of aimless curiosity that characterized Walter's interest in the sermon: "It seems that *Yorick*, who was inquisitive after all kinds of knowledge, had borrowed *Stevinus* of my uncle *Toby*, and had carelessly popp'd his sermon, as soon as he had made it, into the middle of *Stevinus*, and by an act of forgetfulness, to which he was ever subject, he had sent *Stevinus* home, and his sermon to keep him company" (II, 17, 142). And in this spirit, we might add, Tristram and Sterne have popped the sermon into the novel, along with other heterogeneous documents and quotations, some raided from archives and some from favorite compendia such as Burton's *Anatomy of Melancholy* and Chambers's *Cyclopedia*, some pseudo-documents made up for the fiction.

Sermons keep coming up in the history of the novel, often with the function I have before attributed to courts of law in the novel. They allow novelists and their readers to assert the dignity and efficacy of the newly ambitious novelistic form by contrasting it with other authoritative institutions of teaching and psychological insight. It made Fielding angry to hear that Richardson's *Pamela* had been praised by clergymen in the pulpit as if it were a remarkably good sermon. Yet in his own *Joseph Andrews*, Fielding makes his lovable Parson Adams forgetfully leave at home the sermons that he was going to London to publish. The implication is clear: Adams's sermons are dull and do not persuade anyone, but his personal conduct is an effective sermon that Fielding's art makes available to us. But Sterne's sermon functions differently. It is a good sermon, not a failed sermon. It was much admired by its eighteenth-century readers, including Voltaire, who discussed it in his *Philosophical Dictionary*, and even by Richardson, who was generally hostile to Sterne's work. The sermon functions not to prove the superior didactic force of the novel that surrounds it, but to work a peculiarly modern magic: to convert moral writing into literature.

One wonderful transformation of this sort occurs when Dr. Slop cuts his thumb badly as he tries to sever the knots that Obadiah, the Shandys' servant, has tied on his bag of medical instruments. Walter Shandy, angered to hear Dr. Slop abuse Obadiah, offers Slop a really good curse to replace the commonplace invective he has been using, like "the devil take the fellow." Slop, who is a Catholic, is handed a twelfth-century excommunication, composed by Ernulph, Bishop of Rochester. Walter Shandy has an eccentric, antiquarian feeling for old Catholic Europe that mixes a little oddly with the satirical view of Catholicism taken in conventional Protestant discourse. In this appreciation of Catholic society (or at least extension of his text by Catholic means), he bears a family resemblance to our narrator Tristram, who has already introduced a long declaration of the doctors of the Sorbonne on intrauterine baptism as a path to salvation. Walter begs Slop to read the curse aloud because "there is something so whimsical, especially in the latter part of it, I should grieve to lose the pleasure of a second reading" (III, 11, 171). Sterne puts the original Latin on pages facing his English translation with parenthetical comments by the men in the parlor. Words that once dealt eternal death, words that save souls, now yield entertainment and satisfy whimsy and curiosity.

By the texts of Ernulphus and of the doctors of the Sorbonne, Sterne tests his readers' attention and loyalty to his novel. But he mocks the idea that this loyalty should be understood as a high and righteous taste for instruction. Before reading about Catholic prenatal baptism, "Madame," the reader, is rebuked for her inattention to the obscure clues "*that my mother was not a papist*" (I, 20, 56) and is sent back to read over again:

> I have imposed this penance upon the lady, neither out of wantonness or cruelty, but from the best of motives; and therefore shall make her no apology for it when she returns back;—'Tis to rebuke a vicious taste which has crept into thousands besides herself,—of reading straight forwards, more in quest of adventures, than of the deep erudition and knowledge which a book of this cast, if read over as it should be, would infallibly impart with them.—The mind should be accustomed to make wise reflections, and draw curious conclusions as it goes along; the habitude of which made Pliny the Younger affirm "That he never read a book so bad, but he drew some profit from it." [I, 20, 56–57]

The language of penance, infallibility, and rebuke suggests that there is something suspiciously Catholic and tyrannical about didacticism. The passage cleverly slips into an attack on the straightforward, and it swerves into more typically Shandean hints about "curious" conclusions and the joys of bad books. We are invited to join in the divagations of "curious" reading that characterize Walter and Tristram and Sterne. The reader's loyalty to Sterne's book is solicited as an incipient intimacy:

> You must have a little patience. I have undertaken, you see, to write not only my life, but my opinions also; hoping and expecting that your knowledge of my character, and of what kind of a mortal I am, by the one, would give you a better relish for the other: As you proceed further with me, the slight acquaintance which is now betwixt us, will grow into familiarity, and that, unless one of us in fault, will terminate in friendship.—*O diem praeclarum!*—then nothing which has touched me will be thought trifling in its nature, or tedious in the telling. [1, 6, 10–11]

Tristram is not offering to unveil the intimate knowledge of character which is associated with Richardson's novels, the ultimate insight into motives which decides a person to trust (or distrust) another and gives the reader a feeling of privileged access to psychological truth. In Sterne, only the mocking god Momus, the "archcritic," expects to read the heart through a glass window in the breast, to trace (like Pope in the *Dunciad*) all the soul's "maggots from their first engendering to their crawling forth" and then to set down in pen and ink "nothing but what you have seen, and could have sworn to" (1, 23, 74). Tristram promises instead to draw the character of Toby from his hobbyhorse. We learn how it goes when Toby rides it; we "proceed further" with it. The reader catches on to the various family obsessions the way a person is let in on a joke, and from the very first publication readers (even hostile readers) have repeated the jokes and imitated them.[11] The reader learns to do the Shandy. For the

[11]See especially *The Clockmakers Outcry against the Author of the Life and Opinions of Tristram Shandy*, a critical pamphlet published 9 May 1760: "The directions I had for making several clocks for the county are countermanded; because no modest lady now dares mention a word about *winding-up a clock*, without exposing herself to the sly leers and jokes of the family, to her frequent confusion. . . . If a gentleman wind-up his watch in company, and looks affectionately at any particular lady, that is as much as to say that he prefers her to all the rest, and is in love with her: if she wind hers immediately afterwards and reciprocates a look of fondness, it is

appreciative reader, it is like being let into a club, a joking, game-playing club like the Demoniacs, to which Sterne belonged along with his friend and imitator John Hall-Stevenson. Hall-Stevenson, commemorated in *Tristram Shandy* as Eugenius, played host for the club at his Crazy Castle in Yorkshire, and it may be that his family library was a source for Sterne's "curious" learning.[12]

Curiosity in Sterne is not the dangerous political passion that we read about in Hobbes, the specifically human "lust of the mind" (*Leviathan*, I, 6, 124) which "governs" the trains of imagination "by designe" (*Leviathan*, I, 3, 96). In Hobbes, curiosity, armed with language,[13] "hunts" not only the causes of present effects, but also, and more dangerously, the future effects of present causes. This is one reason that humans suffer civil wars but social animals such as bees do not: humans have reason, speech, and curiosity, which lead them to disputes about reforming and innovating government (*Leviathan*, II, 17, 226). Curiosity in Sterne is innocent, even when it is lust in the head, because it does not pursue "designs" in this way. Tristram is very far from Lovelace, another game-playing clubman, whose love of stratagem aids his wish to keep on testing Clarissa. Instead, Sterne's curiosity is agreeable; it is not only a source of pleasure in itself, it is also an attitude that enhances social agreement. Your tolerant curiosity allows other people the liberty to be curiosities, to say or do or read curious things. The stones in Sterne's edifice of state can be more irregular than those in Hobbes's plan, since they do not cause too much trouble or pain. They give aesthetic joy, like Gothic ruins. Sterne likes to give the impression that curiosity is, to use Hobbes's phrase, "compleasant," or "sociable." The eccentricities he indulges may be "superfluous," they may run away with him, but they do not take away anything anyone else really needs. Instead, they produce something new, or at least something more, for everyone to enjoy. Sterne claims he shows

---

as much to say, on her side, that she approves his passion." See Howes, *Critical Heritage*, pp. 70–71. Sterne commented on pamphlets against him, "I wish they would write a hundred such" (*Letters*, p. 107).

[12]See Cross, *Life*, 1:119–27.

[13]Recall the first special use of language (quoted in the epigraph to this chapter): "To Register, what by cogitation, wee find to be the course of any thing, present or past; and about what we find things present or past may produce, or effect."

"complaisance" (the same word as Hobbes's "complesance") to his critics by leaving places "open" for them (II, 2, 84–85).

Not all humor, of course, is enjoyable to all parties. Hobbes's theory of laughter is one more notorious example of competition in power: laughter is a "sudden glory," which is likely to be raised by the "apprehension of some deformed thing in another, by comparison whereof they suddenly applaud themselves" (*Leviathan*, I, 6, 125). Sterne does not always project a sociable image of eccentric humor. Parson Yorick, for instance, has been trapped in a dangerous dynamic of competitive wit, in which jester and jestee are like mortgager and mortgagee; he pays with interest for raising jests at the expense of others. Finally he is mysteriously ambushed and overcome in a "war" provoked by his tactlessness (I, 12, 27–31). Yorick's obscure death early in the novel may be one more way Sterne kills the dangerous practicality of language. Momus, a patron deity of satire, is not the god of this book. Insofar as Yorick's "war" may refer to Sterne's engagement in political controversy in the1740s, and 1750s, Sterne may be killing off his politics in order to raise a more purely literary identity. But Sterne needs first to invoke satire to show that he has renounced, or at least domesticated, its awesome powers.

Yorick's demise in a war of words and Ernulph's condemnation of a soul to eternal death call to mind the mythic origins of satire discussed by Robert C. Elliott.[14] Traces of the legendary power of poets to rhyme their enemies dead can be found, for example, in Swift's execution of Partridge, the astrologer and almanac maker. Swift's parodic prediction of the death of Partridge, followed by the parodic announcement of the fulfillment of the prophecy, succeeded to the extent that the Stationers' Company struck Partridge's name from the rolls and won the right, over his legal protests, to issue the almanac without him.[15] Sterne's many echoes of satiric writers have

[14]Robert C. Elliott, *The Power of Satire: Magic, Ritual, Art* (Princeton: Princeton University Press, 1960). Following and complicating Elliott, Michael Seidel finds satire precisely in the descent to impotence, the entropic eddying that I have discussed as the nonsatiric "pointlessness" of *Tristram Shandy*. See *Satiric Inheritance: Rabelais to Sterne* (Princeton: Princeton University Press, 1979).

[15]Irvin Ehrenpreis is no doubt correct to insist on the term *hoax*, rather than *satire*, for Swift's Bickerstaff *Predictions* and *Accomplishment*, since they actually fooled people on April Fools' Day, 1708. But the practicality of the practical joke

been recognized from the time of his first publication, and we know that he was writing satire immediately before writing his novel, but in the novel satire pulls its punches. References to local Yorkshire enemies seem residual, private satisfactions of little importance to the larger audience of the novel. The learned controversialist Dr. Warburton heard a rumor that Sterne intended to satirize him, and he may even have bought Sterne off for a while in a civilized way, but the digs at Warburton in the novel have to be dug out:[16] they lack the blunt instrumentality of satire.

The "voluptuous infirmity" of Kunastrokius was perhaps more recognizable to the contemporaries of Dr. Richard Mead, but when rebuked for it Sterne writes a pompous letter defending his right to "attack a dead man who can't defend himself"; he does not justify it as a fierce attack on vice. Instead, Sterne has "most distantly" hinted "at a drole foible in his character" and "smiled" at it, connecting Kunastrokius honorably with Solomon as examples of great men who had ruling passions (*Letters*, 89). Sterne's sentimentality is not a rebellion against satire but a domestication of it.[17] When Uncle Toby, an uncontentious man, is offended by or disagrees with what he hears (for example, the cruel condemnations of the excommunication), he whistles "Lillabullero" as a kind of counter-argument (the *argumentum fistulatorium*). James Work's wonderful footnote on "Lillabullero" deserves to be quoted at length, since he shows that it

---

kept its effect even after the authorship of the hoax was known and its impersonation could be appreciated as skillful satirical irony. People were afraid of being satirized, even though the satire could be recognized as fictitious. See Irvin Ehrenpreis, *Swift: The Man, the Works, and His Age*, vol. 2 (Cambridge, Mass.: Harvard University Press, 1967), pp. 197–204.

[16]See Melvyn New, "Sterne, Warburton, and the Burden of Exuberant Wit," *Eighteenth-Century Studies* 15 (1982):245–74.

[17]Melvyn New has made the most thoroughgoing analysis of *Tristram Shandy* as satire. The vast variety of tones in satire, ranging from raillery to railing, and of subjects (from general to particular) allow the term to be applied even to mild ridicule. Edward Rosenheim's notion of satire as a generic spectrum is very helpful in this case. But New reads Sterne's satiric criticism as quite harsh, a distinct rejection of sentimentality and of the "amiable humour" traced by Stuart Tave. Although I do not agree with many of New's interpretations, his approach has the advantage of reminding us that Sterne creates his impression of playful tolerance by defusing very explosive materials. See Melvyn New, *Laurence Sterne as Satirist* (Gainesville: University of Florida Press, 1969); Edward W. Rosenheim, *Swift and the Satirist's Art* (Chicago: University of Chicago Press, 1963), esp. pp. 1–34; and Stuart M. Tave, *The Amiable Humorist* (Chicago: University of Chicago Press, 1960).

was a comic battle song credited with as much efficacy in the Revolution of 1688 as any battle hymn of a Celtic bard:

> *Lillubullero* (variously spelt) was said to have been the watchword of the Irish Roman Catholics during their massacre of the Protestants in 1641; later it became the name of a nonsense song ridiculing the Irish Papists, which was extremely popular in England and which, according to Bishop Percy, "slight and insignificant as [it] may now seem, had once a more powerful effect than either the Philippics of Demosthenes, or Cicero; and contributed not a little towards the great revolution in 1688" (*Reliques of Ancient English Poetry*, fourth edition [1794], 2.373). Bishop Burnet testified that the "foolish ballad . . . made an impression on the [English] army, that cannot be well imagined by those who saw it not. The whole army, and at last all people both in city and country, were singing it perpetually. And perhaps never had so slight a thing so great an effect" (*History of His Own Time*, 4.792). [69–70]

Toby whistles the song to "vent his passion" without killing anybody with his scorn. He would not even condemn the Devil to death.

Sterne took Swift's "Vive la bagatelle," but left out his fierce indignation, which was never so fierce as when he acknowledged the probable impotence of his satire. *Tristram Shandy* reads like a cheerful and indulgent version of Swift's *Tale of a Tub*, a hopelessly digressive work supposed to be written by a modern hack writer, so impoverished that he threatens like Tristram to go on writing forever even if he has to write about nothing or fill up his book with quotations. Swift's hack writes formlessly, commentary finally enveloping his story in chaos, an effective symbol of the criticism Swift levels at a whole conglomeration of enemy ideas—Cartesian, mechanical philosophy; mysticism and astrology; Catholic and Calvinist theology; literary critics who denigrate the classics; and many others. Swift's explanation of all these instances, that passions get astride reason and ride for all it is worth, gives rise to Sterne's theory of hobbyhorses.

Sterne takes a forty-five-degree turn on Swift's criticism by rendering it unintimidating. Uncle Toby's miniature fortifications reinvoke Lilliput in *Gulliver's Travels*, but in an affectionate, fanciful mood. Walter's mysterious theories are too eccentric to carry anyone with him (even though Tristram hints there might be some truth in them). Walter would "move both heaven and earth, & twist & torture every thing in nature to support his hypothesis" like the bad people in the

*Tale of the Tub*; but unlike them he has no bad effects. Indeed, he has begun by entertaining his theories as jokes: "he had a thousand little sceptical notions of the comick kind to defend,—most of which notions I verily believe, at first enter'd upon the footing of mere whims, and of a vive la Bagatelle" (I, 19, 53).

Swift's ultimate term in the *Tale of the Tub* for words run away with by the passions is *madness*, the inspiration and the goal of the hack's literary art and other world-subduing enterprises. In *Tristram Shandy* madness reappears as eccentric originality. One Yorkshire use of the word *shandy* recorded in the seventeenth century is "wild"; an eighteenth-century source says,"a little crack-brained, somewhat crazy."[18] Sterne's famous "Lockean" psychology is not the intellectual self-discipline recommended in the *Essay concerning Human Understanding* or in *The Conduct of the Understanding*. In betting on the literary resources of hobbyhorses, Sterne generalizes Locke's theory of madness, the association of ideas, which Locke added in the fourth edition of the *Essay* (Book 2, Chapter 32). The importance of this transvaluation is made clearer when Sterne attacks Locke's conventional opposition between wit (the associative operation of mind) and judgment (the activity of discrimination).[19] Sterne argues that the two go together, and since judgment is so often given superior weight, this amounts to standing up for wit or, rather, sitting down for it. Sterne compares wit and judgment to the two knobs of a chair—a chair he happens to occupy!—and so illustrates the value of wit by a capricious association.

To Locke's insistence that the judgment should strive for "clear and distinct ideas," we may assume that Sterne opposes "the motley emblem of my work" (III, 36, 226), the marbled page, a unique if unreadable design. Sterne teases us about not being able to "pene-

[18]See Kenneth Monkman and J.C.T. Oates, "Towards a Sterne Bibliography," in *The Winged Skull*, p. 280.

[19]See *Tristram Shandy*, "The Author's Preface" (III, 20, 192–203); and John Locke, *An Essay Concerning Human Understanding*, ed. Peter H. Nidditch (Oxford: Clarendon, 1975), p. 156 (bk. II, sec. xi). Contemporaries of Sterne recognized that Locke's doctrine of wit and judgment had also been developed by Hobbes and that both had emphasized the importance of judgment as a curb on wit. See Owen Ruffhead's review of vol. III and IV in the *Monthly Review* 24 (1761):103, as noted in *The Florida Edition of the Works of Laurence Sterne*, vol. 3, ed. Melvyn New, with Richard A. Davis and W. G. Day (Gainesville: University of Florida Press, 1984), p. 238.

trate the moral" of the marbled page or the black page that had followed the account of Yorick's death. In the chapter on wit and judgment Sterne hinted that the literary problem of his time was not that wit was running away with judgment, but rather that both had been drying up until "all of a sudden the sluices shall break out, and take a fit of running again like fury" (III, 20, 197). The contribution of the marbled page and the black page is not more moral but more ink. Sterne's urgency about keeping the ink running has something to do with his openly friendly attitude, so unlike that of Hobbes or of Locke, toward quotation, imitation, and plagiarism.[20] In a parody of Locke's theory of property, Tristram describes Walter's appropriation of opinions from his wide reading as a matter of "mixing up" your own labor with what you find in books. The motley mixture of ink makes an original, unique and crack-brained, which nevertheless shares a family resemblance with other originals.

Far from teaching us to draw a moral from books, some of Walter's odd theories present parodic versions of the idea that words influence lives. His theory of the lifelong influence of proper names is a theory of the moral effect of words. By a set of accidents poor Tristram ends up baptized with the name his father thinks has the worst effects on the people who hold it. The worst effect of the theory that words run lives is the suffering Walter goes through because of his opinion that Tristram's name will ruin his life (remember the epigraph of the novel: not actions but opinions disturb men). Later Walter tries to produce an education for Tristram through the power of auxiliary verbs. The suggestion is that Walter Shandy might write a work on education, his *Tristrapoedia*, but Sterne would never do that.

Sterne ridicules the notion of applying words to make life better in the clerical consulation at the visitation dinner, when Walter and Yorick try (and fail) to get Tristram's name changed. The recalcitrant Phutatorius is burned by a hot chestnut dropped into his breeches.

[20] As Work points out, Sterne parodies attacks on plagiarism by plagiarizing from Burton's attack on plagiarism (V, 1, 342). In an earlier passage, Sterne pretends to long for a time when the arts were not so near perfection, so that a literary man might have a chance to make his mark, but that would be a time when the perfection of writing had ended writing and the end of writing had ended reading and "we shall all have to begin over again" (I, 21, 164). In a doubly silly fantasy he puts his own begetting in this *ab ovo* of culture.

Phutatorius is given advice to apply to his tender part a page of text freshly printed, for the soothing power of the ink is spread out by the type in "sanative particles," more effectively than when applied by a spatula (IV, 28, 325). Unfortunately the text available to Phutatorius is from the second edition of his treatise on concubines, a chapter on "the thing of a concubine."[21] Yorick advises he would do well to stay out of it. People think that Yorick chucked the hot chestnut at Phutatorius "as a sarcastical fling at his book—the doctrines of which, they said, had inflamed many an honest man in the same place" (IV, 27, 323). People believe this, but they are mistaken.[22] This is typical of Sterne's bawdy jokes. It does not function to take us back to any lusty, basic animal nature by breaking down the barriers of modern propriety. Instead, it makes us feel that reading is after all only reading, and writing is only writing, so it is silly for folks to get all worked up about it.

The only act writing affects is the one it effects—more writing. The novel has a way of growing character and action out of its own rhetoric, and this procedure shows how rhetoric makes book not life.[23] Stretching the whole length of the book is the bawdy tease about where Toby got his wound in the groin. Because friends keep asking solicitously about where he got his wound, Toby keeps working on finding a really good map of the battle of Namur, and that leads him to his hobbyhorse of miniature fortifications. The last story of the book, the courtship of Widow Wadman, carries the joke further. Once again Toby produces the map to show where he got his wound.

[21]I have accepted the translation of Sterne's phrase *de re concubinaria* in the Florida edition, 3:327.

[22]Cash identifies Phutatorius, the vengeful leader of the conspiracy against Yorick and the keeper of concubines, as Sterne's uncle. Jaques Sterne, who had died a year and a half earlier, disappointed Sterne by leaving all his money to his mistress. But, as Cash notes, if this identification were made, everyone at York was too discreet to mention it. See Cash, *Laurence Sterne*, p. 289. I find this too coy for satire; or, rather, the satire has modulated from the punitive to the self-expressive and self-pitying.

[23]The most important study of rhetoric and play in *Tristram Shandy* is Richard A. Lanham, "*Tristram Shandy*": *The Games of Pleasure* (Berkeley: University of California Press, 1973). Lanham argues that Sterne combines the rhetorical treatise with domestic fiction to create a deliberate incongruity of public terms and private life which makes language a "*ludus*, a knowing public display of rhetoric, a game" and man an incorrigible role player (p. 29).

The sentimental praise of Toby's good nature, which so many readers have been willing to accept as the teaching of the book, appears in the form of overliteralizing a figure of speech. Tristram writes that Uncle Toby "had scarce a heart to retaliate upon a fly":

> Go—says he, one day at dinner, to an over-grown one which had buzz'd about his nose, and tormented him cruelly all dinner-time,—and which, after infinite attempts, he had caught at last, as it flew by him;—I'll not hurt thee, says my uncle *Toby*, rising from his chair, and going a-cross the room, with the fly in his hand,—I'll not hurt a hair of thy head:—Go, says he, lifting up the sash, and opening his hand as he spoke, to let it escape;—go poor devil, get thee gone, why should I hurt thee?—This world surely is wide enough to hold both thee and me.
>
> I was but ten years old when this happened; but whether it was, that the action itself was more in unison to my nerves at that age of pity, which instantly set my frame into one vibration of most pleasurable sensation;—or how far the manner and expression of it might go towards it;—or in what degree, or by what secret magic,—a tone of voice and harmony of movement, attuned by mercy, might find a passage to my heart, I know not;—this I know, that the lesson of universal good-will then taught and imprinted by my uncle *Toby*, has never since been worn out of my mind: And tho' I would not depreciate what the study of the *Literae humaniores*, at the university, have done for me in that respect, or discredit the other helps of an expensive education bestowed upon me, both at home and abroad since; —yet I often think that I owe one half of my philanthropy to that one accidental impression.
>
> ☞ This is to serve for parents and governors instead of a whole volume upon the subject. [II, 12, 113–14]

One way to read this passage is that the idea of literature as moral education is the product of words run away with themselves. Even a more forceful reading of this passage preserves the notion of books as play and ends up by letting Walter off the hook: though he is a negligent father who only fools with words and does not educate his son, his son gets an education by shorthand. Either way, you do not have to waste words on morality; you can use them instead to make pure book.

Sterne has told Pitt, in the dedication to the second edition of Volumes One and Two, that "I live in a constant endeavour to fence against the infirmities of ill health, and other evils of life, by mirth."

This image of a life of writing to fence against life is read by many critics as a flight from death, an ultimate meaning or purpose for the text.[24] But a memento mori that teaches the forgetting of death rather than the remembering of it is not very likely to use death instructively to remind us to live well. Tristram's flight from death in Book Seven is the most sheerly parodic part of *Tristram Shandy*: the instructive purposes of a travel book are mocked, and instead it threatens to collapse into a list; important places are not worth describing, and even a famous tomb turns out not to be there. For all its parody the book becomes more bookish when it flees death. A fence against death is also a fence against life.

However much Sterne's "scenes of play" remind us of the later romantic creation of an aesthetic realm, they are more explicitly coordinated with conventional authority and conventional morality. The scene of play in Sterne is so free because we are constantly reassured that someone else somewhere else (like Pitt when he is not relaxing in the country) is taking reasonably good care of things, looking after the state. Not everyone is retired. It is important to understand that the book does not claim that its "play" is a model of the whole of reality. The sermon drifts into the scene of time-killing leisure, but it came from the hands of a member of the established clergy, and it eventually got back into the pulpit, Sterne's own pulpit, as he hints, when he names the place and date of its first delivery and publication:

> Can the reader believe, that this sermon of *Yorick's* was preach'd at an assize, in the Cathedral of *York*, before a thousand witnesses, ready

[24]For the "tragic" humanist version of this reading, see W.B.C. Watkins, *Perilous Balance: The Tragic Genius of Swift, Johnson, and Sterne* (Cambridge, Mass.: Boar's Head, 1960), pp. 99–156. William V. Holtz argues that a fruitful, picture-making imaginative evasion of the journey to death dominates *Tristram Shandy*, except in Volume Seven, where narrative progress threatens the final ending until distance from death and narrative is regained in Volume Eight. See *Image and Immortality*, pp. 127–34. James E. Swearingen distinguishes between Walter's evasion of death as an empirical necessity and Tristram's reflexive, ontological understanding of the dimensions of his being and the mystery of things which reaches beyond the boundaries of finitude. For these reasons Swearingen believes that Tristram's book is "about the domain of potency, freedom, and the future as transcending actuality, necessity and the past" (p. 255). My view is that these impressions of freedom make the book literary but not ontological. In any case Swearingen would agree that Sterne is not in the usual sense "ethical." See *Reflexivity in "Tristram Shandy": An Essay in Phenomenological Criticism* (New Haven: Yale University Press, 1977), pp. 97–139.

> to give an oath of it, by a certain prebendary of that church, and actually printed by him when he had done,—and within so short a space as two years and three months after *Yorick's* death.—*Yorick*, indeed, was never better served in his life!—but it was a little hard to male-treat him before, and plunder him after he was laid in his grave.
>
> However, as the gentleman who did it, was in perfect charity with *Yorick*,—and, in conscious justice, printed but a few copies to give away;—and that, I am told he could moreover have made as good a one himself, had he thought fit,—I declare I would not have published the anecdote to the world;—nor do I publish it with an intent to hurt his character and advancement in the church;—I leave that to others;—but I find myself impelled by two reasons, which I cannot withstand.
>
> The first is, That, in doing justice, I may give rest to *Yorick's* ghost —which, as the country people,—and some others, believe,—*still walks*.
>
> The second reason is, That, by laying open this story to the world, I gain an opportunity of informing it,—That in case the character of Parson *Yorick* and this sample of his sermons is liked,—that there are now in the possession of the Shandy family, as many as will make a handsome Volume, at the world's service,—and much good may they do it. [II, 17, 142–43]

Of course this is a shameless plug. It gives you clues to identify the author of the novel with Parson Yorick and to interest yourself in his other publications, especially his sermons. In the course of publishing *Tristram Shandy*, Sterne does bring out four volumes of his sermons as the sermons of Mr. Yorick, and he is rewarded for his literary accomplishments by the promotions in the church he hinted at in this passage. However much Sterne's novel may parody the moral ideal of books making life, it does recognize the economic effect: that books make livings. Sterne wants this novel and the sermon in it to go into circulation. The playful mechanisms, surprises, and hints in Sterne's book create a curious public of consumers who want to be let in on the joke, and from the beginning of his novelistic career Sterne uses his identity as another odd joke for those who like to be in the know.

Sterne was an excellent self-advertiser, beginning with the letter he wrote impersonating his actress friend Kitty Fourmantel so that she could effectually recommend the first two volumes to Garrick and get him to recommend them to all of London. Sterne suggests (in her name) that a scandal rages over this clergyman who wrote a book the graver people say is "not fit for young ladies to read" (*Letters*, 86). Sterne knew that association with famous people like Garrick and Hogarth would improve his own fame, and he showed particular interest in circulating copies of his portraits by Reynolds and Carmontelle. Impressed by the unusually extensive report on Sterne in the *Royal Female Magazine*, Wilbur Cross was led to claim, "Sterne was in truth the first writer about whom people cared much to know how he lived, how he looked, and what he did when among his friends" (*Life*, 1:201).

However much it functioned as commercial expedient, the identification of the author of *Tristram Shandy* as a clergyman is made political by the sermon on the abuses of conscience, because the sermon recognizes the authority of law over the conscience. In the sermon Sterne dramatizes different ways conscience is made untrustworthy by passion, including two prominent accounts of the ways it has been perverted by the doctrines and practices of the Catholic church: "O Popery! what hast thou to answer for?" (II, 17, 131). Originally delivered in 1750, the sermon can be seen as a remnant of the anti-Catholic propaganda organized through the state church to consolidate the nation against the Jacobite upraising of 1745. The point of the two long diatribes against Catholicism is that the authoritarian institutions, including the "black tribunal" of the Inquisition, interfered with the "sacred court" of conscience. This authoritarian attitude is illustrated by Dr. Slop's initial objections to the "liberty of the press" taken by the sermon in disputing the words of Saint Paul.

Arthur Cash describes the "Sermon on the Abuses of Conscience": "By a clergyman who is also a justice of the peace, it is written for an assembly of judges, yet it comments on the inadequacy of human laws and the obligation to obey the higher, unwritten laws of reason and religion."[25] But the Protestant emphasis on conscience as a better guide than law does not exclude the force of law, especially not the laws that enforce Protestantism: "human laws not being a matter of original choice, but of pure necessity, brought in to fence against the mischievous effects of those consciences which are no law unto themselves" (II, 17, 133). At the end of the sermon, we reach a

[25]Cash, *Laurence Sterne*, p. 234.

typically English compromise: "your conscience is not a law:—No, God and reason made the law, and have placed conscience within you to determine;—not like an *Asiatic* Cadi, according to the ebbs and flows of his own passions,—but like a *British* judge in this land of liberty and good sense, who makes no new law, but faithfully declares that law which he knows already written" (II, 17, 140). Freedom of conscience is safe because it will declare what the law has already written. The position is not exactly authoritarian, but it is not antiauthoritarian, except by comparison. The British judge will keep out the law of the papist and so leave the conscience free.

One of Sterne's sources for the sermon, Swift's sermon "On the Testimony of Conscience," is much clearer about the political realities of conscience.[26] Swift makes the distinction, conventional in Anglican apologetics, between the knowledge of moral law necessary for salvation and available to conscience and the knowledge of points not available to conscience and not absolutely necessary to salvation (largely matters of religious ritual), which must be prescribed by authorized teachers. Like Hobbes, Swift reassures his readers that liberty of conscience, in the sense of knowing one's own thoughts, can never be taken away; but he condemns liberty of conscience in the sense of propagating private beliefs and overthrowing "the Faith which the Laws have already established."[27] In leaving these sections behind, Sterne was not abandoning the authority of the church establishment over papists and Protestant sectarians. He was taking it so much for granted that he assumed it did not require a defense, only the usual fences.

The sermon appears as play in the novel, but it assures us that the free play of the novel is circumscribed by law. We are reminded that there are times and places for law as well as for play. Furthermore, the sermon in the living room aids the political project. The social rather than religious setting forces Dr. Slop the Catholic to listen, with however many captious remarks, to an Anglican sermon. But the atmosphere is the golden haze of English liberalism. Dr. Slop

[26]On plagiarism in Sterne's sermons, see Lansing van der Leyden Hammond, *Laurence Sterne's "Sermons of Mr. Yorick"* (New Haven: Yale University Press, 1948).

[27]Jonathan Swift, *Irish Tracts and Sermons*, ed. Herbert Davis and Louis Landa (Oxford: Blackwell, 1963), p. 151.

falls asleep during the first impassioned indictment of his religion, and he is later moved to sympathize with Trim's sadness over his brother's imprisonment by the Inquisition. We can have the scene of play because the state is settled, the Catholics are reasonably comfortable in their place, which is to say, they are kept out of political places.

The "compleasance" of the scene in the parlor, the ability of all parties to make room for differences of opinion and experience and even enjoy them, is contained by complacency about the establishment. Walter's "frank acknowledgment" of the sinners in the Protestant church brings Dr. Slop to admit that a man in the Romish church might live as badly, but then they begin to skirmish over the value of the last sacrament. Toby breaks it up with an innocent curiosity:

> Pray, how many have you in all, said my uncle *Toby*,—for I always forget—Seven, answered *Dr. Slop*.—Humph!—said my uncle *Toby*; tho' not accented as a note of acquiescence,—but as an interjection of that particular species of surprize, when a man, in looking into a drawer, finds more of a thing than he expected.—Humph! replied my uncle *Toby*. Dr. Slop, who had an ear, understood my uncle *Toby* as well as if he had wrote a whole volume against the seven sacraments. [II, 17, 129]

Toby's polite forgetfulness and his unworried surprise relegate Catholicism further to the sidelines than elaborate polemics could have done. Walter and Tristram are closer to conventional satire in their ironic antiquarian appreciation of Catholic oddments. Toby's more unreflective demotions have the effect of keeping the peace on Protestant terms without making war. Whistling "Lillabullero" was probably safer when Sterne was writing in 1759, after the decisive victory over the Jacobites in 1745, than it was in 1718, the fictional date. Sterne has projected the stability of the 1750s back onto the earlier period as if it were a set of soldierly good habits (the good conscience pronounces like the British magistrate).

In Volume Five, during the reading of the *Tristrapoedia*, Yorick interrupts Walter's philosophical derivation of political authority from paternal authority to say he can read all about the honor due to parents in the catechism without following Walter through Justinian's Institutes. Trim shows his knowledge of the catechism by running through from the beginning to the Fifth Commandment as a demonstration of the manual of arms under the command of Toby. Walter, reasonably enough, wants to test this rote knowledge: "What do'st thou mean, by '*honouring thy father and mother*'? Allowing them, an' please your honour, three halfpence a day out of my pay, when they grew old." Yorick pronounces authoritatively on this answer, "Thou art the best commentator upon that part of the *Decalogue*; and I honour thee more for it, Corporal Trim, than if thou hadst had a hand in the Talmud itself" (v, 32, 393). This chapter reduces the image of living by moral law to habit. As in Hobbes's theory and in the state church Sterne knew, patriarchalist justifications of monarchy are replaced by a customary association of filial reverence with political obedience. There is no Lockean possibility of the dissolution of government. The laws of the catechism are too familiar to be quoted, much less debated. The asterisks that Sterne inserts in place of the earlier part of the catechism are among Sterne's least suggestive asterisks.

John Traugott has argued that Sterne's parodic investigations of weak places in Locke's epistemology and theory of language led him toward Hume's emphasis on the constitutive role of association of ideas (especially that kind of association of ideas known as sympathy) in the formation of customary beliefs.[28] Although Traugott chiefly refers to Books One and Two of Hume's *Treatise*, his argument could be extended to the treatment of ethics and politics in Book Three and in the essays. As a critic of Locke's theory of original contract, Hume argues a more gradual and less formalized process of socialization. Governance and obedience begin in the family, so consent becomes a gradual awareness of the advantages of social habits. Hobbesian compleasance, the sanding down of the rough stones in the social edifice, is more a set of practices than an explicit law:

> The parents govern by the advantage of their superior strength and wisdom, and at the same time are restrain'd in the exercise of their authority by that natural affection, which they bear their children. In a little time, custom and habit operating on the tender minds of the children, makes them sensible of the advantages, which they may reap from society, as well as fashions them for it, by rubbing off

[28] John Traugott, *Tristram Shandy's World: Sterne's Philosophical Rhetoric* (Berkeley: University of California Press, 1954), pp. 19, 48, 73–74, 156n.

> those rough corners and untoward affections, which prevent their coalition.[29]

Similarly, in Hume's account of the origin of property, explicit promises are not necessary; there are many ways to "express" a general sense of common interest in observing the rules of property, "since the actions of each of us have a reference to those of the other, and are perform'd upon the supposition, that something is to be perform'd on the other part. Two men, who pull the oars of a boat do it by agreement or convention, tho' they have never given promises to each other" (*Treatise*, III, II, ii, 542). This image of a conventional rule that is understood as a practice does not seem very far from Trim's muscular Christianity and connects to his expressive physical dexterity throughout the novel. Like Hume, Sterne wants to show that beliefs that are held as habits rather than as articulated conclusions of reason nevertheless serve the purposes of life.

In its emphasis on custom Hume's picture of morality seems closer to Sterne than to Richardson. Although moral discourse is an important medium of morality for Hume, he does not resemble Richardson in putting explicit reasoning about rules at the center of ordinary moral activity. To expect this sort of continuous rational activity seems unrealistic to Hume. In "Of Original Contract" Hume argues, "Obedience or subjection becomes so familiar, that most men never make any enquiry about its origin or cause, more than about the principle of gravity, resistance, or the most universal laws of nature," and that many people "suppose themselves born under obligations of obedience to a certain sovereign, as much as under the ties of reverence and duty to certain parents."[30] Although Hume invokes such common views as a rebuke to refined philosophers such as Locke for their unrealistic and impractical claims about consent, he does not stand with the customary belief in the way Sterne and Yorick do. In Hume customary beliefs do not all have the same philosophical status; he makes an especially sharp distinction between the immediate propensity toward family obligations on the

[29]David Hume, *A Treatise of Human Nature*, ed. Ernest C. Mossner (Harmondsworth: Penguin, 1969), III, II, ii, 538.

[30]"Of Original Contract," in *Essays Moral, Political, and Literary*, ed. T. H. Green and T. H. Grose (London: Longmans, Green, 1875), 1:446.

one hand and on the other the artificial rules of property and government that have social utility as their sole consideration.

Making distinctions between different ways sympathy operates (immediately or by reflection on individual or social utility) and between different degrees of utility allows Hume to negotiate very turbulent political waters in "Of Original Contract, "which was published in 1748, only a few years after the Jacobite uprising of 1745. The obligation to political allegiance is absolutely necessary for the subsistence of society, even though it cannot be derived from more universal rules of morality such as keeping promises or obeying fathers, so this part of Hume's argument reinforces the position of the Hanoverian government, but on anticontractual grounds. Yet Hume's reasoning about the arbitrary laws governing succession and the particular objects of allegiance suggests that, at the very least, Jacobite loyalty to an established succession is based on a principle not more unnatural or immoral or politically dangerous than the Whig principle of consent. The settlement of the Glorious Revolution appears in this account as a very modest alteration in the succession of the monarchy, which is relatively safe because the democratic and aristocratic parts of the government maintain a "sufficient stability." Hume's non-Christian antirationalism pares down the philosophical and historical claims of the establishment, suggests a sympathetic explanation of the attitudes of its opponents, and at the same time manages to side with the use of innovations in the interests of liberty.[31] A comparable tolerance for Jacobite errors, though vague and unargued, may be detected in Sterne's assigning to Trim the name James Butler, which was the name of the Duke of Ormond who fled to the Jacobites when he was accused of treason in 1715. But perhaps Sterne's point is only, once again, Protestant loyalty, since Ormond was a Jacobite who never converted to Catholicism.

We cannot describe Sterne's use of customary belief as Humean in the sequence we have been examining in Volume Five, where the patriarchal political philosophy of the *Tristrapoedia* (Chapter 31) is replaced by the practical filial reverence of Trim's catechism (Chap-

[31]Duncan Forbes suggests that Hume was trying to replace vulgar Whiggism with "scientific Whiggism." See *Hume's Philosophical Politics* (Cambridge: Cambridge University Press, 1975).

ter 32). Customary morality often appears in *Tristram Shandy* as an antiphilosophical part of soldierly brusqueness, a brief and reassuring reminder that the heart of the author is in the right place and that the laws are in place.[32] Sterne supports liberty in Hobbes's sense, the wide discretion in "cases where the Sovereign has prescribed no rule." In the last volume of the novel Toby interrupts Walter's discourse on the two kinds of love to say, "What signifies it, brother *Shandy*, . . . which of the two it is, provided it will make a man marry, and love his wife, and get a few children" (VIII, 33, 585–86). Walter promises to be like a father to the hypothetical children, Toby squeezes his hand, and Yorick once more praises the soldierly "plain sense." Sterne's incipient debate on the value of sexual love is replaced by the marriage contract, which makes "plain sense."

The reduction of speculative power in Sterne's morality is particularly visible in the treatment of gender. In the course of arguing with Walter's patriarchal political theory (V, xxxi), Yorick opens up the question of the mother's authority over the child. Although Walter cites Politian and Justinian, Yorick's objections follow the path of Hobbes and Locke in their refutation of Filmer. This question, which was so important tothe moral debates of *Clarissa*, disappears in the next chapter, when Yorick approves of Trim's practical divinity. Sterne may invite us to laugh at Walter for trying to monopolize authority by leaving the mother out of procreation, but laughing at this strategy does not mean abjuring it, since Walter has already laughed at the legal judgment "*that the mother is not of kin to her child*" (IV, 29, 328). Like Walter, Sterne laughs at such misogyny, but he also enacts it. Tristram's mother, like all the Shandy women except Aunt Dinah, "had no character at all," and so hardly at all belongs to the Shandy family of originals, "I mean the males" (I, 21, 65). Having no hobbyhorses, "my mother" has nothing to pass on to Tristram in the way of opinions. She is not exactly all there during his engendering, since she was thinking about the clock, so she does not know what her husband means when he weeps, "*My Tristram's misfortunes began nine months before he ever came into the world.*"

[32]See Toby's religious consolations when Walter grieves over Tristram's nose; e.g., Walter: "There is a secret spring within us—Which spring, said my uncle *Toby*, I take to be Religion" (IV, vii, 278–79).

Tristram and Toby know, but "she knew no more than her backside what my father meant" (I, 3, 7).

To know her backside is not to know nothing. Women in *Tristram Shandy* are as sexually alert as the men are sexually inattentive (being more concerned with riding hobbyhorses), and the rights that interest them are conjugal rights, narrowly defined. "My mother" has not much use for words, but her body sense refutes Walter's elaborate arguments for technological male midwifery. His arguments in favor of cesarean sections she refutes by turning pale as ashes (II, 19, 153). In their negotiation over the merits of a man-midwife:

> What could my father do? He was almost at his wit's end;—talked it over with her in all moods;—placed his arguments in all lights;—argued the matter with her like a christian,—like a heathen,—like a husband,—like a father,—like a patriot,—like a man:—My mother answered every thing only like a woman; which was a little hard upon her;—for as she could not assume and fight it out behind such a variety of characters,—'twas no fair match;—'twas seven to one.—What could my mother do?—She had the advantage (otherwise she had certainly been overpowered) of a small reinforcement of chagrin personal at the bottom which bore her up, and enabled her to dispute the affair with my father with so equal an advantage,—that both sides sung *Te Deum*. [I, 18, 48]

Even Toby understands her "chagrin personal at the bottom": "My sister, I dare say, added he, does not care to let a man come so near her ****" (II, 6, 100).

Walter resents the female rights of birth: "From the very moment the mistress of the house is brought to bed, every female in it, from my lady's gentlewoman down to the cinder-wench, becomes an inch taller for it" (IV, 12, 284). Walter, it has been explained, feels in many ways short. But there is no special maternal authority that derives from the authority of "my mother's" body. Even though Walter's absorption in the *Tristrapoedia* leaves Tristram to his mother's care, our narrator shows nothing of her influence. When Walter seeks her advice about Tristram's breeches, speaking no doubt peremptorily like the French king in a "bed of justice," "my mother" echoes all of his assertions quite patiently in a way that frustrates his love of argument. Her lack of eagerness to participate in the male Shandy project of protracting discourse has something to do with the time of month; it is the first Sunday of the month, when Walter habitually brings all his family concernments into order. The women have the honor of potency denied to the men; they can bring forth something. But it is not the honor associated with moral action; theirs is activity in the service of body. Women have been referred back from culture to nature. The women's bodily instincts are cast as the polar opposites of the men's wordy play: the women keep biology going, the men keep the book going, and the two do not very often go together (no more than once a month).

Walter's wish to keep women and their matters in their place is helped along by the narrative pattern of the book. The wonderfully long extended joke about Tristram's difficult four-volume birth consigns the women to the childbed for two years and keeps them out of the parlor where they might mix in conversation with the men. This segregation of women from men seems anachronistic. The polite modern culture of the early eighteenth century boasted of the new mingling of women and men in the audience for the essay and the novel, an audience supposedly too civilized for the things that go on in the Shandy parlor—pedantry, bawdy, and smoking. Only the narrator's references to "Madame" and "Jenny" preserve that sense of mixed company, and they seem like provocative invitations for ladies to peer in on a male club. With the exceptions of his embarrassing, uncultivated mother and sister, who hounded him for money, Sterne's own relationships with women were usually of the modern, civilized variety, sentimental flirtations with women of some intellectual pretensions. In spite of difficulties with his wife, Sterne seems to have enjoyed writing letters to her, and he drew from these letters for the *Journal to Eliza*.

It would seem, therefore, that the misogyny of *Tristram Shandy* is a deliberate anachronism, something new, rather than the unbroken lineage of something old. Rather than attributing this effect to the tradition of learned wit or satire, or calling it masculinity, it should probably be called something like "remasculinization." The modern domesticated male, who fears that his civilized polish and sensitive feeling is a kind of womanishness, finds a new way of asserting his masculine superiority over the women he comes close to. So in *Tristram Shandy*, as in much modern art of male sentimentality, sentimental man excludes sentimental woman.[33] The domestic couple that focuses our sentimental feelings is not husband and wife but the two brothers, or in different scenes, Toby and Trim. We are even led to feel outraged that Widow Wadman would fake an interest in fortifications to horn in on the older, more established relation. When Toby asks Trim to write down her perfections and put "humanity" at top of the list, it is the last straw. Humanity? Women only want one thing.

It is a strength of Hobbes's system that he stressed competition, not just in property and status, but more broadly competition in honor. If sensitivity and modesty become cherished social values, there will be competition for these honors. For Hume, any sort of vanity was a promising social emotion; that competition in humanity or sensitivity could be destructive would have been inconceivable to him, but not to Hobbes. Eventually we will see Burke forge a powerful new reactionary rhetoric of male sensitivity.

Trim might well be jealous of Toby's mistaken belief that the Widow Wadman's concern for his wound is compassion, since he and Toby have enacted real compassion at the bedside of Le Fever. In this episode, a great favorite with the original reviewers, a sequence of male nurses and comforters replaces the traditional female figures. First the compassionate landlord of the village inn comes to Toby's house to beg a glass or two of sack for the sick lieutenant. He arouses compassionate curiosity about the lieutenant, especially when he mentions the affecting circumstance of the young son who "has not stirred from the bedside these two days" (VI, 6, 417). When Trim arrives at the inn, he tenderly takes over the toasting fork from the hands of the dutiful son, whose tears he arouses by the mention of the military connection: "his honour will not like the toast the worst for being toasted by an old soldier" (VI, 7, 420).

The sole female figure in the scene, the landlady, serves only as a neutral chorus, who sets the scene by announcing the probable death of the lieutenant. The landlord informs Trim and the curate, who sits

[33]The argument on remasculinization draws on Carol Kay, "Canon, Ideology, and Gender: Mary Wollstonecraft's Critique of Adam Smith," *New Political Science*, no. 15 (1986):63–76. Examples of this structure in our time could be found in movies that show men "fathering," such as *Kramer versus Kramer* and *Ordinary People*. The sensitive father is conceived as mother, and if the father mothers, then there is no need for the mother, so she must be sent away as inadequate or unnecessary.

by the fire at the inn and offers no "comfort," that the boy has made preparations for assisting his father's prayers. In the gap between the landlord's detection of these preparations for prayer and Trim's observation of the signs that the prayers have taken place, Trim defends the piety of soldiers against the curate's superior airs. This speech is perhaps even more successful in exemplifying soldierly piety than was Trim's demonstration of the catechism, since its vigor contrasts with the weakness of the soldier on his deathbed, and yet it lends the whole sequence a particularly masculine air:

> A soldier, an' please your reverence, said I, prays as often (of his own accord) as a parson;—and when he is fighting for his king, and for his own life, and for his honour too, he has the most reason to pray to God, of anyone in the whole world— . . .— But when a soldier, said I, has been standing for twelve hours together in the trenches, up to his knees in cold water,—or engaged, said I, for months together in long and dangerous marches;—harassed, perhaps in his rear today;—harassing others tomorrow;—detached here;—countermanded there;—resting this night out upon his arms;—beat up in his shirt the next;—benumbed in his joints;—perhaps without straw in his tent to kneel on;—must say his prayers *how* and *when* he can. [VI, 7, 421]

Christian worship has been reimagined without priesthood (a good piece of Protestantism), but also without women. The next scene brings Toby to the deathbed to mother the orphaned boy. At the moment of his father's death, the boy turns to Toby, having "taken hold of the breast of his coat and . . . pulling it towards him" (VI, 10, 426).

The exclusion of the comforting mother is effected with an astonishing turn on Toby's modesty. Le Fever had identified himself to Trim as an officer in Toby's regiment, but more memorably as a figure in a romantic story. He was "the ensign at Breda whose wife was most unfortunately killed with a musket shot, as she lay in my arms in my tent" (422). Reminded of this story by Trim (perhaps in a considerately censored version), Toby remembers "that he, as well as she, upon some account or other (I forget what) was universally pitied by the whole regiment" (423). For once, Sterne has succeeded in making sexuality a touching index of human fragility, rather than a funny exposure of weakness, and Toby's typical repression of sexual knowledge seems to strike just the right note of sad forgetfulness.

Trim's delicate concern for Toby throughout the episode frames and repeats the comfort both of them have given to other men.

The special achievement of masculine solidarity in tenderness seems impossible when the mother is alive. The sentimental reminiscence about the death of Le Fever's wife in the arms of her husband repeats in a different mood the more evasive and comical allusions of Walter Shandy, when he responds to the news of the death of his son Bobby by taking refuge in a quotation. Walter ends a long list of ways of death with Cornelius Gallus, who died, "as **************—And if it was with his wife, said my uncle *Toby*—there could be no hurt in it.—That's more than I know—replied my father" (V, 4, 357). In the hall Tristram's mother overhears the word *wife* and bends her head to listen at the crack of the parlor door like the "listening slave." In this undignified position Tristram leaves her for several chapters while he praises Trim's funeral oration for Bobby, forgetting his mother (who still knows nothing of Bobby's death), "as if Nature had plaistered me up, and set me down naked upon the banks of the river *Nile*, without one" (V, 11, 367). In the parlor Walter launches into a convincing performance of Socrates' oration before his judges. "My mother" listens with composure and a vague sense of familiarity until she hears Walter pronounce the part of the oration that Socrates had said should not be affecting, that "I have three desolate children":

> Then, cried my mother, opening the door,—you have one more, Mr. *Shandy*, than I know of.
>
> By heaven! I have one less,—said my father, getting up and walking out of the room. [V, 13, 370]

This abrupt comedown from the oratorical heights of Walter's quotations and Trim's spontaneous eloquence is less a comic deflation than a hard thing delivered in an unhappy marriage, a step onto the threshold of a very different sort of novel. A brief chapter follows in which Toby "most kindly" but also absolutely silently leads "my mother" out to meet her husband to hear the news, and then in the next chapter Tristram draws our attention to his narration with manic fiddling, as if to drown out the memory of what has just preceded. "My mother's" silence is never endowed with the affecting humanity of Toby's incapacity for speech. The omission of her mourning makes the novel do what Walter did: keep her out of the parlor and turn its back on her when she comes in.

Indulgent anachronism, "remasculinization," as I have called it, is not just a matter of keeping play and politics in their separate places (letting sleeping dogs lie, as Sir Robert Walpole put it). It is play that can be used in a new politics. The most important bearer of this political potentiality is the sentimental soldier, Toby Shandy. Disputes about whether Toby should be read satirically or sentimentally rarely weigh the many kinds of evidence in *Tristram Shandy* that Sterne likes war. Walter tells Yorick that if anyone else but Toby had conducted those imitation battles, "it would have been looked upon by the world as one of the most refined satyrs upon the parade and the prancing manner in which *Lewis* XIV from the beginning of the war, but particularly that very year, had taken the field" (VI, 23, 446–47). That is, the satire, if there is any, can only be on the war as conducted by the enemy. The elaborate order of the book was first shown to be orderly, not chaotic, because a chronology of events can be constructed upon the framework of dated battles that Toby participated in as a soldier or as a play-pretend soldier.[34]

The late seventeenth-century wars in which Toby participated protected the Glorious Revolution and Protestant William against the growing power of the French king and his support of the exiled Catholic kings of England. The Duke of Marlborough, England's greatest military hero, is an important figure for the action of the novel because Toby's second retirement is caused by Marlborough's political defeat at the hands of Swift and other Tories, who dismissed him from his generalship and brought his wars to an end with the much execrated Treaty of Utrecht in 1713–14. Toby, who has been eagerly following Marlborough's progress in the newspapers and mounting his battles in the bowling green, is now without his occupation and becomes vulnerable to the Widow Wadman. Once again, Sterne is on the other side from the Augustan satirists.

Sterne's father was a soldier of Marlborough's, and Sterne was born in 1713, just in this period of decline for the English army. After the demolition of Dunkirk, Sterne's father was stationed in Ireland in poor quarters that were Sterne's first memories, and he

[34]See Theodore Baird, "The Time-Scheme of *Tristram Shandy* and a Source," *PMLA* 51 (1936):803–20.

died of fever in Jamaica, an unheroic and unhealthy setting. The displacement of the narrative from Tristram, born in 1718, to Toby's and Walter's lives enacts political nostalgia for the time when Whigs were warrior-heroes fighting for the Protestant succession, not Walpole Whigs trading offices like Sterne's Uncle Jaques. To end the book in 1713 is to bring it up to the date of Sterne's birth and thus almost entirely to exclude the political history of his own time. Can the window's "circumcision" of Tristram, which caused such rumors, be coordinated with Walpole's rise to power in the early 1720s? Tristram's European travels in 1741 take him away from the scene of Sterne's own Walpolean campaign. In any case, it is striking that whenever Sterne touches down on politics, it comes to the sentimental unity of the nation at war. Even in his brief period as a Whig propagandist (1741–42), Sterne was able to defend an administration at war, for Walpole had finally given in to Tory objections to his policy of conciliating Spain and had gone to war in 1739. So Sterne could charge the Tories who complained about Walpole's war with hypocritical antipatriotism.[35]

In 1760 Sterne dedicated the reprint of the first two volumes of *Tristram Shandy* to William Pitt, the extremely popular minister who had been conducting another war since 1757. Pitt had been a member of the opposition group of "Boy Patriots," and he had maintained a reputation for integrity when others of his group appeared to be bought off by office in 1742. Walpole had made him a martyr by dismissing him from a cornetcy, and as paymaster of the forces he had refused the usual large revenues. When he entered administration to conduct the war he had a reputation for patriotism above party and personal interest. We can imagine the kind of psychological satisfaction Sterne would take in himself rising above party to hail this popular hero, whose greatest victories began in 1759, the year of the first volumes of *Tristram Shandy*. In Volume Three Sterne delicately hints that the gushing out of wit and judgment which might be associated with his book could be linked to the new, world-transforming military successes: "in writing and fighting and twenty other gallant things, we drive all the world before us"

[35]See the text of Sterne's "first book," his election pamphlet *Query upon Query, Being an Answer to J.S.'s Letter Printed in the York Courant* (York, 1741), esp. queries 2 and 3; in Curtis, *Politicks*, 47–58.

(III, 20, 197). The last volume of *Tristram Shandy* is dedicated to Pitt, by then become Lord Chatham, but by 1767 some interesting changes had come about in Chatham's career and life.

Sterne's triumphant trip to London in 1760, when he found his book so popular, gave him a political jolt. George III had succeeded to the throne and threatened to topple the system of Whig oligarchic political management. Though George's ideal of the patriot king developed from the sort of opposition anticourt patriotic ideals that Pitt was identified with and that had been developed by Swift's ally Viscount Bolingbroke, George and his former tutor Lord Bute were hostile to Pitt and to his war, and they were working toward peace. You can hear in Sterne's letters a confusion that afflicted him and everyone else of his generation: after the twenty years of Walpole's wheeling and dealing, succeeded by Newcastle's management of Walpole's "Old Corps" Whigs, it suddenly seemed the rules would be changed.

Sterne writes to his friend Stephen Croft:

> I wish you was here to see what changes of looks and political reasoning, have taken place in every company, and coffee-house since last year; we shall soon be Prussian and anti-Prussians, B[ute's] and anti B[ute]s, and those distinctions will do just as well as Whig and Tory—and for ought I know serve the same ends.—The king seems determined to bring all back to their original principles, and to stop the torrent of corruption and laziness.— . . . The present system being to remove that Phalanx of great people, which stood betwixt the throne and the subjects, and suffer them to have immediate access without the intervention of a caball—(this is the language of others): however the K[ing] gives every thing himself, knows every thing, and weighs every thing maturely, and then is inflexible—this puts the old stagers off their game—how it will end we are all in the dark. [*Letters*, 126]

Sterne expresses excitement at the notion of a patriot king without endorsing the attack on the Whig oligarchy ("the caball") that he has served.

Later he feels disappointment at the sudden popularity of the idea of peace and has some sympathy with the debates in Parliament which compared the shameful projected peace to the shameful Treaty of Utrecht in 1713, which gave away so much of the territory Marlborough had won (*Letters*, 129). In Volume Three of *Tristram*

*Shandy* there may be a brief cautious reference to the new order under George III: "Our government has been turning on its hinges" (III, 22, 204). The debate over the cost of the war may appear in Walter's caution, "Take my word,—dear *Toby*, they will in the end quite ruin your fortune and make a beggar of you.—What signifies it if they do, brother, replied my uncle *Toby*, so long as we know it is for the good of the nation" (III, 22, 205–6). The debate on the fall of Strasbourg to the French at the end of "Slawkenbergius' Tale" also hints at the debates about the war (particularly about the controversial continental theater). One side claims that the fear of standing armies exposed Strasbourg to the French, another that the weakness came from excessive national debt (IV, 271), but Sterne backs off from the debate and attributes the fall of Strasbourg to curiosity about noses. A little later he warns us against thinking he means by uncle Toby's character the "militiating spirits of my country" (IV, 22, 301).

At stake in Pitt's career is a struggle for possession of a new national political imagery that would engage the affections and represent the wishes of people who felt excluded by the politics of the Whig oligarchy.[36] Pitt was in trouble in 1760 because the king could bear that symbolism more easily than he could. Pitt therefore intended to resign the political field and marred his image as a patriot by accepting a pension, but the resulting, widespread criticism was so humiliating that he started wheeling and dealing with opposition Whigs. By recognizing and acceding to the king's refusal to deal with the party groupings, he achieved personal control over the ministry for a brief period at the time the last volume of *Tristram Shandy* was dedicated to him. The language of Sterne's dedication acknowledges Chatham's tarnished image as a patriot and offers respect regardless of his change of title and place. Sterne's own political career would make him welcome a hero who had been somewhat demeaned by accepting office.

In the volumes of *Tristram Shandy* published in 1762 (Volumes Five and Six) you can hear some serious defense of soldiers who want to go on fighting, which tentatively links Toby's regret about Utrecht

[36]See John Brewer, *Party Ideology and Popular Politics at the Accession of George III* (Cambridge: Cambridge University Press, 1976).

to Pitt's politics in the 1760s—tentatively because no one was quite sure exactly what those politics were. Interpreters of these passages who read the book satirically are sure that Toby is dangerously muddled;[37] they fail to consider that the muddle might be Sterne's. Recall the beginning of "*My uncle* Toby's *apologetical oration*": "I am not insensible, brother *Shandy*, that when a man, whose profession is arms, wishes, as I have done, for war,—it has an ill aspect to the world;—and that, how just and right soever his motives and intentions may be,—he stands in an uneasy posture in vindicating himself from private views in doing it." But he goes on to assert: "For what is war? what is it, *Yorick*, when fought as ours has been, upon principles of *liberty*, and upon principles of *honour*—what is it, but the getting together of quiet and harmless people, with their swords in their hands, to keep the ambitious and turbulent within bounds?" His conclusion is unequivocal: "And heaven is my witness, brother *Shandy*, that the pleasure I have taken in these things,—and that infinite delight, in particular, which has attended my sieges in my bowling green, has arose within me, and I hope in the corporal too, from the consciousness we both had, that in carrying them on, we were answering the great ends of our creation" (VI, 32, 459, 462).

Not sure of where politics is going, Sterne at least wants to establish that it is not actually immoral to wish for war, and Uncle Toby's well-known humanity serves that purpose—to link the refined readers to the soldiers and politicians through the vicarious enjoyment that characterizes reading political news and reading novels. This is a kind of politics that is also play, modern national image making of the sort John Brewer demonstrates Pitt was very good at.

From Pitt, the story of this new politics moves to John Wilkes, around whom flowed some of the first effective, modern democratic organizing. Wilkes inherited the old Tory and Opposition Whig lines about standing above party and for the Constitution which had been associated with Pitt, but he brought a new sophistication in the use

[37]See New, *Laurence Sterne*, p. 166: "Toby's vaunted sympathy may well feel the miseries of war, but his hobby horse has carried him so far down the path of unreason that he is unable to accept the peace which ends them." For another interpretation, which tries to recover the political context, see Wolfgang Zach, "'My Uncle Toby's Apologetical Oration' und die politische Sinndimension von 'Tristram Shandy,'" *Germanisch-Romanische Monatsschrift* 58 (1977):391–416.

of propaganda to enlarge the importance of his challenge to authority.[38] In 1763 his arrest on a general warrant for number 45 of the *North Briton* (which attacked George's peace negotiations) established an enduring identification of "Wilkes and Liberty." Wilkes eventually took refuge in Europe, but returned in 1768 to run for Parliament. When he was elected, Parliament refused to seat him (and instead seated his defeated rival) because of his earlier libel. The resulting constitutional controversy raged nationwide in the press, in petitions, in street demonstrations, and led to new challenges to the aristocratic bias in the system of representation and to new forms of political organization (notably the Society for the Support of the Bill of Rights).[39]

Like Sterne, Wilkes was an effective self-advertiser and merchandiser of his works, all the more so because he was also like Sterne in playing the part of the scandalous jester. He was a roué clubman, always in debt. One reason for his departure to France, his judicial condemnation, and his expulsion from Parliament in 1763 was the discovery of printer's proof of his obscene imitation of Pope, an *Essay on Women*, which was read aloud in Parliament by the Earl of Sandwich. Opposition supporters of Wilkes in 1763 were quick to point out the political cynicism behind the high moral tone of the ministry, since Sandwich had been with Wilkes a member of the Monks of Medmenham Abbey, the rakehell club that had inspired Sterne's group at York. Wilkes's ugly squint and his sexual reputation made him an ideal lord of misrule, and he became a popular character in masques and jest books. His ability to make politics festive marshaled (that is, organized as well as elicited) political strength from traditional scenes of popular license—feasts, drinking bouts, maypoles. The number 45, associated with the prosecution of issue number 45 of the *North Briton*, became a symbol that ordered these activities and provided a label for marketing Wilkite memorabilia. A feast might begin forty-five minutes after the hour, include forty-

[38]Lucy Sutherland anticipated Brewer's genealogy of Pitt and Wilkes. See "The City of London in Eighteenth-Century Politics" (1956), in *Aristocratic Government and Society in Eighteenth-Century England: The Foundations of Stability*, ed. Daniel A. Baugh (New York: New Viewpoints, 1975), pp. 157–82, esp. 168–70.

[39]See George Rudé, *Wilkes and Liberty* (Oxford: Clarendon, 1962).

five gentlemen eating forty-five pounds of beef, dancing forty-five dances, and so forth.[40] When Sterne died, Bishop Warburton linked him to Wilkes: "Poor Sterne, whom the papers tell is just dead, was the idol of the higher mob, who have left the care of the public to Wilkes and the lower. . . . He found a strong disposition in the many to laugh away life; and as now everyone *makes himself*, he chose the office of common jester to the many" (quoted in *Letters*, 96).

Sterne probably became acquainted with Wilkes during his first trip to London, since Wilkes subscribed to the first two volumes of Sterne's sermons. Wilkes, who was declared an outlaw for failing to return from France to stand trial for libel, saw a good deal of Sterne in Paris in 1764, and rumors of their friendship drifted back to newspapers in England (*Letters*, 212). Wilkes, finally serving a term in prison in England in 1769, offered to write for Sterne's daughter a life of Sterne in collaboration with Sterne's old friend John Hall-Stevenson, but the project came to nothing. It is not unreasonable to speculate about Sterne's attitude if he had lived to see the development of radical politics around Wilkes in the later 1760s and early 1770s. Traveling in Europe with Wilkes's fervent disciple Horne Tooke, Sterne showed how too much pompous talk of "Wilkes and Liberty" bored him (Cross, *Life and Times of Laurence Sternes*, 2:79–80). Even though he was unlikely to throw himself into a political cause, Sterne's usual political connections might have drawn him for a time into Wilkite protest.

Since the remnants of the "Old Corps" Whigs under Newcastle, Pitt, and various other groupings of Opposition Whigs had all suffered under George III, there were attempts to link arms with Wilkes, or at least to draw some of his London support, since ties between the City and the parliamentary opposition had been traditionally strong. At the urging of Edmund Burke, the Marquis of Rockingham, after some hesitation, used his influence in Yorkshire to support the petitioning campaign of 1769 that protested Parliament's declaration of Wilkes's "incompetency" to serve as elected representative of Middlesex. A surprisingly large number of establishment figures joined in the Yorkshire petition, and Sterne's old ally in the

[40]See John Brewer, "The Number 45: A Wilksite Political Symbol," in *England's Rise to Greatness, 1660–1763*, ed. Stephen B. Baxter (Berkeley: University of California Press, 1983), pp. 349–80.

church Dr. John Fontayne "had risen from his sick bed to attend the meeting" (Rudé, *Wilkes and Liberty*, 122). Rockingham's seat at Malton was close to Sterne's livings, and Rockingham became a particular patron in London after the publication of the first volumes of *Tristram Shandy*, so perhaps Sterne would have signed the petition. But the alliance of the aristocratic Rockingham Whigs with London radicals was at best tenuous, and in the next year Burke's party document for the Rockinghamites ("Thoughts on the Causes of the Present Discontents," 1770) dissociated them from radical reform while castigating the ministry for its attempts to repress Wilkes. Chatham had pursued a similar policy of combining criticism of the treatment of Wilkes by the ministry with strong personal dislike of the man, and Wilkes had publicly attacked him for failing to help negotiate a return from France in the 1760s. Middle-class London reformers began to see the limitations of the traditional alliance between popular opposition in the City of London and the aristocratic opposition groups in Parliament. Sterne, like Rockingham, would probably have stopped short of endorsing democratic reformers and popular protests in London. After all, even Wilkes himself was to be found in 1780, musket in hand, defending the Bank of England against the London crowd during the Gordon riots.

Jesting, satire, even riotous play can contribute to a kind of politics, and it particularly interests us in this case because it seems to open up a democratic, antiestablishment politics. Although we should not rule out the traditional "moral economy of the crowd" in the Wilkite demonstrations, the peculiarly modern role of the commercial press in creating a combined demand for political news and entertainment gave the movement a great deal of its modern, national character. In assessing Wilkes's success in extra-parliamentary politics, we confront the ambiguity and mobility of the political imagery he employed. The number 45 was a successful symbol not only because of Wilkes's *North Briton*, but also because it was associated with the Jacobite defeat of 1745 and so with traditional anti-Scottish and anti-Catholic prejudices in the English crowd, prejudices that Wilkes himself battled in the Gordon riots of 1780. This militaristic, nationalistic, anti-Catholic feeling we have called in Sterne a kind of nostalgia, a vicarious participation in the great deeds of the past which can serve the imperialism of the present and the future. John Brewer notes the paradoxically loyalist character of the Wilkite crowds, who combined "ardent support for the crown with allegiance to 'Wilkes and Liberty'" (*Party Ideology*, 190). Perhaps this should not be surprising, since the majority of public fetes and festivals were organized in support of the establishment, and Wilkes could hardly muster an entirely separate counterculture.

In spite of the ambiguity of popular political imagery, serious politics cannot entirely dispense with it. Some forms of vicarious political participation seem inevitable in large modern nation-states, and we should not rule out the probability that even vague gestures toward "liberty" might arouse the political awareness of people excluded from the formal system of representation. My detection of Sterne's establishment loyalties cannot detract from his appeal to a former slave, Ignatius Sancho, who asked him to "give half an hours attention to slavery," for "that subject handled in your own manner, would ease the Yoke of many, perhaps occasion a reformation throughout our Islands" (*Letters*, 282–83). Sancho had been galvanized by what seems like a standard and perfunctory exclamation over slavery in Sterne's sermons: "Consider how great a part of our species in all ages down to this, have been trod under the feet of cruel and capricious Tyrants who would neither hear their cries, nor pity their distresses—Consider Slavery—what it is,—how bitter a draught! and how many millions have been made to drink it" (quoted in *Letters*, 282). Sancho recommends himself to Sterne by the means that Sterne recommended himself to his readers, by his love of books and philanthropy. He displays these good traits in his appreciation of "amiable Uncle Toby!" and of the more plebeian Trim, who particularly drew him out: "I declare I would walk ten miles in the dog days, to shake hands with the honest Corporal" (282).

One wonders whether anyone's yoke was eased by the passage in *Tristram Shandy* which corresponds to the one Sterne promises in his reply to Sancho. It is a conversation between Toby amd Trim about the probability of a poor little Negro girl having a soul. Toby's meditation on England's new worldwide holdings in slavery seems compassionate but not liberationist:

> 'tis the fortune of war has put the whip into our hands *now*—where it may be hereafter, heaven knows!—but be it where it will, the brave, *Trim*, will not use it unkindly.

—God Forbid, said the Corporal.
Amen, responded my Uncle Toby, laying his hand upon his heart. [IX, 6, 606–7]

This little gift of pity for slaves is, in Sterne's phrase, woven into the tale of Trim's brother, who fell subject to the Inquisition because of courting the widow of a Jewish sausage maker. This story in turn is woven into the tale of Toby's courtship of the frustrated Widow Wadman, which is observed by a frustrated, and therefore pitying, Mrs. Shandy. When Walter Shandy speculates about the possibility of Widow Wadman's persuading Toby to get her with child and cries out "Lord have mercy on them," Mrs. Shandy, softly, adds "Amen" and for once Walter echoes her (though it is a loud echo). But when she echoes him with yet another "Amen" that might call to mind Toby's "Amen" of mercy for the slave girl, Mrs. Shandy speaks it "with such a sighing cadence of personal pity at the end of it, as discomfited every fiber about my father" (IX, 11, 613–14) and reminds him that it is that special time of the month.

Lacking any grounding in democratic arguments about justice or in democratic political organizations, particles of pity for slaves, Jews, working men, and women hardly seem fertile seeds for democratic politics, yet we cannot by any means rule out the possibility that the right culture might draw out democratic potential from such scenes. What will count as "liberating" passages in a book depends in part on what else is available. Sancho writes to Sterne that "of all my favorite writers, not one do I remember, that has had a tear to spar[e] for the distress of my poor Moorish brethren, Yourself . . . excepted" (*Letters*, 282). The lively debates among feminist scholars over nineteenth-century American sentimentality suggests that we cannot establish a single formula for the political influence of cultural imagery;[41] rather such imagery provides one more area of conten-

[41]See Ann Douglas, *The Feminization of American Culture* (New York: Knopf, 1977); Jane P. Tompkins, "Sentimental Power: *Uncle Tom's Cabin* and the Politics of Literary History" (1981), in *Sensational Designs: The Cultural Work of American Fiction, 1790–1860* (New York: Oxford University Press, 1985); and Mary Kelley, *Private Woman, Public Stage: Literary Domesticity in Nineteenth-Century America* (New York: Oxford University Press, 1984). Critics interested in the democratic potential of popular culture have been recently turning, with perhaps too much optimism, to Mikhail Bakhtin. See, for example, Terry Castle, *Masquerade and Civilization: The Carnivalesque in Eighteenth-Century Culture and Fiction* (Stanford: Stanford University Press, 1986).

tion for competition in power. As the first writer to popularize the term *sentimental*, Sterne was obviously not content in the long run to manufacture a purely playful text to be interpreted at the whim of his reader; he sought to establish a new line of credit by his coinage.

### *A Sentimental Journey*: Purposeful Play

At the end of *Tristram Shandy*, Walter, who has had early warning of Widow Wadman's "secret articles which had delayed the surrender," holds forth on the evils of women's lust to Yorick and Mrs. Shandy, asserting "that every evil and disorder in the world, of what kind or nature soever, from the first fall of *Adam*, down to my Uncle *Toby*'s (inclusive) was owing one way or other to the same unruly appetite" (IX, 32, 644). Yorick tries twice to speak, once to bring "my father's hypothesis to some temper," then to "batter the whole hypothesis to pieces" when Walter claims that engendering takes place in the dark because "all the parts thereof—the congredients—the preparations—the instruments—, and whatever serves thereto, are so held to be conveyed to a cleanly mind by no language, translation, or periphrasis whatever" (IX, 33, 645).

Yorick is interrupted the first time by the appearance of Toby with his look of "infinite benevolence and forgiveness." Toby's modesty, which has been in the past a refutation of Walter, is here not sufficient to halt Walter on his course of condemnation; in fact, Walter is impelled by resentment on Toby's behalf. The second time, when Yorick is even more determined to speak, Obadiah breaks in with a complaint opposite to Walter's resentment of lust. The Shandy bull has not lived up to his duties and is in danger of losing the reputation of a "town bull." Yorick is allowed to read a lesson in the last words of the book, but it is a lesson against lessons, his praise of the cock-and-bull story. What he might have said to "temper" an attack on lust could not be said in *Tristram Shandy*, even though the display of extremes raises hope for an agreeable middle.

In *A Sentimental Journey* Yorick comes out from the margins into the center of the book, and it is a coming out for Sterne as well. With the publication of four volumes of his sermons as the*Sermons of Mr. Yorick*, Sterne underlined his identification with the character. To bring Yorick into *A Sentimental Journey*, set in 1762, is to make clear that this Yorick is even closer to Sterne than the one in *Tristram Shandy*, who is supposed to have died in 1748.[42] Although Yorick is not to be seen in the pulpit in *A Sentimental Journey* any more than in *Tristram Shandy*, he does remind us at the outset of the kind of coat he wore and that he was not going to leave it behind when he went to France: "The coat I have on, said I, looking at the sleeve, will do" (65).[43] Gardner Stout appropriately links this passage to a letter in which Sterne answers the criticism of a friend. After reading a draft of the first two volumes of *Tristram Shandy*, the friend urged Sterne to avoid gross allusions and remember his character as a clergyman.

Sterne replied, "A Very Able Critick and One of My Colour too—who has Read Over tristram —Made Answer Upon My saying I Would consider the colour of My Coat, as I corrected it—That that very Idea in My head would render My Book not worth a groat—still I promise to be Cautious—but I deny I have gone as farr as Swift—He keeps a due distance from Rabelais & I keep a due distance from him—Swift has said a hundred things I durst Not Say—Unless I was Dean of St. Patrick's" (*Letters*, 76). Although Sterne had not become Dean of Saint Patrick's by the time of *A Sentimental Journey*, he had enjoyed preferment in the church, popularity in the best circles of London and Paris society, and a good deal of literary recognition (even if much of it controversial), so it is reasonable to suppose that there were now some things he did dare say, even if they took him yet farther from Swift than he was in *Tristram Shandy*. He was on his way to exploring the latitude in latitudinarianism.

Sterne's developed sense of literary authority takes him on a different novelistic path from Richardson's or Fielding's, since it led him to

[42]Michael Seidel draws the opposite conclusion about the resurrection of Yorick in *A Sentimental Journey* after his death in *Tristram Shandy*. Instead of coming closer to Sterne as I have said, Yorick in Seidel's view becomes more and more clearly literary, illustrating that "the powers of the narrative and dramatic imagination are never quite ready to give the *coup de grâce* to sucessful inventions." See "Narrative Crossings: Sterne's *A Sentimental Journey*," *Genre* 18 (Spring 1985):7. Seidel's account of the creation of narrative space in *A Sentimental Journey* resembles in some ways my account of the mechanisms of protraction in *Tristram Shandy*, but I see in the later work a significant change in the management of narrative authority.

[43]This and subsequent parenthetical numbers refer to Gardner D. Stout, Jr., ed., *A Sentimental Journal through France and Italy by Mr. Yorick* (Berkeley: University of California Press, 1967).

write a much shorter book than his first. In the perspective of *A Sentimental Journey*, the enormous length and learned wit of *Tristram Shandy* look more elaborately defensive than Toby's fortifications; the insistent play, the nagging of the reader, seem like the strategies of a late bloomer to persuade the company of his unprecedented precocity. With the learned wit pared away, what remains is an astonishing rapidity, a remarkably flexible modulation between reflection and exemplary action. The encumbered narrative of *Tristram Shandy* constantly falls behind, or at least grows backward; in *A Sentimental Journey* Yorick is always ahead of himself. From the beginning his words precipitate him into scenes for which he is not quite prepared. It is not surprising, then, that Yorick should reach the point sooner, more clearly, and more often than Tristram does. He is not totally different from the characters of *Tristram Shandy*, since he is also propelled by defensiveness into somewhat aimless self-extension, but he scores points in this process rather than merely falling into it. *A Sentimental Journey* begins in the middle of an argument because Yorick wants to win it, or at least credential his opinions, by his journey. Yorick in *Tristram Shandy* fell rather thoughtlessly into controversies and contempt, but he did not try to defend his reputation.

Perhaps it is the much-criticized Yorick-Sterne of *Tristram Shandy* and the *Sermons* that the Yorick-Sterne of *A Sentimental Journey* wishes to defend. When we consider the typical English associations with France that might make one speak of things being better ordered there, certain freedoms in the relations of the sexes and freedoms to relate things about the sexes come to mind. Well-mannered flirtation, flattery, frankness about bodily functions, sexy jokes, and cuss words (as well as French maids and adultery) strike the English as very French, and it makes sense that Sterne should take us to France to win his argument against the critics of his bawdry. What results is an unprecedented, and in its own way highly courageous, defense of sex in the head.

Of all the mixed up things that make up the motley pages of *Tristram Shandy*, the mixture of chastity and concupiscence is the most confounding. If the reader tries to clean up a bawdy reference, it spreads the dirt. In a chapter about Walter's learned collection of books on noses, Tristram warns the embarrassingly female reader:

"Now don't let Satan, my dear girl, in this chapter, take advantage of any one spot of rising-ground to get astride of your imagination, if you can any ways help it; or if he is so nimble as to slip on,—let me beg of you, like an unback'd filly, to *frisk it, to squirt it, to jump it, to rear it, to bound it,*—and to kick it, with long kicks and short kicks, till like *Ticketoby*'s mare, you break a strap or a crupper, and throw his worship into the dirt.—You need not kill him" (II, 36, 226). It turns out that getting it off is very like getting it on, but the reader can't get out of it and get on with other things. Like so much of the particolored jesting in *Tristram Shandy*, these embarrassments remind us of a human weakness, but not too severely. Nevertheless, the narrator, who has offered to "halve this matter amicably" (II, 11, 109), so as to allow the reader "something to imagine in his turn," seems especially anxious to blame the reader for immodest thoughts. It is because such thoughts are the natural concomitant of censorship. In "the fragment" on the Queen of Navarre, *whiskers* becomes an indecent word, and it could happen to anything, when "the *extreams* of DELICACY, and the *beginnings* of CONCUPISCENCE" come together: "Chastity, by nature the gentlest of all affections—give it but its lead—'tis like a ramping and roaring lion" (V, 1, 348).

In "Slawkenbergius' Tale" Strasbourg falls because the citizens are absorbed in their curiosity about Slawkenbergius's nose, but in the first story "fragment" in *A Sentimental Journey*, Abdera is saved by sex in the head. The satiric laughter of Democritus has no power of reform, but, it is suggested, only adds "libels and pasquinades" to other kinds of violence, "poisons, conspiracies, and assassinations." Yet the Abderites are converted to love and friendship by the passage from the *Andromeda* of Euripides celebrating the obsessive (even tyrannical) power of Love: "O, Cupid, prince of gods and men." It sexualizes the mind: "nothing operated more upon their imaginations, than the tender strokes of nature which the poet had wrought up in that pathetic speech of Perseus" (131). In this "fragment" Sterne decisively rejects (rather than merely ignoring, as in *Tristram Shandy*) the formative power of satire, and he equally rejects the madness that his source, Burton's *Anatomy of Melancholy*, found in this example of infectious love discourse. The quicksand of sexy thoughts in *Tristram Shandy*, where chastity and immodesty bog down together, has become a scene from a golden age of cooperation and reconciliation: "Friendship and Virtue met together, and kiss'd each other in the street." The men play on their pipes while the women listen "chastly."

The narration has been sent off into Abdera by Yorick's reflections on his newly hired servant La Fleur, a former soldier who practices the utopian morality of making love not war. When the landlord who had recommended La Fleur to Yorick confesses "he is always in love," Yorick replies:

> I am heartily glad of it, said I,—'twill save me the trouble every night of putting my breeches under my head. In saying this, I was not making so much La Fleur's eloge as my own, having been in love with one princess or another almost all my life, and I hope I shall go on so, till I die, being firmly persuaded, that if I ever do a mean action, it must be in some interval betwixt one passion and another: whilst this interregnum lasts, I always perceive my heart locked up—I can scarce find in it, to give Misery a sixpence; and therefore I always get out of it as fast as I can, and the moment I am rekindled, I am all generosity and good will again; and would do any thing in the world either for, or with any one, if they will but satisfy me there is no sin in it.
>
> —But in saying this—surely I am commending the passion—not myself. [128–29]

Yorick asserts his state of continual arousal (or at least frequent arousal) as an ideal condition of charitable responsiveness that leads to moral acts and is clearly bounded by the fences of the moral law. We are not teased with questions about the possible moral ambiguity of "being in love with one princess or another almost all my life." By contrast Tristram always nags us to worry about his relation to his dear, dear Jenny. Is she his wife, mistress, daughter, or friend? The defense of the French sentimental friendship he winds into is too casual and ironic to serve as a moral defense. "Sentiment" here is a set of false alternatives, the pure or the delicious:

> Surely, Madam, a friendship between the two sexes may subsist, and be supported without—Fy! Mr. *Shandy*:—Without any thing, Madam, but that tender and delicious sentiment, which ever mixes in friendship, where there is a difference of sex. Let me intreat you to study the pure and sentimental parts of the best *French* Romances;—it will really, Madam, astonish you to see with what a variety of chaste expression this delicious sentiment, which I have the honour to speak of, is dress'd out. [1, 18, 49]

We may well wonder which are "the sentimental parts" of book or reader. The reader's intercourse with a book is suggested by the range of meaning of the term *sentiment*: it can be an opinion or an idea, a physical or emotional feeling, but it may also be, according to Johnson's dictionary, "a striking sentence in a composition," or according to the Oxford English Dictionary, an epigram or toast. A passage in Sterne's letters which anticipates Yorick's praise of infatuation complains of the vagueness of the term *sentiment*, which he has taken to himself from the French. In the context it is clearly associated with filling up an empty mind:

> I am glad that you are in love—'twill cure you (at least) of the spleen which has a bad effect on both man and woman—I myself must ever have some dulcinea in my head—it harmonizes the soul—and in these cases I first endeavour to make the lady believe so, or rather I begin first to make myself believe that I am in love—but I carry on in my affairs quite in the French way, sentimentally—*l'amour* (say they) *n'est rien sans sentiment*—Now notwithstanding such a potter about the *word*, they have no precise idea annex'd to it—[*Letters*, 256]

Sentimentality is linked to persuasion, which is a kind of make-believe; it does not necessarily make you believe. Sterne quotes his French adage about the necessity of sentiment in the letter La Fleur brings to Yorick to help him write the engaging Fleming, Mme. de L***. It is full of "sentiments," that is, good sentences that anyone might find useful ("vive la bagatelle" as well as "vive l'amour"). The particular sentiments of the sender can remain veiled in these good turns of phrase, especially because Yorick removes the one line that specifies a time for one's "turn." We can say about Yorick's sentimentality what he says about the "French sublime" of the wigmaker: "The French expression professes more than it performs" (159).

The kind of sentimental sex liberation Yorick defends is not geared to performance. The episodic structure maintains an ethos of not going all the way with anyone. It seems odd that so many critics linger over the supposed sexual ambiguity of "the conquest," since Yorick is quite clear that he defends only feeling "the movements which rise" and intends to "govern" them by morality.[44] Judgments

[44]In *The Journal to Eliza* Yorick complains to his surgeons about the diagnosis of venereal disease, "for I have had no commerce whatever with the Sex—not even with my wife, added I, these 15 years." Is it the duty of a critic to disbelieve him?

of tone may differ. In this rather grave, preacherly passage about divinely created nature, I find the sexual references neither snickering nor ironic. They assert a freedom of fantasy and feeling that is bounded by laws governing action:

> If nature has so wove her web of kindness, that some threads of love and desire are entangled with the piece—must the whole web be rent in drawing them out?—Whip me such stoics, great governor of nature! said I to myself—Wherever thy providence shall place me for the trials of my virtue—whatever is my danger—whatever is my situation—let me feel the movements which rise out of it, and which belong to me as a man—and if I govern them as a good one—I will trust the issues to thy justice, for thou hast made us—and not we ourselves. [237–38]

We might take this freedom of feeling to be modeled on the Hobbesian and Anglican freedom of conscience. Thought and feeling are private; actions are the matters that concern the commonwealth. But Sterne goes farther than advocating tolerance; he advocates enjoyment of erotic sentiment, which is the greater because of a recognition of limits: "There is a sort of pleasing half guilty blush, where the blood is more in fault than the man—'tis sent impetuous from the heart, and virtue flies after it—not to call it back, but to make the sensation of it more delicious to the nerves—'tis associated" (234). In the scene of brinksmanship with the *fille de chambre* Yorick would have pleased Hobbes in the readiness with which he takes the coward's role and avoids heroic moral combat. Sentimentality operates as a prophylactic against passion. Because Yorick has Eliza's image in his heart and around his neck, he avoids pursuing the affecting Mme. de L***. The sentimental letter he takes from La Fleur is really a kiss-off.

Yorick's morality is very far from Clarissa's: she struggles to get thoughts as well as actions in line with a high standard and suffers over the slender strand of a "conditional liking" for a man of whom she does not entirely approve. Sterne's monk tells Yorick, "'Twas too late to say whether it was the weakness or goodness of our tempers

---

The *Journal* itself suggests Sterne's preference for the diffusive pleasures of literary fantasy. See Ian Jack, ed., *A Sentimental Journey . . . to which are added "The Journal to Eliza" and "A Political Romance"* (London: Oxford University Press, 1972), p. 141.

which had involved us in this contest" (100), and Yorick compels the gentle traveler to give something to the beggars of France, with the reassurance that "he need not be so exact in setting down his motives for giving them—they will be register'd elsewhere" (132). Yorick's easy conscience, his lack of perfectionism, can be a welcome antidote to Richardson's rigors. Moreover, it is not hard to see that Clarissa, for all her suffering, is a much more dangerous character than Yorick. Yorick, as he tells us, is willing to "give up the triumph, for security" (235).

Coming to France in 1762, before peace has been declared, may not seem the best route to security, but Yorick has come like so many other travelers to perfect the peaceable virtue of compleasance, or as it is more usually called in the context of French culture, "politeness." Smooth, polished manners that enable people to get along, the arts of elegant conversation and compliment, were thought to be the flower of the French court. In his important exploration "Of the Rise and Progress of the Arts and Sciences" (1741), David Hume weighed the value of "modern politeness" and "modern gallantry," both "the natural produce of courts and monarchies" (*Essays*, 1:191). These cultural values arise in modern monarchies rather than in the ancient or modern republics, because in a monarchy the people "must turn their attention upward, to court the good graces and favour of the great," and to be prosperous a man must "render himself *agreeable*, by his wit, complaisance, or civility" (1:186–87).

Hume understands that these court values are not confined to the court, but are diffused throughout a monarchical society, for "a long train of dependence from the prince to the peasant . . . beget[s] in every one an inclination to please his superiors, and to form himself upon those models, which are the most acceptable to people of condition and education" (1:187). So it is not surprising that Yorick need not go to court to find politesse. We might consider the extremely civilized beggars who impress Yorick in Montreuil. As one steps aside, bowing in deference to the female beggars, Yorick exclaims, "Just heaven! for what wise reason hast thou order'd it, that beggary and urbanity, which are at such variance in other countries, should find a way to be at unity in this?" (132). Another beggar offers snuff to those beside him, and Yorick honors him more by taking snuff than by the charity. A soldier's loyalty to the king takes Yorick's fancy. Two more of the beggars are good at compliments ("Mon cher et tres charitable Monsieur," and even better, "My Lord Anglois"). Finally, a man too proud to beg stirs Yorick's charity the most. One female beggar, however, seems outside the circle of politeness and begs only for "the love of God": her dislocated hip disqualifies her for gallantry.

Hume defends gallantry as an extension of politeness. Rather than a degeneracy in masculine virtue, Hume explains gallantry as a civilized form of authority exercised by a modern male over a modern female, "a studied deference and complaisance for all her inclinations and opinions" (1:193). The sexes did not mingle in company in the ancient world, and therefore they lacked the refinement of modern society. We should remember that Hume boasted in his posthumously published autobiography of his own popularity among "modest" women. In the early essay he continues, "what better school for manners, than the company of virtuous women; where the mutual endeavour to please must insensibly polish the mind, where the example of the female softness and modesty must communicate itself to their admirers, and where the delicacy of that sex puts everyone on his guard, lest he give some offense by any breach of decency" (1:194)

Wanting to look good to a woman is an acceptable motive for moral development in the sociology of refinement and politeness, so Yorick's improvement in manners to the monk is not ironized by our perception that he is showing off to a lady; that is the way it is supposed to work. The lady teaches him a further lesson in politesse: he should not call nervous, English-style attention to the special circumstances of politesse, such unchaperoned settings as the remise, where the sexes hold intercourse. But we cannot really expect (and perhaps we would not want) an Englishman to learn politesse perfectly, as Yorick shows in his final discomfiture in the bedroom of an inn alone with a female traveler and her maid.

Yorick, as I have said, does not want to go very far down the road with a woman. There is usually not much conversational intercourse, and it is usually interrupted. Expressive silences and Yorick's skill in translating faces and gestures mean that he does not have to learn much from the woman herself. He cannot attend to the directions of the grisette in the glove shop. Since he has read the love story of Maria as told by Tristram Shandy, he does not need to ask Maria about it; indeed, given her disordered wits, he knows more about it than she does, though she does remember the "pale, thin" Tristram Shandy pitying her and that he "half-promised" to see her again (272). Perhaps Yorick does not need very much sentimental education at the hands of a woman, because he already has all the valuable attributes of a woman. By the process I am calling remasculinization, Sterne has appropriated softness, delicacy, and modesty for his male character.

Yorick's graveyard tears show that he is "as weak as a woman" and deserving of pity (103); his Shandyesque taste for double entendres is interpreted as a strategic cover for extreme modesty: "I have something within me which cannot bear the shock of the least indecent insinuation: in the sportability of chit-chat I have often endeavoured to conquer it, and with infinite pain have hazarded a thousand things to a dozen of the sex together—the least of which I could not venture to a single one, to gain heaven" (217). So Yorick does not need to spend very much time or become very intimate with women. If he did, he might be in danger of crossing over some frontier. The danger of too much intercourse between the sexes may be sexual intercourse, but it may also be the effeminacy of men.

Hume admits that modern politeness, "which is naturally so ornamental, runs often into affectation and foppery, disguise and insincerity" (1:191), but he claims that every social habit contains a negative potential. Yorick of course learns the great secret of flattery from a successful beggar who approaches only women, and with it he keeps his "places" at the tables of people of rank, until he grows ashamed and feels this "dishonest reckoning" is the "gain of a slave" and a "vile prostitution of myself to half a dozen different people" (266).

Perhaps Montesquieu in *The Spirit of the Laws* (1748) is the farthest-reaching analyst of the sociology of politeness under monarchy. A deep moral ambivalence about modern society comes through his defense of modern difference from ancient republican virtue. The guiding principle of a monarchy for Montesquieu is competitive honor, egoistic concern for other people's opinions, rather than the altruistic love of public good which was the virtue of republics.

Politeness may lead people to sociable pleasure in one another, but it is a form of the competitive wish to "distinguish oneself from others." Delicacy of taste develops in the scene of luxury where a multiplicity of goods and constantly varying values make fine discriminations possible (IV, ii). The intercourse of men and women in French society draws Montesquieu out of his philosophic neutrality into a defensive, partisan "we": "If only we could be left as we are" (XIX, vi). The mingling of men with women, their desire to look good in one another's eyes, motivates the increase of taste, "which is the source of the nation's wealth," and the increase of politeness, "which attracts so many visitors to its shores" (XIX, v).[45]

But this sociability that inspires taste and commerce deteriorates the morals. In the *Discourse on the Origin of Inequality* Rousseau's revulsion from the social and political system of the court is tracked all the way back to an early stage of tribal society, when by spending time together and by looking at each other with erotic preferences men and women evolve corrupting principles of competition in honor, along with the arts of singing, dancing, and civility. Inequality originates in politeness even before the invention of private property.

The character type many modern historians think of as bourgeois man, a calculator of advantages, a restless consumer of new values, a competitor above all, turns out to be in Montesquieu primarily the political subject of a monarchy, a participant in commercial culture only secondarily. More recently Norbert Elias has argued that the social psychology of calculating, competitive, polite, and self-controlled individuals appeared first as a "courtly rationality" of the early modern absolutist state before the urban-commercial ethos became culturally important, and then for a long time worked along with it to form the modern personality.[46] Elias is as sympathetic to the "courtly art of human observation" (*Power and Civility*, 274) in Saint-Simon and others as I am to the more abstract theory of Hobbes and Hume. The marketlike model of competitive desire and esteem is never afflicted with the mystifications of "bourgeois individualism":

[45]Melvin Richter, ed., *The Political Theory of Montesquieu* (Cambridge: Cambridge University Press, 1977), p. 271.

[46]Norbert Elias, *Power and Civility* (1939), trans. Edmund Jephcott (New York: Pantheon, 1982), p. 281.

"the individual is always seen in his social context, *as a human being in his relations to others, as an individual in a social situation*" (Elias, 274).

It therefore makes sense for Sterne to send Yorick to absolutist France in order to bring to prominence in his fiction what could strike us as a bourgeois sense of the personality as engaged in "a sentimental commerce."[47] In Yorick's trip we find bourgeois commerce continually resolved into the forms of honor. Yorick's purchases (except for the indispensable French wig) have the quality of gifts that show, in spite of his modest means, his generosity and superiority to need and his intention to give honor as well as to receive it. He hires a larger carriage than he needs, pays wages to a servant untrained but graceful and decorative, buys gloves he cannot wear and ruffles he does not want. The scenes of salesmanship are extremely polite. The grisettes display their gloves and laces quietly and patiently without puffing them. M. Dessein is as adept at compliment as Yorick and foils him in a gentlemanly "duel" of wishing each other well, garnished by courteous bowing. Yorick wishes to relieve M. Dessein of the pain of seeing the ramshackle (and doubtless cheap) *désobligeant* (a kind of carriage), but M. Dessein assures him that the pain of hiring out an unworthy vehicle to "a man of honour" would be worse pain (88).

The scenes not only exemplify Hume's long chain of dependence, which diffuses politeness everywhere; they also point up the peculiar status of the bourgeoisie in an aristocratic society. The people in trade are often in a "client economy" rather than a free market; that is, they are tied to a deferential relation with their aristocratic patrons and forced by their situation to extend large, long-term credit (as well as politesse).[48] Yorick, as a tourist who pays as he goes, has less of this sort of local political power, but the deferential manners of the grisette in the glove shop (and of her husband) suggest the usual attitude toward authority. We might compare the adventure recorded in Boswell's *London Journal*, in which on a "trial of civility"

[47]Arthur Hill Cash, *Sterne's Comedy of Moral Sentiments: The Ethical Dimension of the "Journey"* (Pittsburgh: Duquesne University Press, 1966), chap. 1.

[48]John Brewer, "Commercialization and Politics," in Neil McKendrick, John Brewer, and J. H. Plumb, *The Birth of a Consumer Society: The Commercialization of Eighteenth-Century England* (Bloomington: Indiana University Press, 1982), p. 198.

he sallies forth, an unknown Scot, into a London shop and persuades the tradesman to trust him for the price of a sword because he looks like a gentleman. Boswell sententiously reads the moral of the story to the man: "Sir . . . if you had not trusted me, I should not have bought it from you."[49] Like Yorick, Boswell likes to delude himself that his class privilege is a set of highly personal attributes, so he warns the sword cutter, "Pray don't do such a thing again. It is dangerous." In fact, however, a dealer in such gentlemanly merchandise must adapt his manners to his patrons.

That commerce itself involved agreeable manners was a hopeful article of faith for the new economics of the mid-eighteenth century. We have seen Montesquieu's connection of the polite intercourse of the sexes, taste, fashion, and consumption. Hume's *Political Discourses* (1752), his most popular book, especially in France, asserted, with even fewer hesitations than Montesquieu had expressed, the social values of what had previously been condemned as luxury. "Refinement in the Arts"—that is, the development of industry, commerce, and consumption—ushers in the cultural superiority of people in modern Europe:

> They flock into cities; love to receive and communicate knowledge; to show their wit or their breeding; their taste in conversation or living in clothes or furniture. Curiosity allures the wise; variety the foolish; and pleasure both. Particular clubs and societies are everywhere formed: Both sexes meet in an easy and sociable manner: and the tempers of men as well as their behaviour, refine apace. So that, beside the improvements which they receive from knowledge and the liberal arts, it is impossible but they must feel an encrease of humanity, from the very habit of conversing together, and contribute to each other's pleasure and entertainment. [*Essays*, 1:301–2]

The growth of demand in eighteenth-century England for just such items as wigs and gloves and books has been judged the basis for "the birth of a consumer society,"[50] but how far down the social scale the demand reached has been a matter for speculation. Hume clearly believes that commerce has strengthened the political power of the

[49]Frederick A. Pottle, ed., *Boswell's London Journal, 1762–1763* (New York: McGraw-Hill, 1950), p. 60.

[50]Neil McKendrick, "The Consumer Revolution," in *The Birth of a Consumer Society*, pp. 31–32.

"middling rank of men." Statistics on the increase of wages in the second half of the eighteenth century and on increased industrial output both suggest an increase in consumption; reports of travelers and complaints of social critics such as Fielding suggest that emulation in fashion reached far down the social ladder, although the largest increases came only in the last quarter of the century. However, many plebeian readers might eventually sympathize with Yorick's consumer adventures, in these passages Sterne does not seem to emphasize the democratic potential of commercial sociability.

Two of the most memorable accounts of commerce in *A Sentimental Journey* treat it as a respectable lapse from gentlemanly status. The Chevalier de St. Louis sells pates "without solicitation" (210) near the gates of the palace at Versailles. To all who inquire, he tells the story of his service at the head of a company in war and his impoverishment at the conclusion of the peace, and he refers courteously to the king as "the most generous of princes." As a result, word gets round to the king, so that, without solicitation, the officer is rewarded with a pension that "broke up his little trade" (211). This episode leads into the next story of "the sword." Unlike other French provinces, the special laws of Brittany allow a member of the nobility to suspend his noble rank if he wishes to engage in commerce and to resume it when he declares to a court that he has desisted from this nonnoble activity. The Marquis de E**** resigns his sword and spends nineteen or twenty years of successful application to business in Martinique, yet nonetheless also requires "bequests from distant branches of his house" to enable him to reclaim his nobility and to support it. The characters in these stories do not exactly "earn" a living by commerce; it helps "support" their social dignity, but in indirect ways.

Sterne is surprisingly favorable in these sections to aspects of French polity which for Englishmen typified the tyranny of French government. The officer's roundabout approach to the king suggests the dangers of public criticism or petition. Even the liberal regulations of Brittany show the high legal walls between the aristocratic and commercial class. The social and political segregation of classes was not reinforced by such legal restrictions in England. But the sentimental journey of Sterne, by contrast to the satirical criticism of

Smollett, extends sympathy to things French, even to French styles of authority. At the opera Yorick eagerly places himself beside "a kindly old French officer." The officer reminds him of Captain Toby Shandy, but this is not the Toby who wanted to go on fighting in 1761; *A Sentimental Journey* was written well after the Treaty of Paris in 1763. Yorick's predilection for veterans is a sentimental affection for finding philanthropy in surprising places: "I love the character . . . because I honour the man whose manners are softened by a profession that makes bad men worse" (170). When Yorick's philanthropy is aroused by the sight of a dwarf crowded out by a tall, corpulent German, the sympathetic officer directs a sentinel to attend to it, the German is brought back at musket point, and Yorick claps and cries out, "This is noble." He is only a little embarrassed when the officer reminds him of the political significance of the act: "and yet you would not permit this . . . in England" (179). Perhaps Sterne, like Hume, would have longed for better police control of the crowds during the Wilkite riots. The use of standing armies to control the urban population was one of the hallmarks of French absolutism and the bugbear of English politics, but sentimental philanthropy draws Yorick to approve of it.

The most astonishing extension of Yorick's political sympathies is his imaginative approach to Catholicism. Yorick's typical Protestant attack on monkish sloth and ignorance is not far from the attack on papistry that Sterne issued from the pulpit and in *Tristram Shandy*, but in *A Sentimental Journey* Yorick comes to feel it is bad manners to a "courteous figure." Inspired by his civilized wish to impress a lady, he makes his apologies to the monk with an exchange of snuffboxes. The monk's horn snuffbox then becomes for Yorick an object of superstitious, Catholic-style veneration, a holy relic: "I guard this box, as I would the instrumental parts of my religion, to help my mind on to something better; in truth, I seldom go abroad without it; and oft and many a time have I called up by it the courteous spirit of its owner to regulate my own, in the jostling of the world" (101).

Yorick's sentimental practice is to invest the world with superstition, to perform miraculous acts of transubstantiation with holy relics and rituals. The emblematic chapter titles, "The Desobligeant," "The Remise," lead to "The Supper," and finally to the daring of "The Grace," where Yorick sees religion mixing in the simple peasant dance. But like the sexual liberation of the book, the affection for French authority and religion are an indulgence of personal fantasy and feeling that goes out on a short limb. Yorick never does give money to the monk's convent, and he considers that the monk "took sanctuary, not so much in his convent as in himself" (102). He does not join in Catholic ritual; Catholics join him in sentimental ritual, potentially a subtle vindication of the authority of individual conscience.

The peaceful, ecumenical religious sentiment, like the nostalgia for picturesque philanthropic soldiers, does not obliterate the differences that a war could exacerbate. Yorick's fear of the Bastille, Sterne's best sop to the anti-French prejudices of the English, shows the limits of sentimental fantasy. When he is warned of the dangers of traveling without a passport, Yorick first remembers his joke with Eugenius about getting clapped into the Bastille and living there "a couple of months entirely at the king of France's expense" (196). He tries to extend the spirit of fun in a debunking and reassuring reduction of the Bastille to a word for a tower, and he walks himself easily downstairs, stripping it of its terrors. But the cry of a starling, "I can't get out—I can't get out," and his ineffectual struggle to release it from its cage call back his "dissipated spirits" to reason (198). He walks heavily upstairs exclaiming against slavery and addressing himself to liberty. In his room he exercises his imagination on the plight of one captive, which makes him burst into tears and run off to beg a passport.

This reaffirmation of anti-French politics is not the end of the story, however. The starling, trained by a young English groom, sings a "song of liberty" that is an "unknown language at Paris." So the bird is readily sold to Yorick, but back in England the song of liberty has almost as little credit as in Paris:

> In my return from Italy I brought him with me to the country in whose language he had learn'd his notes—and telling the story of him to Lord A—Lord A begg'd the bird of me—in a week Lord A gave him to Lord B—Lord B made a present of him to Lord C—and Lord C's gentleman sold him to Lord D's for a shilling—Lord D gave him to Lord E—and so on—half round the alphabet—From that rank he pass'd into the lower house, and pass'd the hands of as many commoners—But as all these wanted to *get in*—and my bird wanted to get

> out—he had almost as little store set by him in London as in Paris. [204–5]

In the end the enslaved bird with its desire for liberty finds a resting place as the crest of Yorick's coat of arms, which happens to be the coat of arms used by Sterne, decorated with a starling, or "stern."

I began by saying that in some senses Sterne comes out in *A Sentimental Journey*. As Yorick takes on more teacherly responsibility than Tristram did, he comes out as an advocate for certain freedoms of thought and feeling, and these entail advocacy of certain freedoms and powers of art to move readers. His spokesmanship for religious and sexual tolerance, however hedged about, probably took courage and a considerable degree of the sort of self-criticism allegorized in his episode with the monk. But perhaps most significant, Sterne comes out as someone who can't get out, who cannot sing along with a groom a song for English liberty, because he has been too busy getting in. The vagueness in *Tristram Shandy* about Yorick's "war," which was in that book quickly buried in funereal oblivion, is illuminated in *A Sentimental Journey* by the translation of the starling.

Sterne as a cleric and author is part of the clique of aristocratic rulers, someone who "tells," who gives and seeks favors, and he is also himself a token of honor, a fashionable object of consumption—like a well-hung woodcock passed from one gentleman's larder to another.[51] It is not only in France that he has become good at circulating, and perhaps this recognition of his subjection at home makes him sympathetic to the way they order things in France. Yorick tells the Comte de B**** that the French are polite "to an excess," or at least more polished than he would like to see the English. He takes as his illustration of complaisance that leaves no rough edges the example of much-circulated coins: "by jingling and rubbing up against one another for seventy years together in one body's pocket or another's, they are become so alike you can scarce distinguish one shilling from another" (232). By contrast Yorick

[51]According to Douglas Hay, "Pheasants and hares and sides of venison were . . . so many tokens of social position; game was a special currency of class based on the solid standard of landed wealth, untainted by the commerce of the metropolis." See "Poaching and the Game Laws on Cannock Chase," in Hay et al., *Albion's Fatal Tree: Crime and Society in Eighteenth-Century England* (New York: Pantheon, 1975), p. 246.

claims that Englishmen "keep more apart" than Frenchmen and so preserve a character that is franker, more easily visible, and therefore perhaps more valuable. But the coins Yorick chooses for illustrating the smoothness of the French are "King William's shillings," English coins that have rubbed up against one another so much that they have worn away the features of the defender of English liberty.

# EPILOGUE

# *Burke's Fearful Reflections*

The Libertie, whereof there is so frequent, and honourable mention, in the Histories, and Philosophy of the Antient Greeks, and Romans, and in the writings, and discourse of those that from them have received all their learning in the Politiques, is not the Libertie of Particular men; but the Libertie of the Common-wealth: . . . The *Athenians*, and *Romanes* were free; that is, free Common-wealths: not that any particular men had the Libertie to resist their own Representative; but that their Representative had the Libertie to resist, or invade other people. There is written on the Turrets of the city of *Luca* in great characters at this day, the word LIBERTAS; yet no man can thence inferre, that a particular man has more Libertie, or Immunitie from the service of the Commonwealth there, than in *Constantinople*. Whether a Commonwealth be Monarchicall, or Popular, the Freedome is still the same.

*Leviathan*, II, 21, 266

But as to *our* country and *our* race, as long as the well compacted structure of our church and state, the Sanctuary, the holy of holies of that ancient law, defended by reverence, defended by power, a fortress at once and a temple, still stand inviolate on the brow of the British Sion—as long as the British monarchy, not more limited than fenced by the orders of the state, shall, like the proud Keep of Windsor, rising in the majesty of proportion, and girt with the double belt of its kindred and coeval powers, as long as this awful structure shall oversee and guard the subjected land—so long the mounds and dykes of the low, fat Bedford level will have nothing to fear from all the pick axes of all the levellers of France.

Edmund Burke, *Letter to a Noble Lord*

My reflections on political construction in eighteenth-century fiction come to an end in Burke's *Reflections on the Revolution in France*. It is a work that has deep roots in the British literary and philosophical culture that I have been describing, yet it is in some ways a monstrous mutation, whose progeny transform the national literary ecology. Burke, who drew on Hobbes and Hume, and on many precedents in the eighteenth-century epistle, essay, and satire—forms that also fed the novel—creates a post-Burkean climate in which his predecessors can hardly be read or understood. The rift between the eighteenth and nineteenth centuries in our literary and intellectual histories is not just an accident of disciplinary preserves; it was a creation of that history. Trying to find continuities, you follow tracks that seem to trail off into the desert. Bentham transmitted something of Hume's arguments about utility to John Stuart Mill, but Mill seems never to have gone back and checked for himself, and the loss to his philosophic development was considerable. It is observed that William James never cut the leaves of his edition of Hume. Can anyone plausibly demonstrate a strong influence on George Eliot or Matthew Arnold of Defoe, Richardson, Fielding, Sterne, or Smollett? Or for that matter, of Hobbes, Locke, Johnson, or Hume? Surely not without the intermediaries of Burke, Wordsworth, Coleridge, and Carlyle to fertilize the imagination of an organic culture that has been the locus for both conservative and liberal discourse up to our own time.

It is, I recognize, not Burke who cuts us off from the eighteenth-century past so much as the Revolution he insisted was revolutionary, along with the increasing impacts of industrialism, evangelicalism, and mass culture. I shall not try to bridge this great gap in the history of imagination, but if Burke seems to speak to modernity in ways that his sources do not, then his transformation of them may be instructive. The movement from Hobbes to Burke is often described as the triumph of modern historical and sociological understanding over abstract theory, but it is easy to see that this is one of those judgments that itself proceeds in some roundabout route from Burke's own critique of the enlightenment. I would prefer to argue that to move from Hobbes to Burke is to trace the development of nationalism—the deliberate organization of veneration and identification with the nation—out of arguments about the necessity and authority of states.

It is not hard to see that the two edifices in my epigraphs from Hobbes and Burke have something in common: each represents the power of a nation unified by law. Burke's reassertion of the term *natural* to some extent covers over the secularist premise that he shares with Hobbes and Hume: that justice is an artificial construction originating in human convention: "Man, whose prerogative it is, to be in a great degree a creature of his own making" (189).[1] Burke's argument against the revolutionary doctrine of natural rights sounds particularly Hobbesian. In entering civil society, a person abandons all right to judge for himself, to be his own governor: "that he may secure some liberty, he makes a surrender in trust of the whole of it" (150). And because Burke believes with Hobbes that government is founded on mutable opinion rather than on immutable principles of natural reason, he is peculiarly urgent about exposing the dangerous errors of French revolutionary philosophy and practice. Opinion is to some extent security (97).

For Hobbes, the passion that reliably motivates people to enter into commonwealths and to obey the sovereign law is fear. Fear is certainly one of the emotions that Burke wishes to raise by the publication of the *Reflections*. It is hard to remember that the work was published before the Terror, at a time when English sympathies were widely favorable to the changes in France. The Revolution had condemned many of the things that Englishmen had lambasted so long: absolute monarchy, arbitrary imprisonment, monastic luxury,

[1]*Reflections on the Revolution in France*, ed. Conor Cruise O'Brien (Harmondsworth: Penguin, 1973). Here and throughout this section, parenthetical numbers give pages from this edition.

legal privileges for the aristocracy. Hobbes prided himself on his timidity in being one of the first to leave England when the political conflict was heating up; similarly, Burke could pride himself on being one of the first to be afraid: "whenever our neighbor's house is on fire, it cannot be amiss for the engines to play a little on our own" (92). Burke is not in so good a position as Hobbes to raise the fear of death; instead the emotions he mentions most often and wishes to raise in his readers are "horror and disgust," emotions roused by the violation of sacred things, the disrespect shown a consecrated state. Horror is connected to fear when fear has been stabilized and channeled into religious veneration.

Hobbes had explained that fear of unknown causes and the desire to placate these powers motivated religious worship, and Hume had expanded this account in the *Natural History of Religion* (1757), while removing any rational grounds for the belief in a first cause in his posthumously published *Dialogues concerning Natural Religion* (1778). Through Hobbes's account of the history of religion includes its use by politicians to motivate obedience, his own concern about the sovereign holding sovereignty over the national church seems largely defensive. He wants to block the possibility of any challenge to sovereignty based on claims about unknown spiritual causes and immortal self-preservation. Because these beliefs are motivated by powerful passions, it would not be possible to correct them by reason; rather it is necessary to regulate them by authority. More positive functions of the state church would include teaching respectful obedience to government. Hobbes's experiments in recasting the decalogue and in interpreting biblical history illustrate how Christianity could be used in support of the state, but perhaps the famous frontispiece to *Leviathan* is the closest Hobbes comes to Burke's attempt to create awe and veneration.

The sovereign made of many men is awesome in its power, incomprehensibly greater than that of any individual man, and yet it is a lovely and graceful mustachioed figure that gives the spectator pleasure. Hobbes's idea of the representative or the actor of the commonwealth opens up the possibility of an extensive imaginative identification with political authority, and the model of the theater suggests the aesthetic pleasure associated with a vicarious sense of power. We may use Hanna Pitkin's useful definition of "symbolic" political representation. This kind of representation welds a nation into a unity that rests on "emotional, affective, irrational psychological responses rather than on a rationally justifiable criterion."[2]

Neither Hobbes nor Burke can be described as reducing representation to this wholly affective function, but the potential for it in Hobbes's theory is greatly developed by Burke's emphasis on the admiring sentiments with which we regard the "embodiments" of authority: "These public affections, combined with manners, are required as supplements, sometimes as correctives, always as aids to law. . . . To make us love our country, our country ought to be lovely" (172). Burke's adaptations of Hobbes and Hume resemble Sterne's indulgent adaptations of satire. The humiliation of human reason, which in Hobbes and Hume remains comically humiliating no matter how much they assure us that living by passions is normal and unavoidable, becomes in Burke the enshrinement of prejudice.

Hume's humorous analogy between justice and superstition opens the way to Burke's hallowing of habitual reverence for authority.[3] Hume distinguishes the utility of justice from the utility of priestly superstition, but he draws attention to the similarity in an image that compares the transfer of property and the consecration of an edifice:

> When we abstract from this circumstance [of utility] it must be confessed, that all regards to right and property seem entirely without foundation, as much as the grossest and most vulgar superstition. Were the interests of society nowise concerned, it is unintelligible why another's articulating certain sounds implying consent, should change the nature of my actions with regard to a particular object, as why the reciting of a liturgy by a priest, in a certain habit and posture, should dedicate a heap of brick and timber, and render it, thenceforth and forever, sacred.[4]

Superstitution in this passage is still gross and vulgar, something that is embarrassing to confess. The idea of making our property not only

[2]Hanna Fenichel Pitkin, *The Concept of Representation* (Berkeley: University of California Press, 1967), p. 100. It should be noted that Pitkin does not reduce either Hobbes or Burke to symbolic representation.

[3]For comparisons of Burke and Hume, see George H. Sabine, *A History of Political Theory* (New York: Holt, 1937), pp. 597–620; and Sheldon S. Wolin, "Hume and Conservatism," in *Hume: A Revaluation*, ed. Donald W. Livingston and James T. King (New York: Fordham University Press, 1976), pp. 239–56.

[4]David Hume, *Enquiry concerning the Principles of Morals*, in *Enquiries concerning Human Understanding and concerning the Principles of Morals*, ed. P. H. Nidditch (Oxford: Clarendon, 1975), sec. III, pt. 2, p. 199.

legal but also "sacred" is rendered even more ridiculous by the suspension of the word until the end of the long, complex sentence.

When Burke defends the church establishment as "the first of our prejudices" (188), he makes it the "ground of our social fabric." The church is our ground not because any particular set of natural laws underpins the state and certainly not because priests have divine authority in their liturgy, habits, or posture, but because a state church demonstrates "the uniformly continued sense of mankind, which teaches reverence as well as obedience":

> That sense not only, like a wise architect, hath built up the august fabric of states, but like a provident proprietor, to preserve the structure from prophanation and ruin, as a sacred temple, purged from all the impurities of fraud, and violence, and injustice, and tyranny, hath solemnly and forever consecrated the commonwealth, and all that officiate in it. This consecration is made, that all who administer in the government of men, in which they stand in the person of God himself, should have high and worthy notions of their function and destination; that their hope should be full of immortality; that they should not look to the paltry pelf of the moment, nor to the temporary and transient praise of the vulgar, but to a solid, permanent existence, in the permanent part of their nature, and to a permanent fame and glory, in the example they leave as a rich inheritance to the world. [189]

There is nothing humorous about this passage, yet its exaltation of human creations is deliberately offered as prejudice or opinion or attitude; it is not defended as truth. An unidentified "sense" of humankind with which we identify animates a set of impossible, logically indefensible wishes which culminates in a repeated insistence on permanence that may apply to the soul but that sounds as if it applies to the state. Hume's favorite mechanisms—utility and the love of fame—are not sufficient to insure stability, since they are mechanisms that can operate for change as well as for the status quo.

Burke's Humean legacy is partially apparent in his account of the 1688 Revolution and his refutation of radical claims that found evidence of an original contract entailing a right of revolution. Hume's essay "Of the Original Contract" (1748) might have been lying open before Burke as he composed the *Reflections*. He seems even to have taken from it a disparaging image for the notion that each generation has a right to make the social contract anew. Burke writes: "the whole chain and continuity of the commonwealth would be broken. No one generation could link with the other. Men would become little better than the flies of a summer" (193). In his final revision, Hume had written in "Of the Original Contract":

> Did one generation of men go off the stage at once, and another succeed, as is the case with silk-worms and butter-flies, the new race, if they had sense enough to choose their government, which surely is never the case with men, might voluntarily, and by general consent, establish their own form of civil polity, without any regard to the laws or precedents, which prevailed among their ancestors. But as human society is in perpetual flux, one man every hour going out of the world, another coming into it, it is necessary, in order to preserve stability in government, that the new brood should conform themselves to the established constitution, and nearly follow the path which their fathers, treading in the footsteps of theirs, had marked out to them.[5]

Hume's passage assumes we are not flies, but it reminds us of the animal mortality of every "new brood" of humans and of its low level of rationality. In Burke, Hume's "perpetual flux" of comings and goings becomes "the great mysterious incorporation of the human race," devised "by the dispensation of a stupendous wisdom" (120). Later in the *Reflections*, Burke reverses rhetorical strategies and asserts that "society is indeed a contract," but a kind of contract no group can actually make since it is a partnership "between those who are living, those who are dead, and those who are to be born" (195).

"Treading in the footsteps" of their fathers, following the path "marked out to them," is for Burke inadequate; the images are too low. With them, Hume has deliberately conflated obedience to fathers and mere habit, so that even Locke's notion of "tacit consent" seems to require an improbably high degree of consciousness. Burke does not want to attribute conscious consent as the motive for obedience, but another kind of consent comes into play, consent to use reverential rather than contractual images of obedience. Even our liberties have been described in law as an entailed inheritance: "In this choice of inheritance we have given to our frame of polity the image of a relation in blood, binding up the constitution of our

[5]David Hume, "Of the Original Contract," in *Essays Moral, Political, and Literary*, 2 vols., ed. T. H. Green and T. H. Grose (London: Longmans, Green, 1875), 1:452.

country with our dearest domestic ties; adopting our fundamental laws into the bosom of our family affections; keeping inseparable, and cherishing with the warmth of all their combined and mutually reflected charities, our state, our hearths, our sepulchres, and our altars" (120). We might guess that Burke's addition of a vague Providence to Hume's historical account of government represents an attempt like that in this passage to make institutions cherished, like the inheritance of a home.

The choice of rhetoric makes the difference between Burke and Hume, and it makes all the difference in the world to Burke when he traces the broad outlines of Hume's account of the Glorious Revolution. In the 1688 Revolution, Hume and Burke recognized genuine change, but they emphasize the limited extent of the change, and they assert that revolution cannot be one of the rules of government, it must always be an exception to the rules. Burke follows Hume's essays and his history in assaulting many cherished historical myths of English liberty. For example, they both view the "violent innovations" of Henry VIII as dangerous and undesirable precedents, and both cast doubt on the antiquity and continuity of the ancient Constitution supposedly preserved in Magna Carta. But on these intimations of discontinuity Burke builds an affirmation of historical myth making. The important thing about the common-law lawyers from Coke to Blackstone is not that they "appear to be" right about the continuity of law, but that they demonstrate the "powerful prepossession towards antiquity, with which the minds of all our lawyers and legislators, and of all the people whom they wish to influence, have been always filled" (118).[6] The common-law tradition becomes a necessary rhetoric of reverence which appeals to our inherent tendencies to believe in what is customary. The French revolutionaries have chosen the wrong language; they should not have described themselves as a "nation of low-born servile wretches until the emancipatory year of 1789"; they should have announced that they were "resolved to assume [their] ancient privileges" or the ancient principles of old Europe preserved by their English neighbors (123).

[6]See J.G.A. Pocock, "Burke and the Ancient Constitution: A Problem in the History of Ideas," in *Politics, Language, and Time: Essays in Political Thought and History* (New York: Atheneum, 1971), pp. 202–32. Pocock describes the influence on Burke's historicism of the common-law tradition and takes this as a countertendency to the influence of Hobbes and Hume.

Burke's account of the legal construction of the 1688 Revolution makes clear that the antiquity he praises is an artifice of rhetoric, "a politic, well-wrought veil" (103). Lord Somers, Defoe's hero, appears in the *Reflections* as a master of the art of appealing to political sentiments in his authorship of the Declaration of Right:

> It is curious to observe with what address this temporary solution [i.e., dissolution] of continuity is kept from the eye; whilst all that could be found in this act of necessity to countenance the idea of an hereditary succession is brought forward, and fostered, and made the most of, by this great man, and by the legislature who followed him. Quitting the dry, imperative style of an act of parliament, he makes the lords and commons fall to a pious, legislative ejaculation, and declare, that they consider it "as a marvellous providence, and merciful goodness of God to this nation, to preserve their said majesties *royal* persons, most happily to reign over us *on the throne of their ancestors*, for which, from the bottom of their hearts, they return their humblest thanks and praises." [102]

We could take this mixture of the dry and the ejaculatory as an honorable precedent for the style Burke himself adopted. His pious expressions of patriotic loyalties in the name of the nation bathe his dry historical, political, and economic analyses in the oil of Providence, and his many allusions and verbal echoes help maintain his immersion in continuing traditions: "I am unable to distinguish what I have learned from others from the results of my own meditation" (197). In an introductory note Burke apologizes for the mixed-up form, the incommodious division and distribution of his matter. Though Burke is a member of Parliament, and that credential lends authority to his views, the *Reflections* are not a speech in Parliament, and they are not put before the public as a proposal that might be encoded in law. The book is presented as a private letter written in answer to "a very young gentleman at Paris, who did [the author] the honor of desiring his opinion upon the important transactions" in France, and it grew out of its original structure, "when [Burke's] sentiments had grown into a greater extent, and had received another direction" (84).

Burke takes the epistolary form as a license for formlessness and the expression of powerful personal feelings:

> Indulging myself in the freedom of epistolary intercourse, I beg leave to throw out my thoughts and express my feelings, just as they arise in

> my mind, with very little attention to formal method. I set out with the proceedings of the Revolution Society; but I shall not confine myself to them. Is it possible I should? It looks to me as if I were in a great crisis, not of the affairs of France alone, but of all Europe, perhaps of more than Europe. All circumstances taken together, the French revolution is the most astonishing that has hitherto happened in the world. The most wonderful things are brought about in many instances by means the most absurd and ridiculous; in the most ridiculous modes; and apparently, by the most contemptible instruments. Every thing seems out of nature in this strange chaos of levity and ferocity, and of all sorts of crimes jumbled together with all sorts of follies. In viewing this monstrous tragi-comic scene, the most opposite passions necessarily succeed, and sometimes mix with each other in the mind; alternate contempt and indignation; alternate laughter and tears; alternate scorn and horror. [92–93]

Informality of diction ("It looks to me") mixes with highly patterned sentences, as grammatical parallelism and repetitions of sound and words build to a crescendo of indecorous emotion.

Stylistic mixture is a virtue in Burke and in the Declaration of Right—it is a sign of natural feeling—but it is a vice in the French revolutionary mentality and in the proceedings of the (English) Revolution Society. Burke's *Reflections* presents itself as a letter run wild but also as a piece of rambling literary criticism, first of Dr. Price's sermon, then of the Declaration. But Dr. Price's "very extraordinary miscellaneous sermon" is a "porridge" because it mixes moral and religious sentiments with political opinions and expressions, and the political influence of the sermon on the members of the Revolution Society is a dangerous effluence that makes them come out "reeking" (93).

The satiric language of spreading chaotic mixtures provides a negative way of characterizing a process that has tremendous social importance for Burke, the diffusion of opinions, sentiments, manners throughout a society or from one society to another. This is a process of reflection, of looking at and imitating other people. Sometimes, as in Montesquieu, Hume, and Sterne, this process of cultural interaction is a kind of commerce with more than one reciprocal, mirroring exchange. The French are accepting as English doctrines the natural rights theory that the English radicals try to import as French: "We ought not, on either side of the water, to suffer ourselves to be imposed upon by the counterfeit wares which some persons, by a double fraud, export to you in illicit bottoms, as raw commodities of British growth though wholly alien to our soil, in order afterwards to smuggle them back again into this country, manufacturing after the newest Paris fashion of an improved liberty" (110–11). Yet Burke has in mind for himself just such a trade in counterfeit wares, in a jumbled artifice of politics and history. He is trying to make England into ancien-régime France, the pattern of the old European common law and even of the courtly manners that were always associated with France. In finding a common cultural ground in old Europe, Burke follows Montesquieu and some of the newer Scottish historiography, but in skipping over the history of peculiarly English liberties (not only the Glorious Revolution but even Protestantism) Burke performs a powerful act of conversion.

Like Sterne's sentimental traveler Yorick, the English Burke reads the French a lesson in gallantry. The famous passage on Marie Antoinette makes Burke a flattering courtier who looks up to beauty and rank rather than to virtue. He even tries to recall Frenchmen to their old national habits: "I thought ten thousand swords must have leaped from their scabbards to avenge even a look that threatened her with insult" (170). We should be alert to what Burke is doing to the traditional contrast between France and England as he says, "Oh! What a revolution!" (169). Today it is England that purveys the taste for princesses. The passage on Marie Antoinette struck more than one contemporary reader as "foppery."[7] Burke appears as the would-be masculine protector of female delicacy, but by his process of reflection he also becomes the helpless feminine figure who is overwhelmed by feelings of admiration and pity. Once again, we encounter the sentimental soldier and the aggrandizement of modern male sentimentality which I have described in Sterne. And as in Sterne, this feminization did not exclude militarism. But for the time being Burke only boasts that English passions are ready to serve the

[7]Philip Francis to Burke, 19 February 1790, *Correspondence of Edmund Burke*, vol. 6, ed. Alfred Cobban and Robert A. Smith (Chicago: University of Chicago Press, 1967), pp. 86–87. For an account of Mary Wollstonecraft's feminist response to Burke and of sentimentality as a remasculinization of moral virtue, see Carol Kay, "Canon, Ideology, and Gender: Mary Wollstonecraft's Critique of Adam Smith," *New Political Science*, no. 15 (1986): 63–76.

purposes of the fallen Bastille for punishing those who slander queens.

The most troubling item of reflective commerce in the *Reflections* is commerce itself. Hume says that monarchies export their politeness and import commerce and the rule of law, which originate in republics. Montesquieu agrees that republics (among which he numbers England) promote commerce, except for that commerce in luxuries and fashion which the intercourse of the sexes promotes at monarchic courts. Burke has a peculiarly un-English suspicion of the "traders" in the French assembly; could it even be called a "French" suspicion of traders, since he admits that money and land are more "miscible" in England (210)? He demurs from condemning the third estate in his own voice; it is the manners of the nation that condemn traders, curates, attorneys to a low position of social esteem, and the worst of their effects on the assembly comes from their lack of proper self-esteem. Nevertheless, in denying the sociability of the mercantile classes, Burke deviates from the sociological history of "refinement" in industry, commerce, the arts, and manners which we have seen in Hume. Or rather, Burke is willing to read that history backward: since "commerce, and trade, and manufacture" (174) grew out of the same culture as chivalry, they may not be able to do without their habitual environment of gentlemanly honor, politeness, and religion.

What Burke finds worst in the new influence of the French commercial class is the vast expansion of public credit, the system of paper money founded on the confiscation of monastic holdings. Probably his readiness to predict the worst of public credit stems from the century-long political dialogue in England over the political power that the institutions of public credit fostered, to the benefit of the government and of the "money men." So even the public debt could be seen as an English institution strangely transported to French use; that is, in Burke's mirror, the national debt was something British that the French were mishandling. Hume and Adam Smith, both of whom influenced Burke's economic thought, issued grave warnings about the long-term political and economic effects of a large national debt, yet both saw distinct political advantages to securing the interest of creditors in the Hanoverian establishment. Burke's complaint about the French system of credit is a negative view of this British advantage: "to put every individual in the same bottom and to bind the nation in one guilty interest to uphold this act" (225).[8]

The mythic English bovine figure of the *Reflections* is "sluggish" (181), and it may be that Burke's mustering of custom and reverential spectatorship quells the restlessness that afflicted Hobbesian humanity by hiding the artificiality of institutions, veiling social alternatives, and giving a vicarious sense of power. The sentimental spectator may be the appropriate incarnation of the timid subject that Hobbes was trying to create. The Burkean subject is, for example, a safe consumer of literature because it trains his emotions without providing models of action. English dissidents and freethinkers have, according to Burke, never formed a political cabal like the Encyclopedists for putting their theories into action. The French are not only poor political rhetoricians, they have mistaken satire and fiction for reality. Burke went so far as to claim that Rousseau admitted his philosophic novelties were only intended as a literary innovation to replace the worn-out forms of heathen mythology and chivalric romance (283).

Burke attributes this confession by Rousseau to Hume's testimony, and a great deal of the moral spectatorship I have been discussing in Burke can be found in Hume. Hume's moral theory accounts for moral feelings in relation to moral judgments, but it has little to say about the experience of moral action. My Humean picture of Richardson suggests what several readers have found in *Clarissa*: it represents a life of reading that displaces action. A return to Hobbes from these distant developments of his principles allows some critical detachment from their attractions. The crude explicitness of competition and contracts in his system, which I have also found in the fiction of Defoe, exposes our desire for power and makes us notice when we give it up.

[8]On manners, politics, commerce, and the public debt in Burke, Hume, and Smith, see J.G.A. Pocock, "The Political Economy of Burke's Analysis of the French Revolution," in *Virtue, Commerce, and History: Essays on Political Thought and History, Chiefly in the Eighteenth Century* (Cambridge: Cambridge University Press, 1985), pp. 193–212; and Donald Winch, *Adam Smith's Politics: An Essay in Historiographic Revision* (Cambridge: Cambridge University Press, 1978), pp. 121–49.

# Index


Act of Uniformity 48
Anglican establishment. *See* Political institutions
Alkon, Paul, 90n, 115n, 119n
Allegiance, in Hume, 229. *See also* Consent
Allentuck, Marcia, 209n
Alter, Robert, 109n
Althusser, Louis, 5
Anderson, Perry, 5
Anne, Queen, 53, 60, 62
Annesley, Dr. Samuel, 48
Appleby, Joyce Oldham, 50n, 71, 72
Arendt, Hannah, 5
Arnold, Matthew, 267
Art, aesthetics, viii; as instruction 262; as instruction in Richardson, 9, 127, 129, 141, 158–60, 162, 188–90; as instruction in Sterne, 204; and patriotism, 12, 40–41, 270; as play, 11, 14, 205–6; as play in Sterne, 207–22; political aesthetic, 203–5; in Richardson, 157; in Watt, 9
Atterbury, Francis, bishop of Rochester, 124
Authority: of clergy, 165, 188–89; of Crusoe, 86–91; of Hobbes, 36; to interpret, 35–36; and literature, 8–9; of moral philosophy, 36; of novel in Defoe, 117–19; of novel in Richardson, 141; of novelists and philosophers, 38; of Richardson, 160; of science, 28–29; of sermon vs. novel, 210–12; in Sterne, 262; of teacher, 2 *See also* Family

Bacon, Francis, 25
Baier, Annette C., 131n, 132n–33n
Bank of England, 50
Barrell, John, 137, 138
Barry, Brian, 39n
Battestin, Martin C., 8n
Bentham, Jeremy, 267
Berkeley, George, bishop of Cloyne, 37
Birdsall, Virginia Ogden, 69n
Blackstone, William, 273
Boardman, Michael, 64n, 83n–84n
Bolingbroke, Henry St. John, 1st viscount, 53, 124, 130, 138, 238
Booth, Wayne, 63, 209n
Boswell, James, 161, 257–58
Bradshaigh, Lady Dorothy, 161–62
Braudy, Leo, 119n
Brewer, John, 239n, 240, 244, 257n
Brissenden, R. F., 209n
Burke, Edmund, vii, viii, 7, 23, 233, 242, 265–78
Burton, Dr. John, 199

Canon, 21–23
Carlyle, Thomas, 267
Cash, Arthur H., 197n, 220n, 257n
Castle, Terry, 163n–64n, 245n
Chaber, Lois A., 115n

Charles I, 37
Charles II, 42, 49
Chatham. *See* Pitt, William
Cleary, Thomas R., 8n
Coke, Sir Edward, 273
Coleridge, Samuel Taylor, 267
Competition, viii, 3, 10, 278; among conventions, 193; in Defoe, 59; in Defoe and Hobbes, 64–65, 68, 81; in family in Richardson, 168; in Hobbes, 31; in honor, 233; in laughter, 215
Compleasance, x, 14; in Hobbes, 41–42; in Hume, 227–28; in Sterne, 226; in Sterne and Hobbes, 214–15 *See also* Politeness
Conscience. *See* Religion
Consent, viii, x, 42; in Defoe and Hobbes. 80–81; in Hobbes, 40, 70; in Locke and Burke, 272; in Locke and Hume, 228–29; in Richardson, 192
Construction: character as, 177; defined, 1
Contract, 278; in Defoe, 80–81 85, 88, 93,112; in Defoe and Hobbes, 69–70; in Hobbes 39–40; in Hume, 132–33; in Locke, 40; original contract in Hume and Burke, 271–72
Conventicles Act, 49
Convention, 42; competing conventions, 193; in Hume, 39, 132–33, 135, 228
Counsel, x; and command in Hobbes, 36–37; in Defoe, ix, 114; Defoe as counselor, 52–66; and eloquence in Richardson, 169, 171; in Hobbes, 53–54, 93–94; in *Moll Flanders*, 93–101, 105, 107–9, 114–15, 118–19; reader as counselor, 105; in Richardson, 169; and story-telling, 95, 97, 98; vs. moral discourse in Richardson, 140, 159; and women, 107–8
Cross, Wilbur, 197n, 224
Cumberland, Richard, 67
Curiosity: in Hobbes, 30; in Richardson, 193, 214; in Sterne, 214
Curtis, Lewis Perry, 197n, 201

Damrosch, Leopold, 73n
Davis, Lennard, 62–63
De la Faye, Charles, 123
Declaration of Indulgence, 49, 60
Declaration of Right, 274
Defoe, Daniel, vii, viii, ix, 9, 12–13, 21, 23, 45–119, 123, 169, 267. Works: *And What if the Pretender Should Come?*, 52; *Argument Shewing that a Standing Army is not Inconsistent with a Free Government*, 57; *Compleat English Gentleman*, 54; *Consolidator*, 61, 107–9; *Enquiry into the Occasional Conformity of Dissenters in Cases of Preferment*, 60; *Enquiry into Occasional Conformity Shewing that Dissenters Are no Way Concern'd in It*, 61; *Essay upon Projects*, 55–57, 64–65; *Farther Adventures of Robinson Crusoe*, 90–91; *History of the Union*, 59; *Jure Divino*, 80, 82, 87; *Legion's Memorial*, 51, 92; *Letter to Mr. How*, 60; *Mist's Weekly Journal*, 124; *Moll Flanders*, 92–119; *Review*, 53; *Robinson Crusoe*, 75–92; *Serious Reflections of Robinson Crusoe*, 76, 77, 80–83, 86, 100, 103; *Shortest-Way with Dissenters*, 61; *Tour through the Whole Island of Great Britain*, 65, 126, "True-Born Englishman," 50, 59, 68n. *See also* Hobbes, Thomas; Locke, John
Democratization, 16–18, 23, 240–41, 243–46
Dewey, John, 17n
Dickson, P. G. M., 50n
Doody, Margaret Anne, 123, 124, 146
Douglas, Ann, 245n
Dunn, John, 67n

Eagleton, Terry, 163–64n
Earle, Peter, 72n
Eaves, T. C. Duncan, 123n, 124
Economics, viii, x, 4, 7; Bank of England, 50; capitalism, viii; capitalism and Defoe, 59, 72–73; client economy, 257–58; commerce and cultural exchange, 275–78; commerce in France, 259; consumer society, viii, 257–59; corruption, 130; credit, 108–10; credit in Defoe, 57; Defoe's debt, 51–52; free trade, 71–72; international

Economics (*cont.*)
trade in Defoe, 91; mercantilism and Defoe, 71–72; and novel-writing, 8–9, 223–24; and politics, 13, 116; political influence of commerce, 61–62; public credit in Burke, 277; and religion, 72–73; in Watt, 9. *See also* Politics
Education, x, and art 262; and art in Richardson and Hume, 158; and art in Sterne, 204; authority to teach, 36; and clergy, 188; dissenting academies, 49, 54–55; and guilt, 172; by letters, 190; Lovelace and Clarissa, 179–82; *Moll Flanders* as negative conduct book, 115–16; and rape, 188; in Sterne, 219–21 *See also* Art, aesthetics
Ehrenpreis, Irvin, 215n–16n
Elias, Norbert, 256
Eliot, George, 267
Elliott, Robert C., 215n
Epistemology: and Hume, 28; and knowledge of the future in Defoe, 74–75; and knowledge of the future in Hobbes, 27–28; and politics, 6–7, 36; and science in Hobbes, 27–28; in Watt, 9. *See also* Knowledge of character; Opinion; Politics; Religion

Family, viii, 4, 7; analogy to state, 9, 111,272–73; authority of father, 169, 173,192, 229; authority of husband, 173; authority of mother, 166–67, 169, 230–36; authority of parents, 77; and conflict, 169; in Defoe, 87; in Defoe and Hobbes, 70; duty of children, 141, 229; Fifth Commandment, 163–67; Fifth Commandment in Defoe, 77–78; Fifth Commandment in Sterne, 226–27; in Hobbes, 43; in Hobbes and Locke, 166; husband as sovereign, 157; in Hume, 133, 227; and novel, 9, 43; in state of nature, 69
Fear, 29–30; in Defoe, 114; in Hobbes, 30, 39–40; in Hobbes and Burke, 268–69; in Richardson, 139, 158, 163
Fiction, in Richardson, 158
Fielding, Henry, 8, 9, 21, 58, 130, 138, 142, 211, 247, 267
lmer, Sir Robert, 166, 230
ıntayne, John, 202
Forbes, Duncan, 131n, 229n
Fraser, Nancy, 17n

Garrick, David, 224
Gauthier, David, 133n
Gender: alliance of women, 107; alliance of women in Richardson, 174; authority of mother in Sterne, 230–36; double standard in Hume, 159; double standard in Richardson, 149; female counsel in Defoe, 93–95; female subordination in Defoe, 92–93; feminine reserve in Defoe, 98; feminine reserve in Richardson, 174; remasculinization, 17; remasculinization in Sterne, 232–36; sex in Sterne, 246–53; sex segregation in Sterne, 232; women and law, 10, 138; women and nongovernmental power, 17, 100; women and novels, 17
Generosity. *See* Gratitude
George III, 238, 239
Gierke, Otto von, 67n
Glorious Revolution. *See* Revolution, of 1688
Godolphin, Sidney, 1st earl of, 53, 65
Goethe, Johann Wolfgang von, 205–6
Goldgar, Bertrand A., 8n
Goldsmith, M. M., 27n
Gordon riots, 243
Gramsci, Antonio, 5
Gratitude: in Defoe, 77, 80–82, 86, 88; in Defoe and Hobbes, 69–70; filial, 87; generosity, 170
Grotius, Hugo, 89

Halifax, Lord, 49, 58
Harley, Robert, 52, 53, 58, 59, 61, 62, 65, 123–24
Hay, Douglas, 262n
Henry VIII, 273
Hervey, Lord, 200
Hill, Aaron, 126, 160, 166
Hobbes, Thomas, vii–ix, 6, 12–14, 17, 22–44, 54, 75, 125, 131, 133–36, 138, 140, 141, 146, 158, 159, 163, 166, 171, 172, 192, 256, 267, 269, 270,

Hobbes, Thomas (*cont.*)
278; and Burke, 268; and Defoe, 66–70, 75–77, 79–81, 86–88, 93–95, 100, 102, 103, 107, 108, 112; and Hume, 131–32, 169; model of political analysis, 2–4; on passions, 102–3; and Richardson, 10, 137–38, 140–41, 148, 157–59, 163, 166, 169, 171–72, 182; and Sterne, 197, 214, 219, 225, 230, 233, 278; and Swift, 225. *See also* Authority; Competition; Compleasance; Consent; Contract; Counsel; Fear; Gratitude; Honor; Knowledge of character; Language; Law; Liberty; Morals; Opinion; Politics; Promises; Religion; Reputation; Self-preservation; Vanity; War
Hogarth, William, 207, 224
Holmes, Geoffrey A., 47n, 56n
Holtz, William V., 207n, 222n
Honor, 3, 65, 97; competition for in Hobbes and Sterne, 232
Hornbeck, Catherine Gee, 127n
Howe, Irving, 23
Hume, David, 7, 23, 37, 39, 59, 158, 159, 172, 173, 256, 267, 269, 270, 272, 275, 277, 278; and Hobbes, 28, 32, 169, 268; and Locke, 132. Works: *Dialogue*, 132; *Dialogues concerning Natural Religion*, 269; *Enquiry concerning the Principles of Morals*, 34, 131, 132, 135; *Natural History of Religion*, 269; "Of Original Contract," 228, 271–72; *Political Discourses*, 258; *Treatise of Human Nature*, 37, 131, 132n, 134, 227–28
Hunter, J. Paul, 8n, 74, 77n, 84n, 85
Hutcheson, Francis, 131

Ideology, x, 5. *See also* Opinion

Jacobites, 52, 54, 124
James II, 49, 59, 60, 68n, 169
James, William, 267
Jameson, Fredric, 15n
Jeffreys, George, lord chief justice, 49
Johnson, Samuel, 2, 58, 138, 161, 210, 267

Kelly, Mary, 245n
Kemp Smith, Norman, 28n
Kimpel, Ben D., 123n, 124
Kinkead-Weekes, Mark, 144n–45n, 154n–55n
Knowledge of character, 74–75, 103, 107; in autobiographical fiction, 102–5; in Defoe, 80–81, 88; in family, 128; in Hobbes, 25–27; and law, 117; in letters, 140, 146, 158, 180, 183–85, 274–75; and novel, 24; tests of character in Richardson, 153–56, 158

Language: and anonymity, 115; artificiality of, 34; auxiliary verbs in Sterne, 219; in Defoe, 81; eloquence in Hobbes, 37; figures in Sterne, 221; in Hobbes, 32–38; interpretation and sovereignty, 77; jokes, 13–14, 109, 150, 156–57, 210, 215; modern linguistics, 14; and morality in Hume, 133–135; moral terms in Hobbes, 33–34; moral terms in Hume, 34; names and representation, 40; proper names, 12–14, 93, 97, 113, 115; proper names in Richardson, 178; proper names in Sterne, 219; quotation in Sterne, 219; religious language, 35; rhetoric in Burke, 272–75; and science, 27; as system, 4, 7; titles, 12–14, 99, 101, 143, 148, 173, 175, 257. *See also* Morals
Lanham, Richard A., 220n
Laud, Archbishop, 48
Law, 18, 109; as arbitrary, 51, 112, 116–17; as artificial, 7, 14, 34–35, 268; authority to interpret, 35–36; and family, 164; in Hobbes, 32; indeterminacy of in Defoe, 64; latitude of and Defoe, 106–7; and novelistic authority, 117–19, 185–87, 192; and slander, 109; and women, 100
L'Estrange, Roger, 124
Letwin, Shirley Robin, 131n
Liberty: in Burke, 268, 272, 276; in Hobbes, 32, 41; in Sterne, 240, 261–63; in Sterne and Hobbes, 230, 252; Wilkes and, 241–44

Locke, John, 37, 57, 86, 89, 92, 166, 230, 267; and Burke, 272; and Defoe, viii, 66, 79, 88; and Don Quixote, 29; and Hobbes, 31; and natural morality, 38; social contract in, 40; and Sterne, 206–7, 218–19, 227
London, 50–51, 124, 208, 243
Louis XIV, 51
Lukács, Georg, 206

McIntosh, Carey, 144n
McKee, Patricia, 164n
McKeon, Michael, 15n–16n
McKillop, Alan, 62–63
Macpherson, C. B., 73, 108n
Machiavelli, Niccolò, 25
Magna Carta, 273
Manners. *See* Compleasance; Morals; Political culture
Marlborough, 236, 238
Mill, John Stuart, 267
Miller, Nancy K., 119n
Mintz, S. I., 24n
Monkman, Kenneth, 218n
Monmouth, James Scott, 1st duke of, 49, 127
Montesquieu, Charles Secondat, baron de, 255–56, 258, 275, 276, 277
Moore, John Robert, 47n
Morals: analogy of language in Hume, 135; and discourse in Hume, 133–34; and law, 10; moral discourse, 10, 13, 14; moral discourse in Hobbes, viii, 33; moral discourse in Hume, 34; moral discourse in Richardson, 127; moral philosophy, 15; moral terms, 33–34; and political structure, 191–93; and rules, 13, 148; rules in Hume, 136; rules in Richardson, 128–29 141–43, 174; rules in Richardson and Hume, 136, 159
Morton, Charles, 54–55

Natural law, x; in Defoe, viii, ix, 66–70; in Locke, viii
New, Melvyn, 216n, 240n
Newcastle, Thomas Pelham-Holles, 1st duke of, 238, 242
Nostalgia, viii, and Defoe, 92; and Richardson, 157; and Sterne, 12, 243
Novak, Maximillian, 66–71, 77, 83n, 86n, 114
Novel, 8; and authority to interpret, 75–77; and clergy, 10–11; and political philosophy, 21–24; and politics, 8; and story, 97; and story-telling, 108; vs. legal authority, 185–87; vs. politics, ix–x; vs. sermon, 210–12; and women, 17
Nuttall, A. D., 28n, 206n

Oates, J. C. T., 218n
Occasional conformity, 49
Opinion, x, 7, 102, 111; in Burke, 268; and credit in Defoe, 57; and credit in Richardson, 168; as customary belief in Hume and Sterne, 228–30; in Hobbes, 31–32; as power in Richardson, 142; prejudice, 12, 270–71 and reading public, 37, 52; in Richardson, 165, 170. *See also* Vanity
Ormond, duke of, 229

Parliament. *See* Political institutions
Parties, political, ix, 7, 49, 52, 53, 60, 61, 62, 71–72, 123–24, 125, 130, 138, 170, 240; and Defoe, 51–54 57–58, 61; and Sterne, 198–204, 215, 237–40, 261–62
Passmore, J. A., 131n
Patey, Douglas Lane, 28n
Pelhamites, 202
Penn, William, 60
Pitkin, Hanna Fenichel, 5n, 40n, 269–70
Pitt, William, 10, 11, 12, 204, 221, 222, 237, 238, 239, 240, 242, 243
Play, 10, 246; in Hobbes, 33. *See also* Art, Aesthetics; Political culture
Plumb, J. H., vii, 47n, 56n
Pocock, J. G. A. 6, 38n, 57n–58n, 273n, 278n
Politeness, 232, 253–56, 262
Political construction, in Defoe, 92
Political culture: and commerce, 275–78; in Defoe and Hobbes, 70; festive politics, 241, 243; gallantry in Burke

Political culture (*cont.*)
and Sterne, 276–77; in Hobbes, 197; refinement in Burke and Hume, 277; refinement in Hume, 258–59; remasculinization, 276; veneration of the state in Burke and Hobbes, 269–70. *See also* Compleasance; Natural law; Politeness
Political institutions, ix, 3–5; Anglican establishment, x, 47–49, 54, 60–61, 169, 210, 271; Anglican establishment and Sterne, 222–26, 246–47; aristocracy, x, 9, 269; bureaucracy, 56–57, 64–65; cabinet, 57, 68, 62, 170; City of London, 50–51; common law, 273; established church, 11; magistracy, 113, 148, 167, 224; monarchy 4, 71–72, 268, 274; monarchy in Defoe, 49, 56–59; Parliament, 49–51, 274; petitioning, 51; public debt, 71–72; slavery in Defoe and Hobbes, 79–83; slavery in Sterne, 244–45. *See also* Parties, political
Politics: feminism and the state, 17n; and Marxism, 4–5, 15–16; origin of government, 132, as science in Hobbes and Hume, 135; sovereignty, viii, 3, 12, 37, 70, 86–89; sovereignty, in Hobbes, 38–43; vs. economics, 31, 116, 137; vs. economics in Defoe, 13, 71–72, 86; vs. the social, 1, 3–8; vs. the social in Hobbes, 43–44; vs. the social in Richardson, 129, 187–88. *See also* Parties, political
Pope, Alexander, 130, 200, 213
Poulantzas, Nicos, 5n
Power seeking, 29–30, 85, 278. *See also* Competition
Preston, John, 104n, 183n
Price, Dr. Richard, 275
Price, Martin, 72–73
Promises, 111; in Defoe, 80–81, 88, 99–100, 139; in Defoe and Hobbes, 69–70; in Hobbes, 182; in Hume, 132–33, 228; in Richardson 182. *See also* Contract
Property, viii, 69–70, 86, 132–33; landed estate, 118–119. *See also* Economics
Pufendorf, Samuel, 67

Rader, Ralph, 64n
Religion, viii, 7, 12; Anglican catechism, 167; Catholics, 11, 78, 49–50, 88, 164, 202, 212–13, 224–26, 229, 260; causes in Hobbes and Hume, 269; conscience, 224–26, 252; Dissenters, 47–49, 51, 54, 60–61, 126; fear in Defoe, 85; latitudinarians, 202, 247; and novel, 25; occasional conformity in Defoe, 60; providence in Burke, 14, 272–74; providential signs, 73–74; providential signs in Defoe, 83, 89, 91; providential signs in Defoe and Hobbes, 76; religious war in Defoe, 82–83; salvation in Defoe, 85; toleration, 62; toleration in Defoe, 87–88; toleration in Richardson, 129; veneration in Hobbes and Burke, 269. *See also* Political institutions
Reputation, 13, 101; and credit, 108–10; in Defoe, 99, 108; in Hobbes, 134; in Hume, 134; in Richardson, 151, 165, 168; in Richardson and Hume, 136; slander, 109. *See also* Opinion
Restoration, ix
Revolution, ix; English Civil War, vii, 8; French, vii, ix, 8, 206, 267, 273; and Hobbes and Burke, 23; influence on political theory and novel, 23; Jacobite rebellions of 1715 and 1745, 124, 201, 202, 226, 229; right to 68; of 1688, ix, 50, 92, 119, 217, 236, 271, 273, 274, 276
Revolution Society, 275
Reynolds, Sir Joshua, 161
Richardson, Samuel, vii, viii, ix, 9, 10, 13, 21, 23, 121–31, 136–93, 211, 228, 230, 247, 267, 278. Works: *Clarissa*, 161–93; *Familiar Letters*, 127; *Pamela*, 141–59, 160, 162, 163; *Pamela* II, 162; *Sir Charles Grandison*, 160, 193; works printed: *Daily Gazeteer*, 125; *Negotiations of Roe*, 126; *New Family Instructor*, 126; *Religious Courtship*,

Richardson, Samuel (*cont.*) 126; *Tour through the Whole Island of Great Britain*, 126; *True Briton*, 124. *See also* Hobbes, Thomas; Hume, David.
Richelieu, Armand Jean du Plessis de, cardinal, 58
Richetti, John, 72–73, 114n
Rochester, John Wilmot, 2d earl of, 69
Rockingham, Charles Watson-Wentworth, 2d marquis of, 202, 242, 243
Rosenheim, Edward W., 216n
Rothstein, Eric, 28n
Rousseau, Jean-Jacques, 256, 278
Rudé, George, 241n

Sabine, George H., 67n, 270n
Sacks, Sheldon, 64n
Sale, William Merritt Jr., 123n
Satire, 9, 25, 130, 270, 275; in Burke, 278; in Sterne, 215–18, 249; in Swift, 215–18
Schochet, Gordon, 166n
Schonhorn, Manuel, 56n, 88n
Science, 4, 28–29
Seidel, Michael, 91, 215n, 247n
Self-preservation, 102; in Defoe, 72, 82 86, 114–15; in Defoe and Hobbes, 68–70, 81; in Richardson, 167, and suicide, 171–72
Shaftesbury, Anthony Ashley Cooper, 1st earl of, 49, 127
Shaftesbury, Anthony Ashley Cooper, 3d earl of, 97, 191
Shklovsky, Viktor, 205
Sill, Geoffrey, 71n–72n, 89n–90n
Sitter, John, 8n, 137
Skinner, Quentin, 6, 22n, 24n, 67
Smith, Adam, 172–173
Smollett, Tobias, 21n, 260, 267
Social contract. *See* Contract
Society. *See* Economics; Language; Political culture; Political institutions; Politics
Sovereignty. *See* Politics
Spacks, Patricia Meyer, 144n
Speck, W. A., 47n
Starr, G. A., 63, 78n, 84n, 85, 96, 104n
Sterne, Jaques, 198–202
Sterne, Laurence, vii, ix, 8, 9, 10–12, 13–14, 21, 23, 195–263, 267, 270, 275, 276; and *York Gazeteer*, 199. Works: *Journal to Eliza*, 232; *Political Romance*, 202–3; *Sentimental Journey*, 246–63; *Tristram Shandy*, 204–46. *See also* Burke, Edmund; Hobbes, Thomas; Hume, David
Stewart, Dugald, 39
Stewart, John B., 131n
Stinstra, 125, 160
Stone, Lawrence, 119n
Stout, Gardner, 247
Strauss, Leo, 6, 69n
Sunderland, Charles Spencer, 3d earl of, 53
Sunderland, Robert Spencer, 2d earl of, 58
Sutherland, Dame Lucy, 50n, 241n
Sutherland, James, 47n
Swearingen, James E., 222n
Swift, Jonathan, 130, 225, 236, 238, 247
Sympathy, in Hume, 133–34, 172, 229; in Smith, 172–73

Tave, Stuart, 216n
Taylor, A. E., 38n, 67n–68n
Teaching. *See* Education
Test Act, 49
Test and Corporation Acts, 48
Thomas, Dalby, 56
Todd, Janet, 174n–75n
Tompkins, Jane P., 245n
Townshend, Charles, 2d viscount, 53
Traugott, John, 227

Union of Scotland and England, 59
Utility, in Hume, 229
Utrecht, Treaty of, 236, 238

Van Ghent, Dorothy, 109n–10n
Vanity, 66, 97, 101; in Hobbes, 29, 134; of Hume, 160; love of fame in Hume, 134; love of fame in Richardson, 141–59; of Richardson, 160–62; in Richardson and Hobbes, 182
Voltaire, 211

Walpole, Sir Robert, ix, 53, 54, 58, 123, 125, 130, 199, 201, 237
War: and Defoe, 87; and executive authority, 57, 88; and Pitt, 204; religious, 82–83; sentimental soldier, 276; state of in Hobbes, 31, 35, 39; and state power in Defoe and Hobbes, 68; and Sterne, 204, 236–40; as tool for unity, 68n; and William III, 71
Warburton, William, Dr., 216
Warner, William Beatty, 163n–64n
Warrender, Howard, 38n–39n, 67n
Watkins, J. W. N., 27n
Watkins, W. B. C., 222n
Watt, Ian, 8–12, 62–63, 72
West, Alick, 66n
Wharton, duke of, 124
Wilkes, John, 12, 136, 240–44
William III, 50, 51, 57, 58, 59, 71, 91, 236, 263
William of Orange. *See* William III
Williams, Raymond, 5n
Wilt, Judith, 175n
Winch, Donald, 278n
Winch, Peter, 5
Wolin, Sheldon S., 5, 6, 22n, 270n
Wollstonecraft, Mary, 92
Wordsworth, William, 267
Work, James Aiken, 216–17, 219n

Young, Edward, 160

Zach, Wolfgang, 240n
Zimmerman, Everett, 69n

*Library of Congress Cataloging-in-Publication Data*

Kay, Carol, 1947–
Political constructions : Defoe, Richardson, and Sterne in relation to Hobbes, Hume, and Burke / Carol Kay.
p. cm.
Includes index.
ISBN 0-8014-2043-1
1. English fiction—18th century—History and criticism. 2. Political fiction, English—History and criticism. 3. Defoe, Daniel, 1661?–1731—Political and social views. 4. Richardson, Samuel, 1689–1761—Political and social views. 5. Sterne, Laurence, 1713-1768—Political and social views. 6. Politics and literature—Great Britain—History—18th century. 7. Political science—Great Britain—Philosophy—History—18th century. I. Title.
PR858.P65K39 1988
823'.5'09358—dc19 88-3741